C# Interview Guide

Boost your confidence with answers to hundreds of secret interview questions

Konstantin Semenenko

C# Interview Guide

Group Product Manager: Kunal Sawant

Publishing Product Manager: Nitin Nainani

Book Project Manager: Shagun Saini

Senior Editor: Anuradha Joglekar

Technical Editor: Reenish Kulshrestha

Copy Editor: Safis Editing

Indexer: Subalakshmi Govindhan

Production Designer: Alishon Mendonca

DevRel Marketing Coordinators: Shrinidhi Manoharan

Publication date: March 2024

Production reference: 1070224

Published by Packt Publishing Ltd.

Grosvenor House

11 St Paul's Square

Birmingham

B3 1RB, UK

ISBN: 978-1-80512-046-9

www.packtpub.com

Contributors

About the author

Konstantin Semenenko, a master in C# and .NET technologies, has been a visionary chief technology officer and software developer for over 18 years. His career spans from being the founder and chief technology officer of Managed Code, where he blends advanced technology and AI, to chief technology officer at Winkt, focusing on strategic planning and agile leadership. His expertise covers a wide range of areas, including Xamarin mobile development, Azure AI, Orleans, and Blazor, and he holds multiple certifications such as Azure Developer and Xamarin Developer. Konstantin has also made notable contributions in areas such as generative AI, large language models, and Semantic Kernel. His passion for technology is reflected in his leadership roles and innovative solutions across various companies, demonstrating his commitment to advancing the IT industry.

About the reviewers

Oleksii Sokol is a software developer with a focus on creating web and mobile applications. He volunteers for the Microsoft .NET MAUI Community Toolkit. His specialization in Blazor and MAUI ensures the creation of high-quality, cross-platform mobile applications that provide an optimum user experience and meet business requirements.

Li (Alex) Song is a serial entrepreneur with a significant history in executive roles, including chief technology officer and tech lead, at multiple prominent North American IT consulting firms. He is skilled as a full stack programmer, with particular expertise in backend development, and a seasoned system architect. Li specializes in leading small, agile development teams to rapidly initiate and execute projects. He has a comprehensive and proven track record in the successful development of cloud computing, artificial intelligence, and blockchain projects.

Table of Contents

Part 2: Technical Interview Preparation

3

Fundamentals of C# Programming   41

4

Advanced C# Concepts   59

5

Fundamentals Governing Maintainable and Efficient C# Programming   99

6

Deep Dive into C# Libraries and Frameworks   145

Introduction to Entity Framework and data access   157

7

Overcoming Challenges in C# Technical Interviews and Tips for Tackling Coding Challenges during Interviews   185

8

Building Soft Skills and Expanding Your Network   213

Part 3: Post Interview

9

10

Gaining Expert Insights, Following Up Effectively, and Taking Action   261

11

Launching Your C# Career – Insights   283

Preface

Welcome to *C# Interview Guide*, your comprehensive resource for mastering the C# programming language and acing technical interviews. As a versatile and powerful language, C# is widely used in various fields such as gaming, web services, and enterprise software. This guide is meticulously crafted to help you navigate every step of your job application process, from crafting standout résumés and engaging cover letters to preparing for challenging interviews. It provides in-depth insights into C# fundamentals, advanced concepts, best practices, and the latest frameworks and libraries. Whether you're a beginner looking to make your mark in the world of C# development or an experienced programmer seeking to polish your interview skills, this book is designed to equip you with the knowledge, strategies, and confidence needed to excel in your career and secure your dream job in the ever-evolving tech industry.

Who this book is for

This book is primarily designed for individuals who are aspiring to establish or advance their careers in C# programming and software development. It is an invaluable resource for the following:

- Recent graduates in computer science, software engineering, or related fields, who are looking to break into the technology sector with a focus on C# development

- Junior-to-mid-level C# developers aiming to enhance their understanding of advanced concepts, best practices, and the latest frameworks in C# to progress in their careers

- Seasoned developers in other programming languages who intend to transition to C# or expand their skill set to include this versatile language

- Technical professionals preparing for job interviews, seeking guidance on resume building, interview strategies, and effective communication skills specific to C# roles

- Self-taught programmers with a foundational understanding of programming concepts, looking to formalize and deepen their knowledge in C#

What this book covers

Chapter 1, Crafting a Compelling Resume and Cover Letter, Online Presence, and Interview Preparation, guides you in creating effective résumés, professional online profiles, engaging cover letters, and thorough interview preparation.

Chapter 2, Acing the Interview – Mastering Behavioral Questions and Interview Techniques, focuses on interview preparation, mastering behavioral questions, and presenting yourself professionally in both virtual and in-person settings.

Chapter 3, Fundamentals of C# Programming, introduces the essential concepts, data types, control structures, and object-oriented programming in C# for technical interviews.

Chapter 4, Advanced C# Concepts, explores advanced C# functionalities such as collections, LINQ, async, delegates, lambdas, and multi-threading for complex software development.

Chapter 5, Fundamentals Governing Maintainable and Efficient C# Programming, covers writing clean C# code, implementing SOLID principles, design patterns, and utilizing C# development tools.

Chapter 6, Deep Dive into C# Libraries, Frameworks, and Technical Interview Preparation, discusses essential C# libraries and frameworks such as Entity Framework, ASP.NET Core, and MAUI/Xamarin, along with technical interview strategies.

Chapter 7, Overcoming Challenges in C# Technical Interviews and Tips for Tackling Coding Challenges during Interviews, focuses on MAUI/Xamarin for cross-platform development and strategies for addressing common C# interview questions and problems.

Chapter 8, Building Soft Skills and Expanding Your Network, reviews C# concepts and real-world applications, emphasizing soft skills and networking for successful interview outcomes.

Chapter 9, Negotiating Your Salary and Evaluating Job Offers, guides you on post-interview follow-ups, building professional networks, salary negotiations, and evaluating job offers as a C# developer.

Chapter 10, Gaining Expert Insights, Following Up Effectively, and Taking Action, offers a recap of key C# concepts, interviews with industry professionals, and strategies to adapt to industry changes and emerging technologies.

Chapter 11, Launching Your C# Career - Insights, provides insights into post-interview steps, career-building strategies, and staying updated with C# industry trends for a successful career.

To get the most out of this book

To fully benefit from this book, it's important to have a basic understanding of programming principles and familiarity with **object-oriented programming (OOP)** concepts. Knowledge of basic C# syntax and structure will be advantageous, as the book progresses into more advanced topics. While a background in software development is helpful, it's not essential, as the book starts with foundational concepts before moving on to complex ones. This guide assumes that you are keen to deepen your C# knowledge, improve your interview skills, and are ready to engage with both the theoretical and practical aspects of programming and career development.

Software covered in the book	Topics
Rider	CVs
Visual Studio	Interviews
Visual Studio Code	Cover letters
C#	STAR
MAUI	
OOP	

There are many short code examples in this guide that are provided solely for demonstration purposes, and you do not need to execute these directly.

In order to assist the author in the preparation of this interview guide, participants agreed to be interviewed and to provide information and other materials to be used in connection with this work, including their personal experiences, remarks, and recollections, which are described in Chapter 10, Gaining Expert Insights, Following Up Effectively, and Taking Action.

Conventions used

There are a number of text conventions used throughout this book.

`Code in text`: Indicates code words in text, database table names, folder names, filenames, file extensions, pathnames, dummy URLs, user input, and Twitter handles. Here is an example: "The `args` argument contains an array of strings that is passed to the program upon its launch."

A block of code is set as follows:

```
public class Program
{
    public static void Main(string[] args)
    {
        // program code
    }
}
```

> **Tips or important notes**
> Appear like this.

Get in touch

Feedback from our readers is always welcome.

General feedback: If you have questions about any aspect of this book, email us at customercare@packtpub.com and mention the book title in the subject of your message.

Errata: Although we have taken every care to ensure the accuracy of our content, mistakes do happen. If you have found a mistake in this book, we would be grateful if you would report this to us. Please visit www.packtpub.com/support/errata and fill in the form.

Piracy: If you come across any illegal copies of our works in any form on the internet, we would be grateful if you would provide us with the location address or website name. Please contact us at copyright@packt.com with a link to the material.

If you are interested in becoming an author: If there is a topic that you have expertise in and you are interested in either writing or contributing to a book, please visit authors.packtpub.com.

Share Your Thoughts

Once you've read C# Interview Guide, we'd love to hear your thoughts! Scan the QR code below to go straight to the Amazon review page for this book and share your feedback.

https://packt.link/r/1805120468

Your review is important to us and the tech community and will help us make sure we're delivering excellent quality content.

Download a free PDF copy of this book

Thanks for purchasing this book!

Do you like to read on the go but are unable to carry your print books everywhere?

Is your eBook purchase not compatible with the device of your choice?

Don't worry, now with every Packt book you get a DRM-free PDF version of that book at no cost.

Read anywhere, any place, on any device. Search, copy, and paste code from your favorite technical books directly into your application.

The perks don't stop there, you can get exclusive access to discounts, newsletters, and great free content in your inbox daily

Follow these simple steps to get the benefits:

1. Scan the QR code or visit the link below

https://packt.link/free-ebook/9781805120469

2. Submit your proof of purchase
3. That's it! We'll send your free PDF and other benefits to your email directly

Part 1: Interview Preparation

In this part, you'll learn how to create effective resumes, professional online profiles, and engaging cover letters. You'll also explore strategies to thoroughly prepare for an interview, mastering behavioral questions and presenting yourself professionally in both virtual and in-person settings.

This part has the following chapters:

- *Chapter 1, Crafting a Compelling Resume and Cover Letter, Online Presence, and Interview Preparation*
- *Chapter 2, Acing the Interview – Mastering Behavioral Questions and Interview Techniques*

1

Crafting a Compelling Resume and Cover Letter, Online Presence, and Interview Preparation

Welcome to our detailed guide, designed to be your ally in navigating the complex world of job applications. In this book, we aim to equip you with the essential skills and knowledge to excel in the competitive job market. By the end of this journey, you will have learned how to craft impactful resumes, write effective cover letters, build strong online profiles, and confidently approach job interviews.

In the first chapter, we will dive into several crucial topics. You'll learn how to make a resume that gets noticed and what to include to highlight your skills and experience. Further, you'll understand how to write a cover letter that tells your story and matches the job you want. It's a chance to explain why you're the right fit.

Next, we'll guide you on making a LinkedIn profile that shows your professional journey. It's important for making connections and getting noticed. Finally, for tech jobs, a GitHub profile can show off your coding skills. We'll help you set up a profile that displays your best work and teamwork.

In this chapter, we're going to cover the following main topics:

- Creating a good resume
- Drafting a cover letter
- Utilizing LinkedIn
- Utilizing GitHub

Let's start with *Creating a Good Resume*. In this section, we'll focus on how to make a resume that stands out. You'll learn about the key elements of a good resume, from its structure to how to customize it for different jobs. A well-crafted resume is your first step towards great job opportunities.

Creating a good resume

A **resume** is the first and only thing that the HR manager sees about the candidate, and it's your task to make this information about you compelling enough to catch and hold their attention. Of course, I will provide examples of resumes, CVs, and cover letters later, but let's first understand the difference between a resume and a CV.

Resume versus CV

The alignment of these terms can either be identical or vary, contingent upon the specific region where the job search is being conducted. Therefore, if we consider the regional distinctions, it is important to note that CV and resume may be perceived as distinct concepts.

A resume is needed to provide a brief summary of your work experience, skills, achievements, and education. In other words, a resume is necessary to give the recruiter and employer a general understanding of your work experience.

A **curriculum vitae** (**CV**) contains a story of your experience starting from higher education and academic activity, supplementing information with facts about published works, awards, and merits, the places of your work, details about projects, duties, and more.

The following table gives a more detailed comparison:

	Resume	CV
Document Size	The ideal size is one page and a maximum of two.	Write as much as you need. The size can reach five pages or more.
Structure	It depends on the job description and your capabilities. Mostly, it includes contact information, work experience, skills, and education.	You describe all your activities and achievements, starting from university and ending with all your professional achievements.
Adaptation	The resume should correspond to the vacancy and contain relevant skills.	Your CV is the story of your career and it doesn't change.
Where to Use	In many countries around the world, for example in Australia, India, or South Africa, a resume and CV are the same. But in the US, these are completely different documents.	In Europe, the UK, and New Zealand, the word resume is rarely used, and the word CV refers specifically to the short version.

Table 1.1 – Comparison between a resume and CV

Regardless, let's create a universal mix of a resume and a CV. This will be a template that you can edit to suit the job vacancy.

Let's start with the basic sections:

1. **Contact information**: This should be at the top of your resume and include your name, phone number, email address, and the link to your LinkedIn and GitHub profile.

2. **Objective**: This is a brief statement about your career goals or a summary of your skills and qualifications. This section should be tailored to the specific job you are applying for.

3. **About me**: This section should present a concise and captivating overview of who you are, your main qualifications, and why you are suited for the role.

4. **Skills**: This section should list your key skills and abilities that are relevant to the job you are applying for. You should aim to include both soft and hard skills, such as communication, teamwork, programming languages, or data analysis.

5. **Work experience**: Here you should list your previous jobs in reverse chronological order, with the most recent job first. For each job, include the name of the company, your job title, the dates you worked there, and a brief summary of your responsibilities and achievements.

6. **Education**: This section should list your educational background, again in reverse chronological order. Include the name of the institution, the degree you obtained, and the dates of attendance. If you have recently graduated, you may also want to include relevant coursework or projects.

7. **Certifications (Licenses)**: If you have any professional certifications or licenses that are relevant to the job you are applying for, include them in this section.

8. **Awards and achievements**: If you have received any awards or recognitions in your professional or academic career, list them here.

9. **Languages**: If you are multilingual, it's important to note it on your resume as it's often a highly desirable skill in many fields.

I would advise creating a good basic description and then adapting points 2, 3, and 4 according to the vacancies you are applying for. Let's delve into these points in more detail in the next sections.

The Objective section

This is the first piece of information about you, the objective of your search. This format should highlight your strongest skills, abilities, and ambitions to impress the employer. Here's an example:

*   *Experienced C# developer with more than five years of experience and a deep knowledge of OOP, .NET Framework, .NET Core, Entity Framework, SQL, and web services development*

*   *Known for working effectively in a team and adhering to established schedules and deadlines*

*   *Aim to provide high-level programming and an analytical approach for XYZ company to achieve strategic goals together*

- *Constantly striving for professional growth, learning new technologies, and adapting to rapidly changing technical conditions*

Let's analyze this text and determine how important these points are for an HR manager and how they can be tailored for a specific position:

- **Experience**: Stating your experience of over five years offers immediate proof of your longevity and familiarity in the field. To an HR manager, this suggests a proven track record of handling various tasks and problem-solving scenarios. Depending on the specific role, you could emphasize different aspects of your experience that align with the job requirements.

- **Technical proficiencies**: By listing key technologies, you showcase a strong technical base in your area of expertise. HR managers will look for these specific skills to match the job description. Make sure to highlight those technologies that are particularly relevant to the position you're applying for.

- **Soft skills**: Your capability to work effectively within a team and stick to established timelines are valuable skills in almost all job roles. HR managers are not just looking for technical proficiency but also interpersonal skills and professionalism. Tailor this section to the job by emphasizing those soft skills that the job ad particularly values, such as communication or leadership.

- **Goal orientation**: Expressing your ambition to contribute to the strategic objectives of the company demonstrates your understanding of the larger business context, not just the technical side. This alignment with company goals is attractive to HR managers as it suggests you'll be driven to contribute to the company's success. If possible, try to align your stated goals with the mission or objectives of the company you're applying to.

- **Adaptability and lifelong learning**: These traits are critical in the fast-paced tech industry. To an HR manager, this indicates that you're not only open to changes but actively seek to expand your skill set and stay updated, which is crucial for a company's growth and adaptation to market changes. If the job ad mentions a fast-paced environment or a need for adaptability, make sure to emphasize this aspect in your approach.

All right, we have discussed the Objective part of the resume. Let's move on to the next one, that is, the About Me section.

The About Me section

The **About Me** section in a resume, sometimes known as a **personal statement** or **personal summary**, is a short paragraph that describes your professional skills, goals, and experience. It helps an employer quickly understand who you are as a professional and what you can bring to the company. Here are some tips on how to write this section:

- **Define your professional image**: Start with a brief phrase that describes you as a professional. This could be your strongest specialization or the role you most often perform. For example: *Experienced C# developer.*

- **Highlight key skills**: Include two to three key skills you possess. These could be technical skills (for example, experience with specific technologies) or soft skills (for example, teamwork and leadership).

- **Emphasize important achievements**: Include a brief description of one or two of your most significant achievements in your career. This could be a successful project you carried out or a significant problem you solved.

- **State your goals**: If you have specific professional goals, state them. This could be a desire to work on certain types of projects, use specific technologies, or develop certain skills.

- **Focus on what you can offer the employer**: Your personal statement should be employer-focused. Highlight what you can bring to the company, not just what you want to achieve.

- **Be brief and specific**: Your personal statement should be short and clear. It should be easy to read quickly, so try to keep it within three to five sentences.

Here's an example of a personal statement for a C# developer:

As a passionate technology enthusiast, my interest in coding has shaped my career as a C# Developer. I am known for my dedication to teamwork, meticulous attention to detail, and a knack for problem-solving. A firm believer in the power of continual learning, I'm always on the lookout for new technology and opportunities to further enhance my skills. My commitment to knowledge growth extends beyond my professional life. As an avid guitar player, I have learned the values of discipline, patience, and the pure joy of mastering a new piece. This hobby serves as a creative outlet, providing a balance to my technical pursuits.

Additionally, I enjoy contributing to open source projects, an experience that not only broadens my coding skills but also deepens my appreciation for the collaborative nature of our field. Integrity, collaboration, and the pursuit of excellence are my guiding principles, influencing both my personal and professional life. I am a hard-working individual with a unique blend of technical skills and creative flair, eager to make a significant impact in my future role.

Let's break down the preceding text from an HR perspective:

- **passion for technology**: By stating that you're a passionate technology enthusiast, you highlight that you're not just in the field for a job, but because you genuinely enjoy what you do. This can suggest to HR that you are more likely to be motivated, dedicated, and continually improving in your role.

- **A detail-oriented team player**: Highlighting this quality indicates that you are conscientious and able to work well within a team, both of which are critical attributes in most work environments. This shows HR that you would likely fit well within the existing team dynamic.

- **A continuous learner**: Your emphasis on constant learning is a strong positive signal to HR. It shows that you are proactive, eager to expand your skills, and will likely stay up to date with the latest technologies and trends, contributing to the organization's growth.

- **An interesting person**: Mentioning your hobby of playing the guitar and contributing to open-source projects gives an insight into who you are outside of work. It adds a personal touch to your resume that can help HR to understand you better as a person. It can also demonstrate qualities such as discipline, patience, and creativity.

- **A candidate of integrity, collaboration, and excellence**: These stated values show that you are professional and principled, which can align well with the company's culture and values. It indicates to HR that you have a strong work ethic and are committed to delivering high-quality work.

- **A hard-working and creative individual**: These traits give a quick snapshot of your work style. They suggest to HR that you would be committed to your role and can bring a creative perspective, both of which can be valuable to a company.

While the About Me section is more personal, it should still align with the values and requirements of the job you're applying for. You might want to slightly tweak it for each job application to emphasize the most relevant aspects of your personality and experiences. Next, let's move on to the Skills section of the resume.

The Skills section

Here are some recommendations when crafting the **Skills** section of your resume:

- **Match the job description**: Tailor your skills to the job description as closely as possible. If the job post lists specific technologies or methodologies and you have experience with them, be sure to include them.

- **Distinguish between hard and soft skills**: Hard skills refer to specific technical knowledge and training while soft skills are more related to your behavior and how you interact with other people. Both are important and should be included.

- **Be honest**: Don't embellish or overstate your skills. If you're not proficient in a particular technology, don't claim to be. Honesty is always the best policy, and it's better to learn on the job than to mislead an employer.

- **Don't forget transferable skills**: If you're transitioning from a different career or industry, think about the skills you've gained that can be applied to the job you're applying for. These could include project management, leadership, or communication skills.

- **Be concise but comprehensive**: Aim to include a comprehensive list of your relevant skills but keep the descriptions concise. Each skill should ideally be described in a few words or a short phrase.

- **Consider the order**: The order in which you list your skills can also be significant. Consider putting the most important and relevant skills at the top of the list.

- **Use action words**: Begin each skill with an action word to make it more engaging. For example, instead of *experience with C#*, say *proficient in C#*.

Remember, the Skills section of your resume is your chance to showcase what you're capable of, so make it as tailored and compelling as possible.

Here's an example of the Skills sections for a C# developer:

- **C# programming**: Expertise in core concepts, .NET types, Task Parallel Library (TPL), delegates, and events

- **Frameworks**: .NET Core, ASP.NET MVC, Entity Framework, LINQ

- **Database**: Entity Framework, LINQ-to-SQL

- **Tools**: Visual Studio, NuGet, .NET debugging

- **Testing**: NUnit, MSTest

- **API development**: ASP.NET Core Web API

Having explored all the essential components of your resume, let us now delve into the next section to grasp the concept of a cover letter and learn the process of crafting one.

Drafting a cover letter

A **cover letter**, or an **accompanying letter**, is a document that is typically sent along with your resume when applying for a job. This letter gives you the opportunity to describe your experience, skills, and goals in more detail, as well as indicate why you are interested in the specific vacancy and why you consider yourself a suitable candidate.

Here are some key points to consider when writing a cover letter:

- **Addressee**: Try to find out who will be reading your letter and address this person directly. If you do not know who this is, you can use a general salutation, such as *Dear Employer* or *Dear Hiring Team.*

- **Introduction**: In your introduction, you should indicate the position you are applying for and briefly describe why you are interested in this role.

- **Body**: In this section, you should describe your experience, skills, and achievements that make you a suitable candidate for the specific vacancy in detail. You should demonstrate how your skills match the job requirements.

- **Conclusion**: In the conclusion, you should thank the reader for their time and indicate your willingness to discuss your application in more detail in an interview.

- **Signature**: Conclude your letter with a signature that includes your full name and contact information.

Here is an example of a cover letter for a C# developer:

Dear [company's name] Team,

I am writing to you regarding the C# developer position at your company that I saw on your website (link to the job post).

As an experienced developer with a deep knowledge of C# and .NET Framework, I am very interested in this opportunity.

Over the past five years, I have worked as a C# developer at XYZ Company, where I developed and implemented several high-performing web applications using ASP.NET and SQL.

I was responsible for the entire project development cycle, including requirements analysis, design, coding, testing, and support.

One of my biggest accomplishments was the creation of a web application for automating project management processes, which reduced task completion time by 30%.

I believe that my experience and skills will be a good fit for your team, and I look forward to the opportunity to help your company achieve its goals.

Thank you for considering my application. I look forward to the opportunity to discuss my application in more detail in an interview.

Best regards,

[Your Name]

[Your Contact Information]

From an HR manager's perspective, here's how this cover letter might be analyzed:

- **Opening**: *Dear [company's name] Team* is a good opening. It's professional, friendly, and appropriately addresses the recipient.
- **First paragraph**: The writer provides a clear reason for writing the letter: they're interested in the C# developer position at the company. Including the source of the job posting indicates a proactive approach.

- **Second paragraph**: The writer mentions their experience and technical skills that are relevant to the role. It shows that they have read the job description and understand what is required for the position.

- **Third paragraph**: They provide a detailed account of their past work experience and their responsibilities in their previous role. This gives the HR manager a glimpse of what they could potentially bring to the role in terms of skill set and experience.

- **Fourth paragraph**: They discuss a specific achievement and quantify the result. This highlights their problem-solving skills and ability to deliver results. However, be cautious about including exact percentages if you can't substantiate these claims in an interview.

- **Fifth paragraph**: The writer concludes by expressing interest in contributing to the company's goals, which suggests they are not just focused on personal growth but also on how they can bring value to the organization.

- **Closing**: A respectful and professional sign-off that also expresses eagerness to further discuss their qualifications in an interview.

- **Contact Information**: The inclusion of contact information makes it easier for the HR manager to get in touch.

Overall, this cover letter demonstrates that the writer understands the position, has the necessary qualifications, and is genuinely interested in the role. The HR manager would likely consider them a strong candidate and potentially invite them for an interview. Remember, it's crucial to personalize each cover letter for the specific job you're applying for.

With our cover letter skills polished and ready to impress, it's time to navigate the vast digital world where potential employers may first encounter us. In the following section, we will delve into the intricate workings of LinkedIn, your virtual resume, and how to optimize it for maximum visibility and impact.

Utilizing LinkedIn

Currently, there are two most important platforms for development, namely **LinkedIn** and **GitHub** (we will cover GitHub in the next section). LinkedIn is your online CV, where you can write about yourself. Therefore, it's crucial to pay attention to your profile. Let me remind you once again that your profile is the first and only thing a recruiter sees.

Creating a LinkedIn profile

Your LinkedIn profile is an important tool for job hunting, networking, and professional development. Here are some tips on how you can fill out your profile as a developer:

- **Profile and background images**: Your profile photo should be professional and friendly. The background image can reflect your work or interests in IT. This is important because photos provide the first impression of you.

- **Profile headline**: This is one of the most important elements of your profile. It should clearly reflect your role and specialization, such as C# Backend Developer, JavaScript Developer, or Senior Python Developer. This helps employers and other professionals in the industry to quickly understand what you do.

- **Profile description (About)**: In this section, you can talk more about your skills, experience, and goals. Be clear and specific, focusing on what you can offer employers. You can include information about your professional interests, technologies used, teamwork features, and personal achievements.

- **Work experience**: This is the section where you can detail your work in previous positions. For each position, indicate the company, time of work, your role, and important achievements or projects you worked on. Try to use an active voice and verbs to highlight your contribution.

- **Education**: List your higher education, courses, or certificates related to your profession. This demonstrates your training and education in the field.

- **Skills**: LinkedIn allows you to indicate skills you possess. Emphasize technical skills such as programming languages, databases, and testing as well as soft skills such as teamwork, organizational abilities, and critical thinking.

- **Recommendations**: Ask your colleagues or managers to give you recommendations. They can point out your strengths and successes you achieved while working with them.

- **Volunteering and interests**: If you have volunteering experience, especially related to IT, be sure to include it in your profile. Also, don't forget to add your professional interests such as groups, organizations, or industry events you've joined.

- **Selective projects, publications, and patents**: If you have relevant content, include it in your profile. These can be links to your GitHub projects, scientific works, medium articles, or other relevant works. This will allow you to showcase your real achievements and skills.

- **Languages**: If you speak multiple languages, be sure to include them in your profile. This can be useful, especially if you're interested in working for international companies.

By following these recommendations, you'll be able to create a detailed and attractive LinkedIn profile that reflects your professional experience, skills, and achievements. All these elements will help you attract the attention of employers and other professionals in the industry.

In the next section, I will show you an example of how you can structure your LinkedIn profile.

Structuring a LinkedIn profile

Your resume is great, but think of LinkedIn as your resume that anyone can immediately write to you on! That's why it's also important to have a good LinkedIn profile and include a link to it everywhere. Treat it as the full version of your resume.

Creating an effective LinkedIn profile requires careful consideration of each section. Here's an outlined structure that can serve as a good example:

- **Profile picture**: Choose a professional, well-lit photo where your face is clearly visible.

- **Headline**: Senior C# Developer at XYZ Company | Specializing in .NET Framework and ASP. NET | Open to new opportunities.

- **About**: Experienced C# Developer with a demonstrated history of working in the software industry. Skilled in .NET Framework, ASP.NET, SQL, and Agile Methodologies. Strong engineering professional with a bachelor's degree in computer science from XYZ University.

  I have successfully developed and implemented several high-performing web applications, including a project management tool that improved productivity by 30%.

  I am passionate about problem-solving and continuously improving my skills to stay current with industry trends. Open to new opportunities where I can further apply my skills and contribute to a dynamic team.

- **Experience**:

  Middle C# Developer

  XYZ Company

  Dates Employed: Jan 2018 – Present

  Location: City, Country

  - Develop and implement high-performing web applications using C# and .NET Framework

  - Collaborate with cross-functional teams to define, design, and ship new features

  - Work closely with the QA team to identify and fix bugs

  - Conduct code reviews and mentor junior developers

  Junior C# Developer

  XYZ Company

  Dates Employed: Jan 2016 – Dec 2017

  Location: City, Country

  - Assisted in the development of web applications using C# and .NET Framework

  - Collaborated with a team of developers to implement new features

  - Participated in code reviews and learned best practices in software development

  - Worked closely with senior developers to gain hands-on experience and improve coding skills

  Intern, Software Development

  ABC Company

Dates Employed: June 2015 – Dec 2015

Location: City, Country

- Worked on a team to develop a web-based tool to improve internal communication

- Gained hands-on experience with coding in C# and .NET Framework

- Assisted in troubleshooting and bug fixes

- Learned industry best practices and Agile methodologies

- **Education**:

Bachelor's Degree, Computer Science

XYZ University

Years attended: 2010 – 2014

- **Skills**: .NET Framework, C#, ASP.NET, SQL, Agile Methodologies, Leadership, Team Collaboration, Problem Solving

- **Recommendations**: If possible, ask for recommendations from colleagues, managers, or professors to increase your credibility

To make your profile appear more professional and attractive, it's important to inject some life into it. Here are some essential steps you should consider:

1. **Increase connections**: To add 500 connections or more, start by connecting with people you already know such as colleagues, classmates, and business partners. You can also connect with people in the same industry or profession by using LinkedIn's **People You May Know** feature. Be sure to add HR from the companies you are interested in.

2. **Join groups**: Participating in LinkedIn groups related to your profession or industry is an excellent way to grow your network and stay updated with the latest trends. Engage in group discussions by commenting on posts and offering valuable insights.

3. **Like and share relevant posts**: By liking and sharing content relevant to your profession or industry, you can increase your visibility and engagement. It's also good practice to regularly post insightful content, which can attract more connections and boost your presence.

4. **Improve your Social Selling Index (SSI)**: The SSI (`https://www.linkedin.com/sales/ssi`) is a measure by LinkedIn to rate how effective you are at establishing your professional brand, finding the right people, engaging with insights, and building relationships. To improve your SSI, you can:

   - **Establish your professional brand**: Share accomplishments, skills, and experience in your profile. Regularly post interesting articles or content that shows your knowledge in your field.

   - **Find the right people**: Use LinkedIn's search and research tools to find and connect with the right people in your industry.

- **Engage with Insights**: Share and comment on relevant posts. This shows that you're staying informed about your industry, and it helps to get you noticed.

- **Build relationships**: Cultivate your relationships by maintaining regular contact with your connections. Show genuine interest in their posts and contribute meaningfully to discussions.

- **Fill in all details**: Make sure every section of your profile is filled out, including your education, work experience, and skills. A complete profile gives a better impression of your professional persona.

- **Use a professional photo**: Your profile photo is often the first thing people see, so it should represent you in a professional light. A clear, high-quality headshot is usually a good choice.

- **Customize your URL**: LinkedIn allows you to customize your profile URL. Having a personalized URL makes your profile look more professional and is easier to share.

- **Write a compelling summary**: Your summary is a chance to showcase your achievements, aspirations, and personality. It should be engaging and written in the first person.

- **Keep it updated**: Regularly update your profile with new skills, experiences, and accomplishments. This shows you are active and engaged in your professional development.

Remember, your LinkedIn profile is like your online resume. By following these steps, you can enhance its appeal and make a strong professional impression. Next, we will move on to understanding how to utilize GitHub.

Utilizing GitHub

If you're a developer, it's very important to have a profile on GitHub, but not an empty profile. It's very good to add your projects and contribute to other projects because your code speaks for you better than any resume.

Your GitHub profile plays an important role in demonstrating your experience and skills as a developer. It's a place where you can showcase your actual projects and code. Here are some tips on how you can fill out your C# developer profile:

- **Avatar and username**: Use a professional photo for your avatar. Your username should be easy to understand and remember.

- **Biography**: Provide a short biography that describes you as a professional developer. Include important information such as your main specialization (for example, C# Developer).

- **Include a link to your LinkedIn profile or website**: This will give others the opportunity to learn more about you and your professional experience.

- **Readme**: GitHub allows you to create a README file for your profile, which appears on the main page. You can use this file to describe your work, skills, projects you've joined, or any other information you consider important.

- **Repositories**: Keep your repositories organized and updated. Each repository should have a quality README file that describes the project, its functionality, how to install and use it, as well as how others can contribute.

- **Make your work visible**: Add your projects in which you use C# to your repositories. Don't be afraid to add projects that are still in development.

- **Join organizations**: If you are a member of any GitHub organizations, they will be displayed on your profile. This can show your activity and collaboration in the programming field.

- **Contributions**: Your activity on GitHub is reflected in a contributions graph. Try to be active: commit to your repositories, create branches, pull requests, and respond to issues.

- **Connect with other developers**: Follow other developers you're interested in and interact with them. You may learn something new or even find opportunities for collaboration.

- **Gists**: You can use Gists to store and share small snippets of code. This can be useful for demonstrating specific skills or developing certain solutions.

Remember that your GitHub profile is not just a place to store code – it's your portfolio. It should showcase your skills, experience, coding style, and ability to work on projects.

The GitHub profile should be designed in such a way that it reflects your skills and experience in development. Here's an example of what a GitHub profile might look like for a C# developer:

- **Username**: CSharpDeveloper123

- **Bio**: Experienced C# developer specializing in .NET Framework and ASP.NET. Passionate about problem-solving and continuous learning.

- **The pinned section**: This section allows you to showcase your best or most relevant repositories. As a C# developer, you might pin repositories that contain projects or contributions you've made related to C# or a .NET Framework.

  For example:

  - **ASP.NET web application**: A high-performance web application developed with ASP.NET and SQL for managing project workflows. This application improved productivity by 30% at XYZ Company.

  - **C# algorithms and data structures**: A collection of algorithms and data structures implemented in C#. This repository serves as a reference and a demonstration of my problem-solving skills.

  - **Open-source contribution**: Contributed to ABC Open Source Project by improving the performance of the C# component. This improvement resulted in a 15% increase in the efficiency of the software.

- **Activity overview**: Make sure to keep your activity consistent. Regular contributions and interactions show that you are an active member of the GitHub community.

- **Contribution graph**: This section automatically updates with your contributions to your projects and any other repositories on GitHub. A well-filled contribution graph indicates active engagement with coding and version control.

- **Followers, following, and stars**: Engaging with other users by following them, starring their repositories, or collaborating on projects can demonstrate your involvement in the GitHub community.

- **Organizations**: If you're a part of any organization such as a company or open source project, they can be listed here.

> **Important note**
> Remember, your GitHub profile is an extension of your resume and LinkedIn profile. It's an opportunity to showcase your coding skills, projects, and contributions in a way that can't be conveyed through a traditional resume.

Summary

Throughout this chapter, we've navigated the foundational elements of a job applicant's first impression, from distinguishing between resumes and CVs to optimizing their About Me and Skills sections. With well-articulated cover letters and impactful LinkedIn and GitHub profiles, an applicant's application materials embody the modern digital era, striking a balance between tradition and contemporary appeal.

As this chapter concludes, remember: the techniques and insights gleaned here are just the tip of the iceberg. Up next, in *Chapter 2, Acing the Interview – Mastering Behavioral Questions and Interview Techniques,* we'll pivot from paperwork to interpersonal interactions. Prepare to delve into the nuances of interviewing, mastering the art of memorable responses, and navigating behavioral questions with poise.

2

Acing the Interview – Mastering Behavioral Questions and Interview Techniques

In this chapter, we will focus on the significance of interviews in the workplace and how individuals can effectively prepare and navigate them. Through training and practice, you will be able to confidently respond to behavior-based questions and learn best practices for visually presenting yourself. You'll learn how to dress professionally, make a strong first impression, and successfully conduct virtual or in-person interviews. These skills are extraordinarily useful in today's world of work, where the ability to proficiently conduct an interview could be the key to landing your desired job.

In this chapter, we're going to cover the following main topics:

- Types of interviews
- Introduction to virtual and in-person interviews
- Preparing for virtual or in-person interviews
- Confidently answering common and behavioral questions
- Post-interview actions

By the end of this chapter, you'll know how to ace interviews with confidence and turn your experience into an advantage!

Let's start with exploring the various types of interviews, understanding their unique formats and styles, and how they play a crucial role in assessing a candidate's qualifications and suitability for a job.

Types of interviews

Navigating the landscape of job interviews can be challenging, given the array of formats and styles an interviewer might employ. Broadly, these formats can be categorized into several types: structured interviews, unstructured interviews, behavioral interviews, situational interviews, stress interviews, panel interviews, group interviews, and case study interviews. Each type is designed with specific objectives in mind, intended to assess different aspects of a candidate's qualifications and fit for the role.

Let's delve into the specifics of each interview type and how you, as a candidate, can best prepare for them.

Structured interviews

These interviews offer a systematic approach to candidate evaluation. All candidates are asked the same set of questions, allowing for uniformity and fairness in the interview process. This format lends itself well to objective comparison among candidates.

With a pre-set list of questions, preparation for these interviews involves understanding the job role and the skills required thoroughly. Preparing answers to common questions, with an emphasis on your skills and achievements, can help you stand out.

Remember, each candidate gets the same questions, so your answers need to differentiate you from the competition.

Unstructured interviews

Taking a more conversational approach, unstructured interviews offer greater flexibility. The dialogue might evolve organically, depending on the candidate's responses. This method provides a deeper insight into a candidate's personality, critical thinking, and adaptability.

The free-flowing nature of these interviews necessitates adaptability and excellent conversational skills. Be prepared to discuss a range of topics, from your work experience to industry trends. These interviews can often feel like a professional chat, but remember, each interaction is an assessment.

Behavioral interviews

Rooted in the concept that past behavior predicts future performance, behavioral interviews focus on the candidate's past experiences. The interviewer will probe specific scenarios where the candidate has demonstrated key skills or qualities required for the role.

Preparing for these interviews involves reflecting on your past experiences and identifying examples that demonstrate your skills and qualities. The **Situation, Task, Action, Result (STAR)** method can be highly effective in structuring your responses for these interviews.

Situational interviews

Rather than looking back at past experiences, situational interviews focus on hypothetical scenarios. Candidates are asked to detail their approach to potential future situations, providing insights into their problem-solving capabilities and judgment.

You can prepare for these interviews by considering potential challenges or scenarios you might face in the role. You can showcase your problem-solving process and decision-making skills in your responses. It's less about getting the *correct* answer and more about showing your thought process.

Stress interviews

As the name suggests, these interviews are designed to assess how candidates handle pressure. Through challenging scenarios or rapid-fire questioning, interviewers evaluate a candidate's resilience and capacity to maintain composure under stress.

Mental preparation and resilience are key for these interviews. Practicing mindfulness and stress management techniques can be beneficial. Remember, the interviewer isn't trying to intimidate you – they are trying to assess your resilience and composure.

Panel interviews

These interviews involve multiple interviewers, each with their own area of focus or expertise. This format allows for a comprehensive evaluation from different perspectives within the organization. For these interviews, remember that each interviewer represents a different perspective. Engage with all interviewers, maintain eye contact, and address your answers to everyone. Knowing your audience and adapting your answers to each interviewer's focus can be very effective.

Group interviews

Conducted with multiple candidates simultaneously, group interviews are often used for roles where teamwork is critical. They offer an opportunity to assess a candidate's interaction style, leadership abilities, and teamwork skills in a group dynamic.

Active listening and respectful interaction with other candidates can help you stand out in a group interview. Be a team player, but also look for opportunities to demonstrate leadership. Balancing between not dominating the conversation and not fading into the background is crucial.

Case study interviews

Particularly popular in consulting roles, case study interviews present a business problem to be solved on the spot. This approach tests a candidate's analytical thinking, problem-solving skills, and practical application of their knowledge.

Preparation for these interviews should involve practicing with similar case studies. Highlight your thought process and analysis, not just the final solution. Clear communication, logically structuring your points, and time management are also essential in these interviews.

This concludes our detailed discussion on the various types of interviews and the specialized strategies you can employ to excel in each one.

These strategies can supplement the interview preparation process and improve your performance significantly. By mastering these areas, you can navigate the C# developer interview process more confidently and effectively. In the next section, we will learn about the two most common forms of interview today: virtual and in-person interviews.

Introduction to virtual and in-person interviews

In today's digital age, virtual interviews have become the norm in the hiring process. They present a unique set of challenges, from ensuring a stable internet connection to setting up a professional, distraction-free background. In these interviews, mastering the art of conveying your personality and skills through a screen is vital. It's important to test your technology beforehand and ensure you're familiar with the platform being used.

On the other hand, in-person interviews, while more traditional, are no less demanding. They call for a keen understanding of professional etiquette, from the firmness of your handshake to the appropriateness of your attire. With in-person interviews, you need to be mindful of non-verbal communication cues, punctuality, and navigation of the interview location.

Let's take a look at these two types in detail.

Virtual interviews

The rise of remote work has increased the prevalence of virtual interviews. For these, it's crucial to ensure your technology is in good working order. Test your microphone, camera, and internet connection beforehand to circumvent any technical glitches that might disrupt the smooth flow of the interview. If possible, have a backup device ready.

In a virtual setting, your on-camera presence is integral. Remember, the camera captures only your upper body, but that doesn't mean you should neglect your appearance below the waistline. Dressing professionally from head to toe can not only bolster your confidence but also keep you prepared for unexpected situations, such as needing to stand up during the interview.

When choosing your interview outfit, avoid bright colors or patterns that might be distracting on camera. Opt for neutral tones that come across as more professional and are less likely to clash with your surroundings. Pay attention to your background too – ensure it is tidy and uncluttered as it contributes to the overall impression you present. If possible, opt for a neutral backdrop.

Location is another key aspect of preparing for a virtual interview. Choose a quiet, well-lit location free from possible interruptions – noises or people walking around can distract both you and the interviewer. Make sure the room has ample natural or artificial light to ensure you're visible.

While the comfort of home might make a virtual interview seem less formal, it's crucial to maintain a professional demeanor, just as you would in an in-person interview. Remember to look into the camera when speaking as this simulates direct eye contact. Make sure you mute yourself when you're not speaking to minimize any potential background noise.

Finally, don't forget to prepare your notes and resources. One advantage of virtual interviews is that you can have your resume, cover letter, job description, and any notes right in front of you. Just make sure your eyes aren't constantly shifting away from the camera to look at them.

Virtual interviews might be a relatively new format, but with the right preparation, you can make a lasting impression, proving that distance doesn't have to be a barrier to showcasing your skills and professionalism.

In-person interviews

In-person interviews, although more traditional, require an equally meticulous level of preparation. One of the first considerations should be your arrival time. Aim to arrive early, ideally 10-15 minutes before the scheduled time. This allows you to find the location, deal with unforeseen circumstances such as traffic or parking, gather your thoughts, and walk into the interview feeling composed and unrushed.

Ensure that you bring along multiple copies of your resume, a list of references, and any other relevant documents. This not only demonstrates your preparedness but also provides you with a quick reference point during the interview. It also allows you to provide the interviewer with any documents they might not have at hand.

When it comes to attire for in-person interviews, the key is to dress appropriately for the company culture. If you're unsure about the company's dress code, it's better to err on the side of being overdressed than underdressed. Business professional attire is a safe choice for most interviews. For men, this typically includes a suit and tie, while for women, it can be a suit, professional dress, or skirt and blouse. Regardless of gender, ensure your clothes are clean, wrinkle-free, and in good condition.

Remember, your attire is a reflection of your professionalism and attention to detail and can set the tone for the interview. Avoid overly flashy colors and accessories, opting instead for more conservative, neutral tones. Also, personal grooming should not be neglected. Neat hair, trimmed nails, and subtle cologne or perfume can complement your professional look.

In an in-person interview, your non-verbal cues are as important as your verbal responses. Maintain eye contact, offer a firm handshake, and maintain good posture throughout the interview. These non-verbal cues can express confidence and respect toward the interviewer.

Finally, in an in-person interview, your interaction with everyone you meet matters – from the receptionist to the CEO. Be courteous to everyone as their feedback might play a part in the hiring decision.

With the right preparation and mindset, an in-person interview can be a great opportunity to make a strong impression and showcase not only your skills but also your demeanor, professionalism, and cultural fit within the company.

With this overview of virtual and in-person interviews, let's take a look at some key steps in the preparation process for these interviews.

Preparing for virtual or in-person interviews

Navigating the world of job interviews can be a daunting task. Whether the interview is virtual or in-person, each type comes with its own set of expectations and nuances. However, careful preparation can drastically increase your chances of success, and this starts with understanding what to expect.

Regardless of the format, thoroughly researching the company and role you're applying for is a must. This will allow you to tailor your responses to show how your skills and experience align with what the company is seeking. Moreover, anticipating common interview questions and practicing your responses will help you present your thoughts clearly and confidently.

It's also crucial to prepare thoughtful questions for your interviewer. This demonstrates your genuine interest in the position and gives you a chance to determine if the company is the right fit for you.

In the end, remember that an interview is a two-way process. It's not only about proving your worth to the company but also about assessing if the company and role align with your career goals and values. So, prepare, practice, and walk into every interview with confidence and poise.

Let's dive deeper and discover this process more carefully.

Overcoming interview anxiety

Interviews, especially for high-stakes C# developer roles, can be anxiety-inducing. Therefore, strategies for managing this stress can be invaluable. Breathing exercises can help maintain composure, and visualization techniques can boost confidence. Furthermore, adequate preparation and practice can reduce anxiety significantly. Remember, it's perfectly acceptable to take a moment to gather your thoughts during the interview. An interviewer will appreciate thought-out answers more than hasty responses.

Presenting yourself

Presentation extends far beyond your choice of attire – it encompasses your total demeanor, including body language and communication skills, which can leave a lasting impression on the interviewer. Being mindful of these subtleties can communicate confidence, professionalism, and respect – key attributes that interviewers often seek in potential candidates.

Eye contact is one of the most fundamental aspects of non-verbal communication. Maintaining appropriate eye contact shows the interviewer that you're engaged, interested, and respectful. However, remember that there is a fine line between maintaining eye contact and staring. The aim is to create a connection, not make the other person uncomfortable.

Handshakes can be a quick gauge of your confidence level. A firm handshake – not too tight, not too limp – can convey confidence and assertiveness. Remember to wait for the interviewer to extend their hand first, and make sure your hands are dry and clean. A smile, combined with a confident handshake, can set a positive tone for the rest of the interview.

Posture can also speak volumes about your self-confidence and attentiveness. Sit up straight, but ensure your posture is comfortable and not overly stiff. This displays your interest and enthusiasm in the conversation. Leaning slightly forward can also show that you're actively engaged and interested in the conversation.

Be aware of any nervous habits you may have, such as fidgeting, hair twirling, or leg shaking, as these can be distracting and may convey nervousness or lack of preparedness. Practicing mindful awareness can help you recognize and control these habits.

In addition to non-verbal cues, verbal communication plays a significant role in presenting yourself. Speak clearly and at an appropriate volume. Avoid using jargon or slang and try to articulate your thoughts as succinctly and coherently as possible. Practice active listening, which involves paying full attention to the interviewer, and responding appropriately to their questions.

Finally, remember that presentation is not a one-time thing that ends when the interview concludes. Be sure to follow up with a thank-you note or email, expressing your gratitude for the opportunity. This not only reaffirms your interest in the position but also demonstrates your courtesy and professionalism.

By being mindful of these aspects, you can present yourself as a confident, engaging, and respectful candidate, thereby increasing your chances of making a positive, lasting impression.

Subtleties of non-verbal communication

Non-verbal cues often communicate more than words during an interview. While we briefly touched upon body language earlier, a detailed analysis of this aspect can greatly enhance your interview performance. Good posture indicates confidence and interest while maintaining eye contact displays attentiveness. Similarly, controlled facial expressions can portray a composed and professional demeanor. Learning to use gestures effectively can add emphasis to your words and indicate enthusiasm. However, being a C# developer interview, ensure your hand gestures don't distract from the code or diagrams you might need to explain.

Understanding the company and role

Irrespective of the type of interview, an essential part of your preparation should involve thorough research about the company and the role you're applying for. This understanding can help you align your skills and experiences with what the company is seeking, enabling you to frame your answers effectively during the interview.

Start with the company's website – delve into their mission statement, history, products or services, and company culture. Companies often share their core values and strategic goals on their website, which can provide valuable insights into what they might be looking for in an employee. Understanding these aspects will help you speak confidently about why you are a good fit for the organization.

Apart from the company's website, investigate recent news or press releases about the company. Has the company recently launched a new product or service? Have they been featured in any noteworthy articles or events? Being able to discuss recent company news during the interview not only shows that you've done your homework but also demonstrates your genuine interest in the organization.

In addition to understanding the company, gaining a deep understanding of the role is just as important. Go beyond the job description – seek to understand how this role contributes to the larger goals of the company. What expectations and responsibilities are associated with this role? What skills and experiences is the company seeking for this position?

Connect your skills and experiences to the role's requirements. Consider specific instances where you have demonstrated these skills or met similar expectations. Being able to discuss these examples in the interview will demonstrate your readiness for the role.

Also, investigate the industry in which the company operates. Familiarize yourself with industry trends, challenges, and opportunities. This will not only equip you to discuss the company's positioning within the industry but also highlight your broader awareness of the business environment in which the company operates.

Remember, thorough research and understanding will set you apart from other candidates. It showcases your dedication, initiative, and interest in both the role and the company. Furthermore, it gives you the ability to ask thoughtful questions of the interviewer, turning the interview into a two-way conversation and demonstrating your proactive engagement.

Anticipating interview questions

While it's impossible to know every question you'll be asked in an interview, part of your preparation should involve anticipating and formulating responses to frequently asked questions. These usually revolve around your strengths, weaknesses, prior experiences, and why you are interested in the specific role and company. Develop thoughtful, authentic responses to these questions, including real-life examples from your past experiences to provide depth and context.

To become more comfortable with your responses, consider practicing them out loud. You can do this with a friend, mentor, or even in front of a mirror. Not only does this help you familiarize yourself with articulating your thoughts, but it also provides you with an opportunity to refine your answers and improve your overall presentation skills.

Next, anticipate the possibility of behavioral interview questions. These are designed to delve into your past behavior in specific situations to infer how you might respond to similar scenarios in the future. You might hear phrases such as, *Tell me about a time when...* or *Can you describe a situation where...* These questions aim to uncover your problem-solving skills, decision-making process, and your approach to handling challenges.

A common technique for answering these questions is the **STAR** method. The **STAR** method is about telling a story. That means it needs to have a beginning, middle, and end. By using this method, you can provide a clear, concise, and easy-to-follow narrative that effectively showcases your skills, abilities, and experiences.

Finally, remember that an interview is not just about answering questions but also about asking questions. Prepare a set of thoughtful questions about the role, the team, and the company to ask at the end of the interview. This will underline your interest and enthusiasm and give you a better understanding of what it would be like to work there.

By preparing in this way for both virtual and in-person interviews, you empower yourself with the knowledge and confidence necessary for a successful interview process. The goal is not merely to answer questions, but to engage in a constructive two-way conversation. This approach enables you to showcase your suitability for the role while simultaneously learning more about the company and the team, thereby asserting your value as a prospective employee.

Making a strong first impression

Whether in-person or virtual, first impressions during interviews are crucial. As the adage goes, *you never get a second chance to make a first impression*. Beyond your chosen attire, your demeanor, how you carry yourself, and the way you interact from the very beginning will set the tone for the whole process.

In virtual interviews, your first impression starts from the moment your camera turns on. Ensure your technology works correctly, your video and audio are clear, and your internet connection is stable. Address any potential technical issues in advance to avoid last-minute stress and distractions. This demonstrates your professionalism and respect for the interviewer's time.

Your virtual environment also contributes to your first impression. Choose a clean, uncluttered, and well-lit space to conduct your interview. A tidy background not only minimizes distractions but also conveys your organization and attentiveness to detail.

During the interview, whether virtual or in-person, remember to be courteous to every person you interact with, from the receptionist to the hiring manager. Genuine interest in what others say and good manners can reflect positively on your interpersonal skills. Every interaction, no matter how brief, adds to the overall impression you make.

When you meet the interviewer, greet them warmly and express appreciation for the opportunity to interview for the role. In a virtual setting, maintaining eye contact can be a bit tricky, but try to look into the camera when you are speaking or listening. This is equivalent to maintaining eye contact in an in-person setting and it shows you are engaged and respectful.

Active listening is another vital component of creating a positive first impression. Show genuine interest when the interviewer is speaking by nodding where appropriate, maintaining eye contact, and offering thoughtful responses. This conveys that you're fully engaged and respect the interviewer's input.

Body language is also important, even in a virtual setting. Maintain an upright posture and avoid fidgeting or making distracting movements. These non-verbal cues communicate confidence and enthusiasm for the role.

As we move forward to the next section, we'll explore how to confidently answer common and behavioral interview questions, preparing you to shine in any interview scenario. Remember, the impression you make isn't solely about your responses; your preparation, presentation, and conduct all significantly contribute to creating that solid first impression. This strong impression paves the way for a successful interview, increasing your chances of securing the job.

Confidently answering common and behavioral questions

When you've diligently prepared for the interview, presented yourself professionally, and established a positive first impression, the next major aspect to address is answering the interview questions with confidence. Interviewers typically pose a mix of common and behavioral questions to assess your professional abilities, gauge your personality and work ethic, and understand how you would respond in certain workplace scenarios.

Common interview questions are generally straightforward and revolve around your skills, qualifications, experiences, and interest in the role or the company. For example, *Why are you interested in this role?* or *Can you tell me about a project that you're particularly proud of?* To answer these questions confidently, make sure you understand the job description thoroughly, research the company, and reflect on your past experiences that align with the role's requirements. Have specific examples ready to demonstrate your skills and achievements and ensure that your answers reflect your enthusiasm for the role and the company.

Behavioral interview questions, on the other hand, are designed to uncover how you have handled certain situations in the past, providing insights into how you might perform in similar circumstances in the future.

Some typical behavioral interview questions include, *Have you ever encountered a challenging coworker? Can you share that experience? Describe an instance where you had to complete a task within a stringent timeline.*

For confident responses to behavioral queries, apply the STAR method – a framework that offers a structured approach to showcase your problem-solving skills and results. For a more detailed understanding of this beneficial technique, please refer to *The STAR method* section.

Remember, your confidence comes from preparation and practice. By anticipating the common and behavioral questions and preparing thoughtful responses, you'll be well-equipped to handle any question that comes your way during the interview.

Common interview questions

Common interview questions provide a broad spectrum of information about your qualifications, your interest in the role, your work ethic, and your approach to professional challenges. Some typical examples are as follows:

- *Can you tell me a little about yourself?*
- *Why are you interested in this role?*
- *What are your greatest strengths?*
- *What is a challenge you've faced at work, and how did you deal with it?*
- *Can you describe a situation in which you showed initiative?*
- *Where do you see yourself in 5 years?*
- *How do you handle feedback and criticism?*
- *Why did you leave (or why are you leaving) your last job?*
- *Could you provide an instance where you were faced with a tough decision-making situation in your professional environment?*

To confidently tackle these queries, you should craft precise, thoughtful responses well in advance. Remember that your answers should focus on the skills, experiences, and accomplishments that are most pertinent to the job you're targeting.

When asked about yourself, aim to provide a brief overview of your professional background, highlighting experiences and skills that make you a strong candidate for the role. The goal is not to recite your resume, but to give the interviewer a snapshot of your professional journey and why you're a good fit for the position.

If you're asked why you're interested in the role, discuss what attracted you to the job and how it aligns with your career aspirations. Show your knowledge about the company and the role, and connect it to your skills, values, or passions. This shows the interviewer not only that you've done your homework, but also that you're genuinely interested in the opportunity.

When discussing your greatest strengths, pick qualities that are most relevant to the job and provide specific examples that demonstrate these strengths. This provides concrete proof of your skills and reinforces your credibility.

These questions probe further into your problem-solving abilities, your long-term career aspirations, how you deal with feedback, your reasons for job changes, and your decision-making skills.

To address the question about showing initiative, choose an example where you went above and beyond the expectations of your role to achieve a result. This could be a situation where you identified a problem and took the lead in finding a solution, or when you proposed an innovative idea that had a positive impact on your team or the organization.

When asked about your future aspirations, be honest but also align your ambitions with the role and the company. This shows the interviewer that you're looking at this position as a long-term opportunity and not just as a stepping stone.

In response to how you handle feedback and criticism, share an instance where you received constructive criticism and how you used it for self-improvement. This shows your ability to accept feedback gracefully and your commitment to personal and professional development.

If asked why you're leaving or why you left your last job, be honest and professional. Don't speak negatively about your previous employer or colleagues. Instead, focus on the new opportunities and potential for growth that the job you're interviewing for presents.

For the question about making a difficult decision, choose a scenario that illustrates your sound judgment, analytical skills, and ability to navigate complex situations. Briefly outline the situation, describe the options you considered, and explain why you chose the route you took.

Finally, when asked about a challenge you've faced at work, choose a situation that allowed you to demonstrate problem-solving skills and resilience. Describe the issue clearly, explain your approach to resolving it, and highlight the positive outcome or lessons learned. This will show the interviewer your ability to overcome adversity and learn from experience.

The key to successfully answering these common questions lies in being authentic, prepared, and directly related to the job requirements. Be sure to practice these responses, as this will help you articulate your thoughts more clearly during the actual interview.

Behavioral interview questions

Behavioral interview questions focus on how you've handled specific situations in the past, as this is often the best predictor of how you'll behave in the future. Here are a few more examples:

- *Tell me about a time when you had to solve a complex coding problem. How did you do it?*
- *Tell me about a time when you had to work with other developers on a project. How did you collaborate with them?*
- *Tell me about a time when you had to test and debug code. What methods did you use?*
- *Tell me about a time when you had to document code. What methods did you use?*
- *Tell me about a time when you had to work with a difficult client who kept changing their project requirements. How did you manage to interact with them?*
- *Tell me about a time when you had to make a decision about a project. What factors did you consider?*

- *Tell me about a time when you had to learn a new piece of equipment or technology. How did you do it?*

- *Tell me about a time when you had to work under pressure. How did you handle it?*

- *Tell me about a time when you had to resolve a conflict. How did you do it?*

It's important to note that each of these questions requires a different set of skills and competencies, and how you answer them provides the interviewer with insights into your suitability for the role. You will need to dig deep into your past experiences to provide meaningful answers.

In the next section, we'll break down how to use the STAR method to structure your responses to the aforementioned behavioral questions, ensuring you provide clear, concise, and comprehensive answers that demonstrate your skills and abilities effectively.

The STAR method

The **STAR** method is an invaluable tool for addressing behavioral interview questions, allowing you to give comprehensive, thoughtfully structured answers. This method not only helps ensure that you're providing all necessary information but also allows your responses to showcase how your skills and experiences make you the best candidate for the position. Let's take a look at each attribute in detail:

- **Situation**: Set the scene and provide the necessary details about a specific situation or challenge you've faced – for example, *At my previous company, we were on a tight deadline to deliver a project to a key client, but midway, one of our team members fell sick.*

- **Task**: Next, explain your responsibilities in that particular situation. It could be, *As the team leader, it was my responsibility to ensure the project was completed on time without compromising on the quality of work.*

- **Action**: This is the core of your answer. Describe in detail the specific actions you took to address the situation – for instance, *I reassigned the tasks of the sick team member among the rest of the team and also took on some of his tasks. I ensured clear communication with all members about the changes and recalibrated our work schedule to meet the deadline.*

- **Result**: Conclude your answer by discussing the outcomes of your actions – for example, *We managed to deliver the project on time, maintaining the high-quality standards we pride ourselves on. The client was delighted, and we secured an ongoing relationship with them.*

Applying the STAR method when answering behavioral interview questions can help you paint a vivid picture of your professional experiences. This helps the interviewer understand not only your skills and capabilities but also how you apply these skills in real-world situations.

By thoroughly preparing responses to potential interview questions using the STAR method, you will be able to demonstrate your ability to handle different situations. You'll show the interviewer how you think, how you operate under pressure, and ultimately why you are the best candidate for the job.

Now, armed with these tactics and strategies, you are well prepared to shine in any interview, tackling behavioral questions with confidence and creating a strong, positive impression. Remember, every interview brings you one step closer to your career goals, so embrace the process, prepare diligently, and always learn from each experience.

Utilizing the STAR method for responding to behavioral interview queries not only helps depict your professional journey vividly but also gives interviewers insights into your skills and their practical application. This preparation allows you to showcase your thought process, how you respond under stress, and why you're the ideal fit for the role. With these strategies, you're set to excel in interviews, respond to behavioral questions with assurance, and make a lasting impression. Now, let's dive into some STAR examples for a more concrete understanding.

STAR examples

This section provides practical examples that illustrate the application of the STAR method. We will explore real-world scenarios that are typically presented in interviews, and I'll demonstrate how to effectively structure responses using the STAR framework. These examples will shed light on how to address complex situations, such as dealing with difficult team members, meeting stringent deadlines, making critical decisions, and much more.

Each example aims to showcase the ideal way to encapsulate your experiences, from detailing the context and your responsibilities to your actions and the subsequent outcomes. These scenarios are designed to provide you with a clear, step-by-step guide on how to apply the STAR method effectively in your interview preparation.

Let's begin by examining a common scenario that many professionals encounter – dealing with a difficult team member. This example, along with others in this chapter, should equip you with the necessary tools to confidently navigate similar situations in your interviews:

- *Tell me about a time when you had to solve a complex coding problem. How did you do it?*

  - **Situation**: I was working on a project to develop a new algorithm for image recognition. The algorithm was working well for most images, but it was failing for a small number of images. I needed to figure out why the algorithm was failing and fix the problem.

  - **Task**: My task was to identify the bug in the algorithm and fix it.

  - **Action**: I started by debugging the code. I looked for errors in the logic and the implementation. I also ran the algorithm on a variety of test images to see if I could reproduce the problem. After debugging the code, I still couldn't find the bug. I decided to try a different approach: I used a debugger to step through the code line by line. This allowed me to see exactly what the code was doing and where it was failing. Finally, I found the bug. It was a small mistake in the logic of the algorithm. I fixed the mistake and the algorithm started working correctly for all of the images.

  - **Result**: I was able to solve the problem and the algorithm was working correctly for all of the images. I learned a lot from this experience, and I improved my debugging skills.

- *Tell me about a time when you had to work with other developers on a project. How did you collaborate with them?*

  - **Situation**: At XYZ Software Solutions, I was part of a team of four developers tasked with designing a new feature for our flagship product. We faced challenges in ensuring our code didn't conflict and integrating different parts seamlessly.

  - **Task**: My specific role was to create the feature's core logic while collaborating with teammates handling the UI, database, and testing.

  - **Action**: To ensure smooth collaboration, we set up a shared Git repository. Before diving into coding, we held a joint session to define our interfaces and expectations clearly. Whenever a developer felt a feature might have side effects on others' tasks, we held quick sync-ups to realign. Continuous code reviews were conducted to ensure we all understood the entirety of the code base.

  - **Result**: Through regular communication, code reviews, and collaborative tools, we launched the feature a week ahead of schedule with fewer bugs than previous releases. This experience underscored the importance of open communication and proactive coordination in team projects.

- *Tell me about a time when you had to work with a difficult client who kept changing their project requirements. How did you manage to interact with them?*

  - **Situation**: At my previous job at ABC Software Solutions, we were building a C# desktop application for a client named XYZ Corp. However, they kept revising their specifications and features for the application after we had already begun development.

  - **Task**: My role was to implement the core functionalities of the application, while also ensuring that the changing requirements did not derail our development timeline or affect the quality of the product.

  - **Action**: I initiated a technical meeting with the client to better understand and prioritize the changing requirements. I employed version control rigorously, making use of branches in Git to handle different feature requests, ensuring that our main development branch remained stable. I modularized the application using OOP principles, ensuring that making changes in one section had minimal effects on others. For each change request, I drafted a technical document detailing how the change would impact the current architecture, the additional time needed, and any potential risks. This helped the client understand the implications of their requests.

  - **Result**: With clear communication and structured coding practices, we managed to integrate most of the client's changes without compromising the project timeline significantly. The final application was well-received by XYZ Corp., and they expressed their appreciation for our team's flexibility and transparency. This project reinforced the importance of agile development practices and effective client communication for me as a developer.

These examples are intended to be adapted to your specific experiences. Remember, the STAR method allows you to demonstrate that you can draw on your experiences and transferable skills to meet new challenges. The more you practice using this method, the easier it becomes to structure your responses effectively in an interview scenario.

Being able to handle questions confidently is an essential part of the interview process, but it's not the only aspect. An interview is a two-way street. It's also your opportunity to figure out if the role and the company are a good fit for you. That's where asking your own questions comes into play. It shows your interest in the position and can provide you with valuable insights.

In the next section, we'll discuss asking your own questions during an interview, its significance, and how you can frame insightful questions to make an informed decision about your potential new job.

Asking your own questions

An interview is not just about answering questions – it's also an opportunity for you to learn more about the role and the company. This exchange of information is vital as it not only provides you with a better understanding of the job and the organization but also demonstrates to your interviewer that you have a genuine interest in the role and have taken the initiative to delve deeper.

By preparing and asking thoughtful questions, you can engage more profoundly with your interviewer and distinguish yourself from other candidates. Here are some examples of the questions you might consider:

- *Can you describe a typical day in this role?*

  This question can give you a realistic idea about what your day-to-day responsibilities would look like.

- *What are the growth opportunities for this position?*

  By asking this, you can gauge the scope for personal development and career progression within the company.

- *Can you tell me about the company culture here?*

  This helps you understand the workplace environment and values, and if they align with your own.

- *How would you describe the team I'll be working with?*

  This gives you an insight into the dynamics of the team you'd be joining. Are they collaborative, independent, creative, or analytical? This can impact how you fit into the group.

You may also consider asking more specific questions about the challenges and projects that you might undertake in the role:

- *What are the most immediate projects that need to be addressed in this job?*

- *What kind of obstacles/challenges has the team faced in recent projects and how did they overcome them?*

- *Can you share some examples of the most successful projects that the person in this position would be involved in?*

Asking for feedback during the interview can show your openness to learn and grow. These types of questions also demonstrate your interest in personal improvement and the value you place on constructive criticism. However, do keep in mind that these should be asked thoughtfully, and you should be prepared for honest answers. Here are a few *feedback*-type questions that you might consider:

- *Given what you know about me from my resume and this interview, how well do you think I would fit in this role and your company's culture?*

- *Are there any skills or experiences you think I'm missing for this role?*

- *Based on our conversation today, what aspects of my background do you feel would benefit this role and the team the most?*

- *Do you have any reservations about my fit for this role that I could address?*

Asking these types of questions not only shows your eagerness to improve but also gives you a chance to address any concerns the interviewer might have on the spot. This can help you leave a positive and lasting impression.

As with all your questions, ensure they're asked sincerely and you're ready to listen to and learn from the responses. This way, the interview becomes a constructive two-way conversation, rather than a one-sided assessment.

All these questions will not only help you determine whether the company and the role are a good fit for your career aspirations and working style but also show the interviewer that you've done your research and are proactive and interested in the role and the company.

> **Note**
>
> Remember, interviews are not just for employers to learn about you, but also for you to learn about your potential employer.

Managing challenging queries

There may be times during your interview for a C# developer position when you encounter complicated questions. For instance, you might have to explain gaps in your employment history, discuss a situation where you were let go from a previous job, or address an absence of direct experience with a specific C# framework or technology. In such scenarios, honesty and framing your experiences positively are key. Discuss how you utilized employment gaps for self-improvement, learning, or skill enhancement. If you were let go from a job, focus on what the experience taught you and how it has shaped your professional growth. If you lack direct experience in a specific area, highlight your eagerness to learn, adapt, and leverage your existing C# knowledge to quickly come up to speed.

Post-interview actions

After the interview process, your responsibility doesn't immediately cease. It's crucial to follow up with a thank-you message to the interviewers, expressing your gratitude for considering you for the role. This step further underlines your professionalism and reiterates your interest in the C# developer position.

In the follow-up message, succinctly convey your thanks, mention an insightful point you gathered from the interview, and restress your keenness for the role. However, remember to keep it brief – this isn't the moment to pen down a lengthy justification for why they should select you.

Once you've done this, spend some time reflecting on the interview. Analyze the inquiries that were posed and your responses to them, and note down areas you could enhance for upcoming interviews.

Every interview you participate in serves as a valuable learning experience, aiding you in honing your approach and fostering greater self-assuredness. By mastering these interview techniques and preparing for behavioral questions specifically tailored for C# developers, you're paving your way toward acing the interview and securing your sought-after job.

In addition to the thank-you note, there are other steps you can take post-interview to enhance your prospects:

- **Connect on professional networks**: If appropriate, you might consider connecting with the interviewer or other relevant individuals you've met at the company on professional networking platforms, such as LinkedIn. This could be another way to keep yourself on the company's radar and expand your professional network.

- **Maintain patience**: After the interview, you may experience a waiting period before you hear back regarding the decision. It's important to be patient and keep a positive outlook during this time. Remember, the hiring process can take time, especially if the company is conducting multiple interviews.

- **Keep applying**: Until you have a confirmed job offer, keep your job search active. Apply to other roles that align with your skills and interests as a C# developer. This not only keeps your options open but can also potentially provide additional interview practice.

- **Continue learning**: Use the time after your interview to continue learning and growing your skills. Whether this means deepening your knowledge of certain frameworks or languages, building a new project for your portfolio, or learning new problem-solving techniques, the steps you take to continue your professional growth can make you an even stronger candidate for the next opportunity.

With these strategies, you can effectively follow up your interview and make a lasting positive impression on the interviewers, improving your chances of landing your desired role as a C# developer.

Summary

We looked at various interview types, including structured, unstructured, and behavioral, focusing on how to effectively prepare for each. We also delved into the details of virtual and in-person interviews, discussing their key differences and preparation strategies.

As a C# developer candidate, your mastery of these approaches is only part of the equation. You also need a strong understanding of C# programming principles – and that's what we'll dive into next.

In *Chapters 3* to *5*, we will transition from the interpersonal aspect of the interview process to the technical aspect, starting with the fundamentals of C#. This part of this book is designed to reinforce and deepen your understanding of the core principles of C# programming, allowing you to tackle any technical question confidently.

Advice on answering common and behavioral questions confidently was highlighted, along with tips on professional presentation and making a strong first impression. The chapter concluded with the importance of post-interview actions, emphasizing their role in showing professionalism and interest in the role. By the end, readers are equipped to approach interviews with confidence and turn their experiences into advantages.

In *Chapter 3, Acing the Interview – Mastering Behavioral Questions and Interview Techniques*, we will explore the building blocks of C#, from essential concepts and principles to data types, variables, operators, control structures, loops, and the bedrock of modern C# - object-oriented programming. Whether you're a beginner just getting started or an experienced developer looking to refresh your knowledge, this chapter will provide you with a comprehensive understanding of the fundamentals.

So, get ready to dive deep into the world of C# programming. It's time to switch gears and get technical!

Part 2: Technical Interview Preparation

This part covers technical interview preparation, focusing on mastering C# from its core principles to its more complex features. This part guides you through the practical implementation of design patterns and best practices, as well as exploring libraries, frameworks, and MAUI. Strategies for excelling in coding challenges and technical interviews are explored, along with advice on soft skill development and networking.

This part has the following chapters:

- *Chapter 3, Fundamentals of C# Programming*

- *Chapter 4, Advanced C# Concepts*

- *Chapter 5, Fundamentals Governing Maintainable and Efficient C# Programming*

- *Chapter 6, Deep Dive into C# Libraries, Frameworks, and Technical Interview Preparation*

- *Chapter 7, Overcoming Challenges in C# Technical Interviews and Tips for Tackling Coding Challenges during Interviews*

- *Chapter 8, Building Soft Skills and Expanding Your Network*

3

Fundamentals of C# Programming

Welcome to *Chapter 3*, where we shall dive into the heart of technical interviews, specifically focusing on the fundamentals of C# programming. C# is a widely adopted, robust, and versatile language, used across various domains, including but not limited to game development, web services, and enterprise-level software.

Grasping the essentials of a programming language such as C# is crucial to excel in technical interviews. In this chapter, we will walk you through the vital principles of C#, commencing with essential concepts, data types, variables, and operators, and swiftly move to control structures and loops. Our aim is not just to acquaint you with the syntax but to also ensure that you comprehend the logic behind it, enabling you to write effective and clean code.

Furthermore, we shall delve into the basics of **object-oriented programming** (**OOP**) using C#. Understanding OOP allows you to design and manage complex applications, a skill that is greatly appreciated in the tech industry.

By the end of this chapter, you will possess a solid foundation in C# programming. This knowledge will empower you to confidently tackle coding challenges and demonstrate your problem-solving abilities during technical interviews. This chapter is designed to provide you with a balanced mix of theoretical understanding and practical exercises, thereby ensuring you can apply the learned concepts effectively.

In this chapter, we're going to cover the following main topics:

- Essential C# concepts and principles
- Working with data types, variables, and operators in C#
- Writing control structures and loops in C#
- Exploring the basics of OOP using C#

Essential C# concepts and principles

In this section, we aim to help you deepen your understanding of fundamental C# principles, enabling you to confidently answer the related questions you may encounter during technical interviews. This section is designed as a Q&A in which we will tackle potential interview questions covering a range of topics, from the basics of the C# syntax to key concepts of OOP in C#. We believe this interactive approach will help reinforce your knowledge and prepare you effectively for real-world interview scenarios.

Let's dive in and start exploring the questions you might face and how to approach answering them effectively.

What does the C# language represent, and for which platforms and applications is it intended?

C# is a programming language created by Microsoft and part of the .NET platform. With C#, a variety of applications can be developed, such as desktop applications, web applications, mobile applications, gaming applications (via Unity), cloud computing solutions, and more. C# is supported across various platforms thanks to .NET Core and Xamarin.

What's the fundamental difference between .dll and .exe files in the context of C# projects?

In the context of C# and .NET, an .exe (**executable**) file is an executable that contains an entry point for the program. In other words, when you run an .exe file, the program starts its execution. On the other hand, a .dll (**dynamic-link library**) file is a code library that doesn't have a direct entry point but can be called by another program or application. It's a means of code reuse among different projects.

How does the entry point of a program written in C# look?

The entry point in a C# program is typically represented by the Main() method, which is located in the Program class. This method must be static and serves as the starting point for the program's execution. Usually, its structure looks like this:

```
public class Program
{
    public static void Main(string[] args)
    {
        // program code
    }
}
```

The args argument contains an array of strings that is passed to the program upon its launch.

How is memory management conducted in C#?

In C#, memory management is handled automatically thanks to the **garbage collector** mechanism. It automatically identifies objects that are no longer used by the program and frees the memory they occupy. While the garbage collector simplifies memory management, developers need to carefully manage unmanaged resources that are not controlled by the .NET garbage collector, such as database connections or file streams. If developers do not release these resources, they will persist for the lifetime of the application, potentially causing memory leaks and system strain.

What are the principles of OOP in C#?

OOP is based on four main principles: encapsulation, inheritance, polymorphism, and abstraction. In C#, this means the following:

- **Encapsulation** allows data and methods to be bundled into a unit (class) and restricts access to certain components.

- **Inheritance** permits one class (the child or derived class) to inherit the attributes and methods of another class (the parent or base class). This promotes the reuse of code and establishes a hierarchical relationship between classes.

- **Polymorphism** is the capability of a single function or method to work in various ways based on its inputs or on which object it is called upon. In C#, polymorphism can be achieved through method overriding, using the `override` keyword, and method hiding, utilizing the `new` keyword to hide a method in the base class.

- **Abstraction** allows developers to hide complex implementations and show only the essential features of an object. This means that the user interacts with only what's necessary and the internal workings are kept hidden. In C#, abstract classes and interfaces are tools that can help achieve abstraction.

These principles help in designing robust and scalable applications, allowing for easy maintenance and further development. C# offers a rich set of features to implement and benefit from these principles effectively.

How is error handling done in C#?

In C#, the primary error handling mechanism is based on the use of `try`, `catch`, `finally`, and `throw` constructs. When code in a `try` block causes an error, execution jumps to the corresponding `catch` block, where the exception is handled. The `finally` block, if present, is typically executed after `try`/`catch`, regardless of whether there was an exception or not. However, there are critical exceptions, such as `StackOverflowException` or `OutOfMemoryException`, which can result in a program crash and thus the `finally` block won't be executed.

What does the dependency injection principle mean and how is it implemented in C#?

Dependency injection (**DI**) is a software design approach that reduces tight coupling between system components. At the core of DI is the passing of dependencies (services, objects) to components rather than creating them inside those components. In C# and .NET, DI is often implemented using dependency containers, such as *Microsoft.Extensions.DependencyInjection*, *Ninject*, *Autofac*, and others.

What are boxing and unboxing in C#, and why can they be a problem?

Boxing is the process of converting a value type (e.g., int) to an `object` type or any interface type implemented by that value type. **Unboxing** is the reverse process, where a value from an `object` type is converted back to the corresponding value type. The primary concern with boxing and unboxing in C# is their potential to degrade application performance. Boxing necessitates heap memory allocation and value type copying, thus slowing operations, especially with large datasets or in high-frequency scenarios. Unboxing, if incorrectly managed, can lead to runtime errors due to improper type casting, disrupting program execution. Additionally, these operations can increase the workload on the garbage collector, causing more frequent collection cycles and negatively impacting the application's responsiveness.

What does Entity Framework represent and how is it applied?

Entity Framework (**EF**) is an **object-relational mapping** (**ORM**) framework developed by Microsoft for the .NET ecosystem. It enables developers to work with databases using object models instead of writing direct SQL code. This tool simplifies the process of creating and managing data models, automating database schema migrations, and writing queries that make database interaction more intuitive.

What's the difference between threads and processes in C#?

In an operating system, a process is a distinct execution entity that has its own memory space. A thread is the smallest unit of execution within a process. Each process can have one or multiple threads. In C#, threads can be managed using the `Thread` class from the `System.Threading` namespace. The main difference lies in the fact that threads within a single process can share the same memory area, whereas each process has its own isolated memory context.

What are the main development environments used for C#, and are there alternatives to Visual Studio?

The main IDE for C# is Visual Studio from Microsoft. However, there are alternatives, such as Visual Studio Code (a lightweight code editor with support for C# extensions) and JetBrains Rider. Each environment has its own benefits and features, and the choice depends on the specific needs of the developer:

- **Visual Studio**:

  - *Features*: Comprehensive IDE with advanced tools for large-scale projects and multi-language support

  - *Use case*: Best suited for enterprise-level applications, offering a range of tools for collaborative and complex projects

- **Visual Studio Code**:

  - *Features*: Lightweight, open source code editor with a rich ecosystem of extensions, including C# support

  - *Use case*: Ideal for individual developers or small teams, providing a flexible and extensible environment for various languages and frameworks

- **JetBrains Rider**:

  - *Features*: Cross-platform .NET IDE with powerful tools for .NET development and a rich set of plugins

  - *Use case*: Excellent for cross-platform development, offering consistent experiences and high-quality code analysis and refactoring tools

What programming patterns do you know, and which ones have you implemented in C#?

Programming patterns are proven solutions for common development challenges. They indicate the optimal way to implement a specific task. In C#, I often use patterns such as *Singleton*, *Factory*, *Observer*, *Strategy*, and *Decorator*.

Can you describe different software testing methods and their primary differences?

There are several types of testing, including the following:

- **Unit testing**: Focuses on individual pieces of code, particularly functions or methods
- **Integration testing**: Checks the interaction between different parts of the software
- **System testing**: Tests the entire system

The main difference lies in the level of access and the scope of testing.

How do you determine the best time to conduct unit testing compared to integration or system testing?

Unit testing is best conducted during development when a specific component or function is being created or modified.

Integration testing should be applied after several components have been combined to verify their correct interaction.

System testing should be applied when the entire product or a significant portion of it is ready for release.

What is NuGet, and how can it be used to add libraries to your project?

NuGet is a package manager for the .NET platform that allows developers to easily add, update, and remove external libraries and dependencies in their projects. To add an external library to a project through NuGet, you need to open the NuGet console in the development environment (e.g., in Visual Studio) or use its graphical interface, find the desired package, and install it.

Having mastered the essential concepts and principles of C#, you've already taken a significant step toward understanding this powerful programming language. But the journey doesn't end here. Your next step is to delve into working with data types, variables, and operators in C#. Ready to continue? It's time to dive even deeper!

Working with data types, variables, and operators in C#

When diving into C#, it's essential to grasp data types, variables, and operators—they're the backbone of your applications. In this section, we'll explore these foundational elements, paving the way for more advanced coding. Ready to solidify your understanding? Let's dive in!

What are the basic primitive data types in C#? What is the main difference between value type and reference type?

In C#, there are primitive data types, such as `int`, `float`, `double`, `char`, `bool`, `byte`, and others. The main difference between the *value* type and *reference* type lies in how they are stored and how their memory management. Value types are stored on the stack and directly contain their value, while reference types are stored in the heap and contain a reference to the object in memory.

What is the primary distinction between string and StringBuilder in the context of strings?

The `string` type in C# is immutable, meaning every time the string is modified, a new instance is created. On the other hand, `StringBuilder` is designed for efficiently modifying strings without the need to create numerous new instances.

How do you initialize and interact with one-dimensional and multidimensional arrays? What differentiates "string[][]" from "string[,]"?

A one-dimensional array in C# is initialized like this: `int[] arr = new int[5];`. As for multidimensional arrays, `string[,]` is a two-dimensional array, while `string[][]` is an array of arrays, also known as a *jagged* array.

What are bitwise operations and which operators in C# support these operations?

Bitwise operations allow for manipulations at the level of individual bits of a numerical value. The primary bitwise operators in C# are & (*AND*), | (*OR*), ^ (*XOR*), and ~ (*NOT*).

What is the purpose of "nullable" types in C# and how do you work with them correctly?

`Nullable` types in C# allow representing an absent or uninitialized value for value types. They are typically used when there is a need to distinguish a *zero* value from the absence of a value. To check for the presence of a value, you can use the `HasValue` property, and to retrieve the value itself, you use `Value`.

What is known about operator overloading in C# and why can it be useful?

Operator overloading allows defining the actions of operators for user-defined data types, such as classes. This can be useful, for instance, for easy manipulation of complex numbers, vectors, or other mathematical structures.

How can one overload an operator in C# and could you provide an example?

In C#, operator overloading allows you to redefine the way built-in operators work for user-defined types such as classes and structs. To overload an operator, you define a static method in your class or struct with the `operator` keyword followed by the operator symbol you want to overload. The method must return a result and take at least one parameter of the type you're overloading the operator for.

Here's a simple example of overloading the + operator for a custom `Vector` class:

```
public class Vector
{
    public int X { get; set; }
    public int Y { get; set; }

    public Vector(int x, int y)
    {
        X = x;
        Y = y;
    }

    // Overload + operator
    public static Vector operator +(Vector v1, Vector v2)
    {
        return new Vector(v1.X + v2.X, v1.Y + v2.Y);
    }
}

// Usage:
Vector vector1 = new Vector(1, 2);
Vector vector2 = new Vector(2, 3);
Vector result = vector1 + vector2;   // This will call the overloaded +
operator
```

How do comparison and relational operators work in C#?

Comparison (==, !=) and relational (<, >, <=, >=) operators are used to compare two values. It's important to remember that when comparing reference types, the == operator checks for reference equality, not content.

What is the purpose of logical operators in C#, how do they function, and why is it important to pay attention to operator precedence?

Logical operators, such as && (*logical "and"*), || (*logical "or"*), and ! (*logical negation*), are used for combined logical conditions. It's important to know operator precedence as it affects the order of operations. For example, the expression A && B || C will be interpreted as (A && B) || C, not A && (B || C), which can lead to different results.

When and why should you use "const" variables in C#? What's the difference between them and "readonly"?

const variables should be used when you need to define a variable that doesn't change throughout the program's life cycle. They must have a value assigned at compile time. On the other hand, readonly can be initialized in a class constructor and ensure that its value cannot be changed afterward.

Which method of object comparison in C# is better to use, "==" or "Equals()", and why?

For value types, == and Equals() usually work the same way, but for reference types, == checks for reference equality, not content. Equals() can be overridden for custom classes to ensure content-based comparison. As a rule, if you want to compare the content of objects, it's better to use Equals().

What's the primary distinction between "is" and "as" when converting types in C#?

is checks whether an object is an instance of a certain type and returns a Boolean value. as is used for safe type casting and will return null if the conversion is not possible, rather than throwing an exception.

What do explicit and implicit type conversions mean in C#?

Implicit-type conversion happens automatically when a data type that can hold less information is converted to one that can hold more (for example, from int to double). Explicit-type conversion (casting) is required when there's a risk of data loss during the conversion.

What is the purpose of the "??" operator in C# and in which scenarios should it be used?

The ?? operator is a null-coalescing operator that returns the left operand if it's not null; otherwise, it returns the right one. It's useful for setting default values for potentially null values.

What are tuples, how are they used in C#, and what are their advantages compared to classes?

Tuples in C# are ordered collections of various types. They are useful for representing datasets without creating specific types. Compared to classes, tuples are typically lighter and more convenient for small, temporary datasets.

In this section, we delved into the core components of C#—data types, variables, and operators, which form the backbone of any C# application. We explored the differences between value and reference types and examined string manipulations, alongside the initialization and handling of various arrays. We also discussed the role of bitwise and logical operators, the use of nullable types, and the principles of operator overloading. We touched upon important topics such as object comparison methods, type conversions, and the advantages of using tuples for compact data representation. With this solid foundation, we are ready to advance to the next section, *Writing control structures and loops in C#*, to further enhance our programming skills.

Writing control structures and loops in C#

Control structures and loops are fundamental elements of any program, allowing developers to efficiently manage the flow of code execution. In the C# language, there is a variety of powerful tools for this purpose. In this section, we will delve into various control structures, such as conditional statements and selection, as well as key concepts of looping through data using different types of loops. Through an in-depth study of these elements, you'll gain a solid foundation for writing efficient and structured code in C#. Let's begin!

What are the main loops available in C# and how do you choose the best loop for a specific situation?

In C#, several types of loops are available: for, foreach, while, and do-while. Let's look at each of them:

- for: This is the most commonly used loop when you know the number of iterations beforehand.
- foreach: This type of loop is perfect for iterating through collections or arrays when you need to work with each element sequentially.

- `while`: This loop executes as long as the specified condition is true. It's useful when you don't know the number of iterations beforehand.

- `do-while`: This loop is similar to `while`, but the condition is checked after executing the loop body, ensuring the loop body is executed at least once.

Choosing the best loop depends on the specific situation. If you need to iterate over all elements of a collection, `foreach` would be the most convenient. If you know the number of iterations, `for` would be the most efficient. In cases where you don't know the number of iterations in advance, you can use `while` or `do-while`, depending on whether you want the loop body to execute at least once or not.

How do you use the "if", "else if", and "else" operators in C#? In which situations would you recommend using each of them?

The `if`, `else if`, and `else` operators are used for conditional code execution. `if` checks a condition and, if it's `true`, executes the code block following it. `else if` allows you to check additional conditions if the previous conditions were `false`. `else` executes a code block when none of the previous conditions were met. Use `if` to check a single primary condition, `else if` to check additional conditions, and `else` as a fallback code block to execute.

What's the difference between "for" and "foreach" loops? In which cases is it better to use each?

The `for` loop is used when you know in advance how many times you need to execute the loop. The `foreach` loop is designed for iterating over collections, such as lists or arrays. Use `for` when you have a specific number of iterations, and `foreach` when you need to iterate over all elements in a collection.

What is the "switch" operator and how is it different from a sequence of "if-else" operators?

The `switch` operator allows you to check a variable against multiple values. It is more compact and often more convenient for checking the values of a single variable. An `if-else` sequence, on the other hand, offers more flexibility as it can check different conditions, not being limited to just one variable.

What do the "continue" and "break" operators do in loops, and when can they be useful?

`continue` skips the current loop iteration and proceeds to the next one. `break` exits the loop prematurely. `continue` is useful when some loop iterations need to be skipped, and `break` when you need to terminate the loop execution under a certain condition.

How do you combine multiple conditions in a single "if" statement using logical operators?

You can use logical operators && (*logical "and"*) and || (*logical "or"*) to combine multiple conditions, for example, if (x > 5 && y < 10) {...}.

What is the peculiarity of the "do-while" loop compared to the regular "while" loop?

The primary difference is that in the do-while loop, the condition is checked after the loop body is executed, ensuring that the loop body runs at least once, regardless of the condition.

What does a nested loop look like and why can it be useful?

A nested loop is a loop placed inside another loop. It is often used for processing a two-dimensional array or matrix. See the following for an example:

```
for (int i = 0; i < 3; i++)
{
    for (int j = 0; j < 3; j++)
    {
        Console.WriteLine($"i = {i}, j = {j}");
    }
}
```

How can you prevent a potentially infinite loop execution?

To prevent an infinite loop, it's crucial to ensure that a loop termination condition will be met. This can be done by checking conditions before entering the loop, using execution time limiters, or through internal counters and monitoring tools.

What is recursion in C# and how do you prevent stack overflow when using recursive methods?

Recursion is a technique where a method calls itself. To prevent stack overflow, it's important to have a clear base case that will halt the recursive calls and to limit the recursion depth.

How can you optimize a loop for processing a large amount of data in C#?

To optimize a loop, you can use parallelism, employ efficient data structures, reduce the number of operations within the loop, and utilize caching where possible.

What is "yield return" in C# and when can it be useful?

`yield return` allows you to create iterators without the need to generate an auxiliary collection. It's useful when you want to lazily generate values as you iterate through a collection.

How do you create an infinite loop using "for"?

An infinite loop can be created using `for` in the following manner:

```
for(;;)
{
// loop code
}
```

Here, the condition, initialization, and increment are absent, so the loop will run indefinitely.

In this section, we explored control structures and loops, essential tools for dictating the flow of code in C#. We discussed various loop types, such as `for`, `foreach`, `while`, and `do-while`, highlighting how to select the appropriate one depending on the task at hand. We also covered the usage and applications of conditional operators `if`, `else if`, and `else`. We examined the efficiency of the `switch` operator compared to that of a chain of `if-else` statements, and the roles of `continue` and `break` operators within loops. With this foundation, we are now prepared to delve into more advanced topics.

Exploring the basics of OOP using C#

In this section, we turn our focus toward the basics of OOP using C#. As we venture further, we will unravel the core principles of OOP, a paradigm that facilitates organized and reusable code. Through C#, we will explore key OOP concepts such as classes, objects, inheritance, and polymorphism, fostering a deeper understanding and equipping you with the skills to craft robust and efficient applications. Let's embark on this enlightening journey.

How does C# integrate the principles of OOP?

C# supports all the core principles of OOP: *encapsulation*, *inheritance*, *polymorphism*, and *abstraction*. For instance, classes and interfaces in C# allow for the implementation of inheritance and polymorphism, while access modifiers facilitate encapsulation.

How does encapsulation work in C#?

In C#, encapsulation is ensured through access modifiers such as `private`, `protected`, and `public`. These modifiers determine the visibility of class members, allowing for the hiding of implementation details and exposing only the necessary API.

How is polymorphism implemented in C#?

Polymorphism in C# is realized through the ability to override methods in subclasses using the `virtual` and `override` keywords, as well as through interfaces that allow different classes to have a consistent set of methods.

What does inheritance entail in C#?

Inheritance in C# allows for the creation of a new class based on an existing one, inheriting its attributes and behavior. This is achieved using the `:` keyword, followed by the name of the base class.

What is the difference between a class and its instance in C#?

A class serves as a schematic or prototype that delineates the characteristics and functions of objects. An object (or instance of a class) is a specific representation of that class with a unique set of attribute values.

Why are access modifiers such as "public", "private", "protected", and "internal" used in C#?

These modifiers determine the level of access to class members. `public` makes a member accessible to any code; `private` restricts access to only the methods of the given class; `protected` allows access to the given class and its descendants, and `internal` makes a member accessible to any code within the same assembly.

Can a class in C# inherit from multiple other classes simultaneously?

No, C# does not support multiple inheritance for classes. However, a class can implement multiple interfaces.

How do method overloading and method overriding differ in C#?

Method overloading allows having multiple versions of a single method in one class with different parameters. Method overriding allows a subclass to replace the implementation of a method provided by its base class.

What are the main differences between interfaces and base classes in C#?

Interfaces define a contract (a set of methods without implementation) that must be adhered to by the class that implements it. Base classes contain an implementation that can be inherited and extended. A class can inherit only one base class but can implement multiple interfaces.

Why is composition sometimes considered a better choice than inheritance?

Composition offers greater flexibility, allowing dynamic changes to an object's behavior on the fly, and reduces the risk of issues associated with tight coupling between classes. It also promotes the principle of *composition over inheritance*, suggesting that using composition for the reusability of code is a more desirable approach.

What are properties in C# and how do they differ from fields?

Properties are a special kind of class member in C# that represents access to data with the ability to define logic when reading or writing that data. They allow you to control access to internal fields and can contain additional logic, for instance, for validation. Fields, on the other hand, are variables defined in the class and are used to store data.

What's the main difference between abstract classes and interfaces in C#?

Abstract classes can contain methods both with and without implementation. They cannot be instantiated directly. Interfaces only contain method declarations without implementation. A class can implement multiple interfaces but can inherit only one abstract class.

Why is encapsulating fields important for the SOLID principles?

Encapsulation helps keep the internal state of an object protected and hidden from the external world, which supports adherence to the *Open/Closed Principle* of SOLID. It also helps prevent unwanted state changes that could violate the *Single Responsibility Principle*.

What is the role of delegates in OOP in the context of C#?

Delegates in C# are objects that can point to methods. They allow for the realization of the function pointers concept in a type-safe manner. Delegates are often used to implement events and callbacks.

How are constructors used for object initialization and how do they differ from static constructors?

Constructors help initialize an object at the time of its creation, setting the necessary state or performing any other required setup. Static constructors are used to initialize static members of a class or to perform actions that should occur only once for the class, not for each individual object.

What do aggregation and association mean in OOP, and how are they implemented in C#?

Aggregation and **association** represent two distinct relationships between classes within the OOP paradigm. Association denotes a broader connection between two classes, indicating that one class incorporates the other.

Let me show some examples of how they are implemented:

- Association is a bi-directional relationship between two classes. Here, we demonstrate a one-to-many association between a `Library` class and a `Book` class:

```
public class Book
{
    public string Title { get; set; }
}

public class Library
{
    public List<Book> Books { get; set; }
    public Library()
    {
        Books = new List<Book>();
    }
}
```

In the preceding code, the `Library` class has a list of `Book` objects, illustrating a one-to-many association.

- Aggregation represents a relationship where one class is a part of another class. Here, we illustrate an aggregation between a `Car` class and an `Engine` class:

```
public class Engine
{
    public string Model { get; set; }
}

public class Car
{
    public Engine CarEngine { get; set; }

    public Car(Engine engine)
    {
        CarEngine = engine;
    }
}
```

In this example, the `Car` class contains an `Engine` object, demonstrating an aggregation relationship where the `Engine` class represents a part of the `Car` class.

Through these examples, we can see how both association and aggregation relationships can be implemented in C# using class properties and constructors.

How can multiple inheritance be implemented in C# if there is no direct support?

In C#, there's no direct support for multiple inheritance. However, multiple inheritance can be realized using interfaces. A class can implement multiple interfaces that may come from different sources.

What does the principle of "composition over inheritance" mean and when is it useful?

Composition over **inheritance** is a software design approach that encourages the use of composition (where objects utilize other objects) over inheritance for code reusability. It can be useful when a class's behavior requires dynamic changes or when inheritance might lead to undesired rigid coupling between classes.

Why are exceptions in C# considered objects, and how do you create your own exception class?

In C#, exceptions are implemented as objects that inherit from the base `Exception` class. This allows for passing additional information about the exception and creating custom exception types. To create your own exception class, simply inherit it from the `Exception` class or one of its subclasses.

What is the purpose of the "base" keyword in the context of inheritance in C#?

The `base` keyword allows you to call members from the base class when in a derived class. It is most commonly used in derived classes to call the constructor of the base class or to access other base class members that were overridden in the derived class.

How is the "this" keyword used in C#?

The `this` keyword points to the present instance of the class. It is often used to point to the fields or methods of the current object, especially when method parameter names overlap with class field names.

We've reached the end of our journey through the basics of C# and OOP in this chapter. With a strong foundation established, you're well-equipped to tackle the most common C# coding scenarios in your technical interviews.

Summary

In this chapter, we dove deep into key concepts, explored data types, variables, and operators, dissected control structures and loops, and discovered the basics of OOP. However, becoming proficient in C# is a continuous learning journey.

As we turn the page, we'll start navigating the more advanced terrain of C# programming in the next chapter. *Chapter 4, Advanced C# Concepts*, will bring light to the advanced facets of C#, including working with collections, LINQ, exception handling, debugging, asynchronous programming, and a lot more.

We will unravel the complexities of C# and learn how to make the best use of its capabilities to solve more intricate problems and enhance application performance. From creating reusable code with generic classes, methods, and interfaces to diving deep into multithreading and garbage collection, we'll gear you up for a higher level of programming challenges. Remember, each concept is a stepping stone, leading you to master the art of C# programming. So, buckle up for the next exciting chapter in your learning journey!

Additional reading

- *C# 12 and .NET 8 – Modern Cross-Platform Development Fundamentals - Eighth Edition,* by Mark J. Price

  ```
  https://www.packtpub.com/product/c-12-and-net-8-modern-cross-
  platform-development-fundamentals-eighth-edition/9781837635870
  ```

- *Refactoring with C#,* by Matt Eland

  ```
  https://www.packtpub.com/product/refactoring-with-c/9781835089989
  ```

4

Advanced C# Concepts

As we journey deeper into the realm of C# programming, it becomes apparent that the language, under its seemingly straightforward facade, harbors a wealth of advanced functionalities designed to address complex software development needs. This chapter delves into these sophisticated facets of C#, equipping you with the knowledge to craft efficient, flexible, and robust applications.

From the intricacies of collections and the power of **Language Integrated Query** (**LINQ**) to the nuances of asynchronicity, we'll embark on an enlightening expedition that transcends basic programming constructs. We'll explore the realm of delegates and lambdas, unravel the mysteries of garbage collection, and tread the intricate paths of multithreading and concurrency.

While these topics might initially seem daunting, remember that mastering them is what separates a novice programmer from a seasoned developer. By the end of this chapter, you'll be well versed in the following areas:

- Efficiently manipulating data using collections and LINQ
- Debugging your code effectively and gracefully handling exceptions
- Enhancing user experience through asynchronous programming
- Harnessing the power of delegates, events, and lambda expressions for more streamlined and adaptive code
- Crafting reusable code with generics
- Mastering the complexities of multithreading and ensuring smooth concurrent operations
- Optimizing performance by understanding and managing garbage collection

Ready to elevate your C# expertise? Let's embark on this exciting journey!

Working with collections and LINQ

In the vast landscape of C# programming, **collections** stand as foundational structures, serving as versatile containers for data. But what if we could query and manipulate these collections with the elegance and power akin to database operations? Enter **LINQ**. This section unveils the synergy of collections and LINQ, guiding you through the art of efficiently organizing, querying, and manipulating datasets. Whether you're dealing with a simple list of items or complex nested structures, the combined prowess of collections and LINQ will transform the way you handle data in C#. Prepare to explore techniques that will not only elevate your coding prowess but also dramatically enhance the efficiency and clarity of your applications.

What are the key differences between the "IEnumerable" and "ICollection" interfaces? When is it optimal to use each?

Both `IEnumerable` and `ICollection` are interfaces in the .NET Framework designed for handling collections of data, but they serve different purposes:

- `IEnumerable` provides the basic capability to iterate over a collection. It exposes an enumerator, which supports a simple iteration over a non-generic collection. Essentially, if you only need to enumerate over items, `IEnumerable` is sufficient.

- `ICollection` extends `IEnumerable` and provides additional methods for manipulating the size of the collection and for adding, removing, and checking the existence of elements in the collection.

In practice, do the following:

- Use `IEnumerable` when you simply want to iterate over a collection without needing to modify it

- Use `ICollection` when you need to manipulate the collection itself, such as adding or removing items

How does the "deferred execution" principle work in LINQ, and how does it impact performance?

Deferred execution in LINQ means that actual data processing or computation does not occur until the results are enumerated. When you construct a LINQ query, it just creates a query definition. The actual execution is delayed until you iterate over the query result, such as by using a `foreach` loop or converting the results with methods such as `ToList()` or `ToArray()`. This can enhance performance by avoiding unnecessary computations. However, it's important to manage the moment when the data is actually *materialized* – that is, fetched and loaded into memory. Materializing the data too early can sometimes consume more resources, especially when the data source is substantial, such as a database. You might want to append more conditions or filters to the query before deciding to materialize the results to optimize resource usage and performance.

What are the primary differences between the "Where" and "Select" LINQ methods, and when is it best to use each?

Both `Where` and `Select` are extension methods provided by LINQ, but they serve different purposes:

- `Where`: This method is used for filtering collections based on a given predicate. It returns a new collection that includes only those elements that satisfy a specified condition.

- `Select`: This method is used for projecting or transforming the elements of a collection. It returns a new collection with elements that have been transformed based on a specified function or projection.

In practice, do the following:

- Use `Where` when you want to filter a collection and retain only those elements that meet certain criteria

- Use `Select` when you want to transform the elements of a collection, such as extracting a specific property or converting the data in some way

What are the differences between the "All" and "Any" LINQ methods, and how do they behave when applied to an empty collection?

Both `All` and `Any` are LINQ methods used to evaluate collections against specific criteria. Here are their differences:

- `All`: Checks if every element in the collection satisfies a particular condition. Use `All` when you need to ensure that all elements of a collection meet a specific criterion.

- `Any`: Checks if at least one element in the collection satisfies a particular condition. Use `Any` when you need to determine if there are any elements that fulfill a specific criterion.

When the collection is empty, the following happens:

- `All`: Always returns `true` because there are no elements that would violate the condition. This might seem counter-intuitive, but in the absence of any elements to check, it defaults to `true`.

- `Any`: Always returns `false` since there are no elements present to satisfy the condition.

For instance, if you want to verify that all numbers in a list are positive, you'd use `All`. If you're going to check if there's a negative number in the list, you'd use `Any`.

What distinguishes "FirstOrDefault" from "SingleOrDefault", and when do these methods return "null"?

Both `FirstOrDefault` and `SingleOrDefault` are used to retrieve an element from a collection, but they serve slightly different purposes:

- `FirstOrDefault`: Returns the first element that matches a condition or the first element if no condition is specified. If no matching element is found, it returns the default value (typically `null` for reference types).

- `SingleOrDefault`: Returns the only element that matches a condition but throws an exception if there's more than one matching element. If no elements match the condition, it returns the default value.

In terms of returning `null`, the following applies:

- For reference types, both methods return `null` when no matching elements are found in the collection

- However, for value types (such as `int` and `double`), they would return the default value of the type (such as 0 for `int`)

What are the primary collection types in .NET you consider, and what are their key differences?

.NET provides several primary collection types:

- `List<T>`: A dynamic array of elements. It maintains order and allows duplicate elements.

- `Dictionary<TKey, TValue>`: A collection of key-value pairs. It does not have a defined order, and keys must be unique.

- `HashSet<T>`: A set of unique elements. It does not maintain any specific order.

- `Queue<T>`: A collection supporting **First-In-First-Out (FIFO)** operations.

- `Stack<T>`: A collection supporting **Last-In-First-Out (LIFO)** operations.

What are the differences between "List<T>" and "Dictionary<TKey", "TValue>"?

The primary distinction between `List<T>` and `Dictionary<TKey, TValue>` lies in how you access elements. In `List<T>`, elements are accessed by their index, whereas in `Dictionary<TKey, TValue>`, elements are accessed by their key.

How can you optimize the execution of LINQ queries when dealing with large datasets?

Optimizing LINQ queries, especially with substantial datasets, can be achieved through several approaches:

- Utilize *deferred execution* whenever possible, ensuring that queries are only executed when the result is genuinely required. This avoids unnecessary computations.

- Choose the most efficient collection type tailored for your specific use case, as the underlying data structure can impact performance.

- Limit the size of the resulting dataset when feasible using methods such as `Take` to avoid processing more data than necessary.

- Avoid or judiciously use nested queries. They can lead to performance issues due to multiple rounds of data retrieval or computations.

- Use methods such as `ToArray` or `ToList` to materialize results into memory if you anticipate multiple operations on the data. This can prevent repeated execution of the same LINQ query.

What are the key differences between the "IEnumerable" and "IQueryable" interfaces? Explain their implementation and usage scenarios.

`IEnumerable` and `IQueryable` are two primary interfaces representing collections in .NET. This is what they do:

- `IEnumerable`: Operates at the object level in memory. When you execute LINQ queries against an `IEnumerable` interface, operations are performed in memory. It's suitable for working with in-memory collections such as arrays or lists.

- `IQueryable`: Designed for interacting with external data sources (for example, databases). Queries made with `IQueryable` get translated into queries specific to the data source (such as SQL for relational databases). This interface allows for deferred execution and **out-of-memory (OOM)** data querying, making it efficient for large datasets, especially in databases.

The main distinction between these two interfaces lies in the execution location: `IEnumerable` processes data in memory. Meanwhile, `IQueryable` allows the construction of an expression tree that can be translated into a query suitable for an external data source, such as SQL for databases. Then, it sends the parsed query for processing to the data source and fetches the results as `IEnumerable`.

What's the key difference between an array and "List<T>" in C#? When is it optimal to use each of these structures?

The primary distinction lies in flexibility and size. Arrays have a fixed size once defined, while List<T> can dynamically resize as elements are added or removed.

Arrays are typically faster for indexed access compared to other data structures, and they can be more memory-efficient since there's no overhead associated with storing additional metadata or maintaining unused capacity, which is often the case with lists. Arrays are particularly suitable when the number of items is known upfront and remains constant, as they cannot dynamically resize as lists can.

On the other hand, List<T> provides a host of useful methods for manipulation and can grow or shrink as needed. It's an optimal choice when the collection size is uncertain or if you need the added functionality and methods that List<T> provides over arrays.

In essence, while arrays are more lightweight and efficient for static collections, List<T> offers more versatility for dynamic collections.

In which scenarios should one prefer "HashSet<T>" over "List<T>"?

HashSet<T> maintains a collection of unique elements and is optimized for operations that require fast lookups, insertions, and deletions, as well as ensuring uniqueness. Use HashSet<T> when you need to prevent duplicates or when frequent lookup operations are carried out.

On the other hand, List<T> is an ordered collection that can contain duplicates and is useful when the order of elements matters.

The choice between the two largely depends on the specific use case and the operations you intend to perform more frequently.

What is the key distinction between "LinkedList<T>" and "List<T>" in C#? In which scenarios is it optimal to use "LinkedList<T>"?

LinkedList<T> is a doubly linked list, where each node has references to the previous and next nodes. In contrast, List<T> is a dynamic array. The fundamental difference lies in how the data is stored and how it can be modified. LinkedList<T> is optimal for insertion and deletion operations in the middle of the list, given its node-based structure, which allows for efficient node addition or removal without shifting other elements. Conversely, List<T> is efficient for indexed access due to its array-backed nature.

When frequent insertions or deletions are expected, especially in the middle of a collection, LinkedList<T> can be more efficient. However, if the primary operations involve indexed access or if the collection size remains relatively static, List<T> might be a better choice.

What does "Dictionary<TKey, TValue>" represent in C#, and what are typical scenarios for its use?

`Dictionary<TKey, TValue>` in C# is a collection of key-value pairs where the keys are unique. This data structure allows fast lookups, insertions, and deletions based on keys. Typical scenarios for its use include storing configuration settings, caching data, and scenarios where you need to quickly retrieve a value associated with a unique key, such as a lookup table or a dictionary.

What are immutable collections in C#? What are their advantages and disadvantages?

Immutable collections in C# are collections that cannot be modified after they are created. Instead of modifying them directly, any operation that would change the collection returns a new instance of the collection with the desired changes. Advantages of using immutable collections include thread safety (since there's no risk of another thread modifying the collection unexpectedly) and the assurance that the data remains unchanged throughout its life cycle. On the downside, they can be less performant than mutable counterparts, especially when frequent modifications are needed, as each modification results in a new collection being created. This can also lead to increased memory usage.

As we conclude our discussion on collections and LINQ in C#, you are now better prepared to handle data with increased efficiency and flexibility in your C# endeavors. The knowledge acquired here lays a solid foundation for tackling complex data-related tasks in your upcoming projects.

Next, we venture into the vital realms of exception handling and debugging in C#. These skills are pivotal in enhancing the robustness of your applications, aiding in swift error identification and resolution. Stay tuned for insights and strategies to navigate through errors and exceptions adeptly in the next segment.

Exception handling and debugging

Every software, regardless of its complexity, is susceptible to unexpected behaviors and errors. Navigating through these unforeseen challenges requires a robust set of tools and techniques, and this is where exception handling and debugging come into play. This section delves deep into the intricacies of identifying, understanding, and resolving anomalies in your C# code. From gracefully managing unexpected scenarios using exception handling to probing your code with the precision of a surgeon through debugging, we'll equip you with the skills to ensure your applications run smoothly and efficiently. Embrace the journey of turning pitfalls into learning opportunities and ensuring the resilience and reliability of your software solutions.

What's the difference between using "throw" and "throw ex" inside a "catch" block?

When you use throw without any argument, you're essentially rethrowing the current exception, preserving the original stack trace. This allows for easier debugging as you maintain the information about where the exception was originally thrown. On the other hand, when you use throw ex, you reset the stack trace to the current catch block, potentially losing valuable information about where and how the exception originated. Therefore, in general, it's recommended to use throw by itself within a catch block if you intend to rethrow the caught exception.

What are the primary types of exceptions in C# and under what conditions do they typically arise?

C# features a wide variety of exception types to cater to different exceptional scenarios. Here are a few key ones:

- ArgumentNullException: This is thrown when an argument passed to a method is null when a non-null value is expected
- ArgumentOutOfRangeException: This occurs when an argument's value is outside the permissible range
- DivideByZeroException: This is thrown when there's an attempt to divide by zero
- InvalidOperationException: This arises when the state of an object doesn't permit a particular operation
- FileNotFoundException: This occurs when a file that's being attempted to be accessed doesn't exist
- StackOverflowException: This is thrown when there's a stack overflow due to excessive recursion or other reasons
- NullReferenceException: This occurs when you try to access a member on an object reference that is null

What does the "finally" block do in a "try-catch" structure, and are there scenarios where it might not execute?

The finally block ensures that the code inside it gets executed regardless of whether an exception was thrown in the preceding try or catch blocks. This is particularly useful for cleanup operations, such as closing files or database connections.

In most cases, the `finally` block will execute. However, there are rare circumstances, such as program termination or catastrophic exceptions (for example, `StackOverflowException` or a process termination), where the `finally` block might not get executed because these critical errors can disrupt the normal flow of program execution, and the app will stop, leaving no opportunity for the `finally` block to run.

What is an "inner exception", and how can it be used to improve debugging?

An **inner exception** refers to a previous exception that led to the current exception being thrown. It's especially useful when the current exception arises as a result of another exception. By examining the inner exception, developers can trace back to the root cause of a problem, providing a clearer picture of the sequence of events leading up to the final exception. This can be invaluable during debugging, as it helps pinpoint the primary source of the issue and, potentially, cascading failures that led to the current state. When throwing a custom exception, you can include the original exception as the inner exception, preserving this chain of causality.

What is a "stack trace", and how can it be beneficial in tracing exceptions?

A **stack trace** provides a snapshot of the method call sequence leading up to the point where an exception was thrown. It essentially shows the hierarchy of method calls that the application went through before encountering the exception. This can be instrumental for developers as it offers insights into the execution flow and context in which the exception occurred. By analyzing the stack trace, developers can often pinpoint the exact location and reason for the exception, making debugging and resolving the issue more efficient.

What is the essence of a "conditional breakpoint" in Visual Studio, and when is it beneficial to use?

A **conditional breakpoint** is a specialized breakpoint that pauses the execution of your code only when a specific condition is met. Instead of halting execution every time a particular line of code is reached, it only does so if the condition you've specified evaluates to `true`. This is particularly useful in scenarios where an issue arises only in certain circumstances or with specific data. By using a conditional breakpoint, developers can efficiently debug complex problems without having to manually pause and inspect the program state multiple times.

How can we handle or avoid an "unhandled exception"?

An **unhandled exception** occurs when an exception arises in your code that isn't caught by any `catch` block. To prevent this, do the following:

- Surround potential exception-throwing code with appropriate `try-catch` blocks, ensuring that you are catching specific exception types or a general exception if necessary.

- Utilize global exception handlers, such as `AppDomain.UnhandledException` for .NET Framework applications or `TaskScheduler.UnobservedTaskException` to handle exceptions from unobserved tasks. This provides a safety net, ensuring that any uncaught exceptions are still addressed in some manner.

- Always validate and sanitize inputs, and be aware of potential exception sources such as I/O operations, database access, and third-party library calls.

What is the difference between "Debug" and "Release" configurations?

In Visual Studio, the two primary build configurations are `Debug` and `Release`. The `Debug` configuration is tailored for code debugging. It usually includes additional debugging information, doesn't apply certain compiler optimizations, and might have different code paths (such as more verbose logging) enabled by using preprocessor directives. This ensures that the debugging experience is seamless, allowing developers to step through code, inspect variables, and use breakpoints effectively.

On the other hand, the `Release` configuration is optimized for the final deployment of the application. The code is compiled with full optimization, removing any debugging information, which leads to better performance and often a smaller binary size. Additionally, certain debug-specific code paths might be excluded, ensuring that the final product is lean and efficient.

Understanding and choosing the right configuration is essential as it can significantly impact both the performance and behavior of the application.

How can one deliberately trigger an exception?

You can use the `throw` keyword to programmatically generate an exception. For instance, executing `throw new Exception("Test exception");` will raise an exception with a `"Test exception"` message. Deliberately triggering exceptions can be useful in situations where you want to enforce certain conditions or validate assumptions in your code.

What's the distinction between using "Assert" and "Throw" in unit test development and debugging?

`Assert` is primarily used to validate conditions that are expected to be true at specific points in the code. If the condition is not met, an assertion failure typically halts the execution, alerting the developer of the discrepancy, especially during debugging sessions. It's a tool to ensure code correctness and assumptions during development.

On the other hand, `Throw` is employed to raise exceptions, indicating error conditions or unexpected scenarios. These exceptions can be caught and handled further up the call stack.

While both can be used to identify and address issues, their primary purposes and usage contexts differ: `Assert` is more about validating code logic during development, whereas `Throw` is about handling exceptional runtime scenarios.

How should one handle exceptions in "Task"? What's the difference between "async void" and "async Task" in the context of error handling?

When dealing with exceptions in `Task`, there are several approaches. One can use the `ContinueWith` method on a task to handle exceptions, or use the `await` keyword and wrap the awaited task inside a `try-catch` block to catch any exceptions it might throw.

The distinction between `async void` and `async Task` methods is crucial when it comes to exception handling. `async void` methods don't return a task, so exceptions thrown from such methods get thrown directly into the thread pool. This can lead to unobserved exceptions which, at best, could crash the application if not caught, and at worst, might silently fail without any indication to the developer. `async Task`, on the other hand, returns a task that encapsulates the operation, and exceptions can be observed and handled by awaiting the task or inspecting its result.

As we conclude our deep dive into exception handling and debugging in C#, a segment where we mastered the craft of diagnosing and rectifying code discrepancies, we are poised to step into the dynamic domain of asynchronous programming with `async` and `await`.

The upcoming section promises to bolster your C# programming capabilities, unlocking the potential for simultaneous operations and paving the way for more responsive and efficient code execution. Let's seamlessly transition from becoming adept at troubleshooting errors to harnessing the power of concurrency and parallelism inherent in modern C#. Gear up for an enthralling learning curve ahead!

Asynchronous programming with async and await

In today's fast-paced digital world, responsiveness is paramount. Users demand applications that are quick, smooth, and most importantly, non-blocking. Enter the realm of **asynchronous programming** with C#'s `async` and `await` keywords. This section illuminates the transformative power of asynchronous operations in enhancing application performance and responsiveness. We'll journey through the mechanics of executing tasks concurrently without stalling the main thread, ensuring a seamless user experience. By mastering `async` and `await`, you'll unlock the potential to perform complex operations behind the scenes, letting your applications remain swift and user-centric. Dive in to harness the future of efficient coding and elevate your applications to new heights of efficiency and interactivity.

What is the purpose of the "async" and "await" keywords in C#?

The `async` and `await` keywords in C# are used to denote and execute asynchronous operations, allowing for non-blocking code execution. The `async` keyword indicates that a method may contain asynchronous code, while `await` is used to asynchronously wait for a task to complete without freezing the main thread. This enables writing more responsive applications, especially when dealing with I/O-bound operations or long-running computations.

What's the main difference between multithreading and asynchronous programming?

Multithreading involves running multiple threads concurrently in a single process to optimize execution. It's about using multiple threads to achieve parallelism. **Asynchronous programming**, on the other hand, focuses on allowing code to continue its execution without waiting for long-running operations (such as I/O) to complete. Asynchronous code can run on a single thread, utilizing mechanisms such as an `event` loop to handle non-blocking operations efficiently.

What does an "async" method return?

An `async` method can return `void`, `Task`, `Task<T>`, or `ValueTask<T>`. However, it's generally recommended to avoid returning `void` from `async` methods, except in event handlers, because it makes error handling difficult; exceptions thrown in an `async void` method can't be caught by the caller, leading to unhandled exceptions, which can crash the application. Returning `Task` or `Task<T>` allows the caller to await its completion or chain other continuations.

What pitfalls can arise from the careless use of "async" and "await"?

Careless use of `async` and `await` can lead to several issues:

- **Deadlocks**: Especially when mixing synchronous and asynchronous code
- **Thread starvation**: Over-relying on the thread pool can lead to situations where all threads are consumed, causing delays in processing

- **Performance overheads**: Unnecessary usage can introduce performance overheads
- **Debugging complexity**: Asynchronous code can be more challenging to debug due to its non-linear execution flow

What is a "deadlock" in the context of asynchronous programming, and how can it be avoided?

In the context of asynchronous programming, a **deadlock** occurs when asynchronous code inadvertently gets blocked waiting for another operation to complete, which in turn is waiting for the original operation. This creates a situation where neither operation can proceed. Deadlocks often arise when mixing synchronous and asynchronous code or when awaiting tasks inappropriately. To avoid deadlocks, follow these guidelines:

- Avoid synchronously waiting on asynchronous methods (for example, avoid using `.Result` or `.Wait()`)
- Use `ConfigureAwait(false)` judiciously to prevent marshaling the continuation back to the original context, which can be a source of deadlocks, especially in UI applications

How does asynchrony impact the call stack?

Asynchrony can fragment the call stack into several segments. When asynchronous methods are invoked, they return almost immediately, often before the work is complete. This means the traditional call stack might not represent the full sequence of execution, complicating debugging. Tools such as the **Tasks** window in Visual Studio can help developers understand the state and flow of asynchronous operations.

What's the difference between "Task", "Task<T>", and "ValueTask<T>"?

Let's have a look at what the differences between these types are:

- `Task` represents an asynchronous operation that doesn't return a value. It's essentially a promise that some work will be completed in the future.
- `Task<T>` represents an asynchronous operation that returns a value of type `T` upon completion.
- `ValueTask<T>` is a newer type optimized for scenarios where the result might be available synchronously, potentially avoiding heap allocation. It's particularly useful for high-performance scenarios to reduce overhead, but it should be used with care as misuse can introduce subtle bugs or decrease performance.

How can multiple asynchronous operations be executed concurrently and awaited for their completion?

You can use `Task.WhenAll()` to execute multiple asynchronous operations concurrently and await their completion. This method returns a single `Task` object that completes when all of the provided tasks have been completed. It's a way to initiate several tasks at once and then continue execution when all of those tasks are done.

What issues might arise when using asynchronous methods in class constructors or finalizers?

A few issues may arise, such as the following:

- Using asynchronous methods in constructors can complicate object initialization since constructors can't return a `Task` object. This means you can't call `await` an asynchronous method directly inside a constructor, making it challenging to perform asynchronous operations during object initialization.

- Using asynchronous methods in finalizers may lead to a problem because the object might get garbage collected before the asynchronous operation completes. Finalizers are not meant to have asynchronous code, and doing so can lead to unpredictable behavior.

How are exceptions handled in asynchronous methods?

Exceptions in asynchronous methods can be handled using standard `try-catch` blocks. However, it's important to note that exceptions might not be thrown until the task becomes *faulted*. This means that the exception will be thrown at the point where you call `await` for the task. If an exception occurs in an awaited asynchronous method, it will propagate to the calling method, just as with synchronous code. It's also worth noting that if multiple exceptions are thrown by concurrent tasks awaited with `Task.WhenAll()`, all exceptions will be bundled into an `AggregateException` exception.

What is "synchronization context" in asynchronous programming, and what is its significance?

Synchronization context represents the environment in which asynchronous operations run. It ensures that asynchronous code can interact correctly with environments that have specific requirements, such as UI threads in Windows Forms or WPF applications. This is crucial to ensure that operations interacting with the UI are executed on the appropriate thread. In essence, synchronization context acts as a bridge between asynchronous code and its execution context, allowing for thread-safe updates to UI or other thread-specific resources.

How does "ConfigureAwait" work, and why is there a recommendation to use "ConfigureAwait(false)"?

ConfigureAwait allows developers to specify whether or not to return the execution to the original *synchronization context* after an asynchronous operation completes. Using ConfigureAwait(false) indicates that the continuation code shouldn't run in the original context, potentially preventing deadlocks and improving performance, especially in library code. This ensures that the asynchronous method does not attempt to marshal the continuation back to the original context, which might be unnecessary or even detrimental.

What is "task continuation", and how is it used?

Task continuation allows you to specify a segment of code to execute after a Task instance completes. It's often used via methods such as ContinueWith on a Task instance, allowing developers to chain operations without nesting callbacks. Continuations can be useful to define the logic that should run after an asynchronous operation without blocking the thread, making it easier to sequence asynchronous operations or handle results.

How do asynchronous methods interact with threads?

Asynchronous methods don't inherently spawn new threads. Instead, they use mechanisms to execute code asynchronously on the current thread, leveraging the thread pool for compute-bound operations when necessary. The key benefit of asynchronous methods is that they allow potentially blocking operations, such as I/O-bound work, to yield control, freeing up the current thread to perform other tasks. This leads to more efficient use of system resources, especially in scenarios where many operations might be waiting on external factors such as network responses or file reads.

What is "TaskCompletionSource" in the context of asynchronous operations?

TaskCompletionSource provides a way to manually control the completion of a task. It's particularly useful in scenarios where you need to integrate asynchronous code with other asynchronous mechanisms that don't natively use the Task pattern. Essentially, with TaskCompletionSource, you have the ability to directly set the result, exception, or cancellation state of its associated task.

What is a "cancellation token", and how is it used?

A **cancellation token** provides a mechanism to request the cancellation of an ongoing operation. It's typically passed into an asynchronous method, which can periodically check the token to see if a cancellation has been requested, allowing the operation to gracefully terminate early. This is especially important for long-running operations where you want to give the user or calling code the ability to interrupt and stop the operation.

What's the difference between "Parallel" from TPL and "async/await"?

`Parallel` is designed for parallel execution of code across multiple threads, focusing on CPU-bound operations that can be executed concurrently. It's about optimizing CPU usage by distributing computations over multiple cores.

On the other hand, `async/await` is designed for the non-blocking execution of code, particularly for I/O-bound operations. It's about improving responsiveness and scalability by allowing a thread to perform other tasks while waiting for a long-running operation to complete.

What are Parallel loops in TPL, and how to control them?

In TPL, there are two main `Parallel` loops: `Parallel.For` and `Parallel.ForEach`.

You can control the number of threads by using `ParallelOptions` and setting `MaxDegreeOfParallelism`. The default value of `MaxDegreeOfParallelism` is set to `-1`, indicating that TPL automatically decides the number of threads to use, typically based on the number of processor cores. However, you can modify this value to limit the maximum number of threads. This can be useful in scenarios where tasks are resource-intensive and you don't want to overload the system.

To manage loops, you can use the `Break()` and `Stop()` methods, as outlined here:

- `Break()`: The `Break()` method indicates the need to cease the current iteration's execution.

  Here's an example:
  ```
  var options = new ParallelOptions { MaxDegreeOfParallelism = 2
  };
  Parallel.For(0, 10, options, (i, state) => {
      if (i == 5) {
          state.Break();
          return;
      }
      Console.WriteLine($"Processing item {i}");
  });
  ```

  In the preceding example, `Parallel.For` processes numbers from 0 to 9. If it encounters the number 5, it uses `Break()` to halt further processing in the iteration.

- `Stop()`: The `Stop()` method halts execution as quickly as possible. This method is essential for controlling the loop's state.

  Here's an example:
  ```
  Parallel.ForEach(dataCollection, (data, state) => {
      if (someCondition) {
          state.Stop();
          return;
  ```

```
        }
        // Process data
    });
```

In the preceding example, if you're processing a large list of data and encounter a critical error, you can use `Stop()` to immediately cease processing.

How to use Parallel.ForEachAsync, and what is the difference between it and Parallel.ForEach?

`Parallel.ForEach` is a synchronous method used for executing iterations in parallel.

`Parallel.ForEachAsync` supports asynchronous operations within iterations. This is useful when you need to perform asynchronous requests or operations with waiting times, such as interactions with databases or web services.

Here's an example:

```
await Parallel.ForEachAsync(dataCollection, async (data,
cancellationToken) => {
    // Asynchronous processing of each data item
    await ProcessDataAsync(data);
});
```

In the preceding example, `Parallel.ForEachAsync` allows each item in the data collection to be processed asynchronously, which is beneficial for tasks that involve latency, such as database queries or calls to web services.

When is it appropriate to call an asynchronous function without using await, and how does this affect execution?

You can invoke an asynchronous function without `await` if you do not need to wait for its completion before moving to the next line of code. However, this can lead to issues such as untracked errors and difficulties in managing thread execution. The method's execution continues irrespective of the state of the asynchronous operation, potentially leading to unpredictable behavior, especially if it affects shared resources or the application's state.

Also, an asynchronous function can be called without `await` when you need to initiate several asynchronous tasks simultaneously. However, without `await`, you cannot catch exceptions that might occur during task execution, and the result of the operation will be ignored.

Here are some examples:

- Here, it's ignoring the result:

```
    _ = DoSomeAsync();
```

- Here, it's running tasks in parallel:

```
public async Task ProcessDataAsync(IEnumerable<Data> dataList) {
    var tasks = new List<Task>();
    foreach (var data in dataList) {
        tasks.Add(ProcessSingleDataAsync(data));
    }
    await Task.WhenAll(tasks);
}

public async Task ProcessSingleDataAsync(Data data) {
    await Task.Delay(TimeSpan.FromSeconds(1));
    return data;
}
```

In the second example, `ProcessDataAsync` initiates several asynchronous tasks in parallel and waits for their completion using `Task.WhenAll`. This approach is useful for efficiently processing multiple tasks concurrently.

What are "asynchronous streams" in C# 8.0, and how can "IAsyncEnumerable" transform real-time data processing?

Introduced in C# 8.0, **asynchronous streams** allow you to asynchronously iterate over collections using `await foreach`. `IAsyncEnumerable` is an interface that facilitates creating data streams that can be read asynchronously. This is particularly beneficial when dealing with large data streams or data sources that produce data asynchronously. It provides a way to process data as it becomes available, rather than waiting for the entire dataset, making it especially valuable for real-time applications.

How can you use "SemaphoreSlim" for asynchronous synchronization of resource access?

`SemaphoreSlim` offers a `WaitAsync` method, which allows for asynchronously obtaining a semaphore. This is advantageous when you need to limit concurrent access to a shared resource in asynchronous code without blocking the executing thread. By using `SemaphoreSlim`, you can ensure that a limited number of tasks can access a particular resource or section of code at the same time, providing a mechanism for throttling or controlling access.

What is "asynchronous disposal" in C# 8.0 with the use of "IAsyncDisposable"?

Asynchronous disposal in C# 8.0 provides a mechanism for objects to release resources asynchronously. The `IAsyncDisposable` interface introduces the `DisposeAsync()` method, which can be implemented to perform asynchronous cleanup operations. This is particularly beneficial for resources that require asynchronous interactions for their disposal, such as network streams or database connections. By allowing asynchronous disposal, resources can be released more efficiently, and it helps prevent potential deadlocks or blocking scenarios, especially in contexts that heavily rely on asynchronous operations.

As we conclude our journey through the dynamic world of asynchronous programming with `async` and `await`, where we unlocked the potential of parallel operations and enhanced code efficiency, we now stand at the threshold of another significant topic: delegates, events, and lambda expressions.

The forthcoming section promises to further enhance your proficiency in C#, offering insights into the powerful programming constructs that enable event-driven programming and functional programming styles. Prepare yourself to delve deep into the intricacies of delegates and experience the responsiveness facilitated by events and the concise code enabled by lambda expressions, as we continue to expand our C# programming horizons.

Delegates, events, and lambda expressions

Peeling back the layers of C# reveals a sophisticated tapestry of mechanisms designed to facilitate advanced coding patterns and techniques. Central to this are **delegates**, **events**, and **lambda expressions**. This section delves deep into these constructs, shedding light on their intertwined relationships and essential roles in the .NET ecosystem. Delegates empower developers to encapsulate methods as first-class entities, providing a foundation for events and fostering dynamic method invocation. Events, in turn, offer a robust communication system, allowing objects to interact seamlessly without rigid dependencies. Meanwhile, lambda expressions infuse elegance and brevity, enabling concise function definitions on the fly. Together, these three pillars form the backbone of many modern programming patterns in C#. Embark on this exploration to discover how you can harness their combined potential, crafting flexible, maintainable, and expressive code with ease.

What are "event accessors" in C#, and how can they customize subscription or unsubscription logic?

In C#, **event accessors** are the `add` and `remove` methods that define custom actions for subscribing to or unsubscribing from an event, respectively. They grant developers the capability to incorporate additional logic or validation when working with events. For example, you might want to limit the number of subscribers to an event or log every subscription. Customizing these accessors provides greater control over event behavior and interactions.

How does .NET implement lambda expressions at the compilation level? Do they become actual methods of a class?

During compilation, lambda expressions are transformed into either anonymous methods or class methods, depending on their usage context. If a lambda captures only local variables, it might be represented as a static method. However, if it captures variables from its surrounding scope (closure), the compiler generates a special class to hold these captured variables, and the lambda becomes a method of this generated class. This transformation ensures that the lambda functionality is preserved while integrating seamlessly with the .NET type system.

What are the primary differences between lambda expressions and expression trees, and what opportunities does working with expression trees provide?

While lambda expressions are functional constructs that can be executed directly, expression trees represent code as a structured data format. In other words, while lambdas execute logic, expression trees describe logic. Expression trees allow for the introspection, modification, or even dynamic generation of code at runtime. This capability is especially beneficial for scenarios such as **object-relational mapping (ORM)** systems, where one might want to convert LINQ queries into SQL queries, or for building custom compilers or interpreters.

Why can "multicast delegates" be problematic in modern applications, and what alternatives exist?

Multicast delegates allow multiple handlers to respond to a single event. This can introduce complexities in management and debugging and can lead to unexpected side effects if not handled correctly. It becomes challenging to ensure the order of execution or handle exceptions thrown by individual delegate targets. An alternative is the use of events or the **Observer** pattern, which provides more structured and controlled ways to notify multiple subscribers.

How can one dynamically create functions based on lambda expressions at runtime?

By using expression trees (`Expression<TDelegate>`), one can dynamically construct, modify, and compile lambda expressions at runtime. Expression trees represent code as data and can be transformed or inspected before being compiled into executable code using the `Compile` method.

What is understood by "closure" in the context of lambda expressions and anonymous methods, and how does it affect captured variables?

A **closure** in the context of lambda expressions and anonymous methods refers to the ability of these constructs to *capture* and retain access to variables from their enclosing scope. The captured variables are stored in a way that they remain accessible and mutable even after the method in which they were declared has finished executing. This can lead to unexpected behaviors if not understood correctly, especially in multithreaded environments, where closures can introduce shared state across threads.

What can be the consequences if one of the event subscribers throws an exception during the event invocation? How does it impact other subscribers of that event, and what approaches can be employed for the graceful handling of such scenarios?

If one of the event subscribers throws an exception during its execution, the subsequent subscribers in the invocation list won't be executed. This means that other subscribers might miss the event notification. To mitigate this, one can invoke each delegate in the event's invocation list separately, wrapped in a `try-catch` block. This ensures that an exception in one subscriber does not prevent the others from being invoked. Handling exceptions appropriately also ensures that the main logic isn't interrupted unexpectedly.

What's the difference between delegates and events, and how do they interoperate?

While delegates are essentially type-safe function pointers that can point to one or more methods, events are a mechanism that allows a class to notify other classes or objects when something of interest occurs. Events use delegates behind the scenes to maintain a list of subscribers and to specify the signature of methods that can handle the event. In essence, events encapsulate delegates, adding an extra layer of protection and ensuring that only the owning class can raise an event.

How can lambda expressions be used in C#, and what are their advantages over delegates?

Lambda expressions in C# are concise representations of anonymous methods using a clear and succinct syntax. They are often used with LINQ queries and other scenarios where short, inline methods are desirable. The primary advantages of lambda expressions over traditional delegate syntax are brevity and clarity. Lambda expressions provide a more readable and compact way to define inline methods without the need for explicit delegate instantiation.

What is the difference between "Func<T>", "Action<T>", and "Predicate<T>" in C#, and when should each be used?

In C#, `Func<T>` is used for delegates that return a value, `Action<T>` for delegates that don't return a value, and `Predicate<T>` for delegates that return a Boolean value. Specifically, do the following:

- Use `Func` when you need to compute or retrieve a result
- Use `Action` when you want to perform an operation or action without expecting a return value
- Use `Predicate` when you want to evaluate a condition and get a `true` or `false` result, typically for filtering or checking conditions

What challenges might arise when working with events, and how can they be mitigated?

Working with events in C# presents several challenges, such as the following:

- **Memory leaks**: If subscribers don't unsubscribe from events, it can lead to memory leaks, especially if the publisher has a longer lifetime than the subscriber

- **Multithreading Issues**: Accessing events from multiple threads can introduce race conditions, a situation where two or more threads attempt to modify shared data simultaneously, leading to unpredictable and erroneous outcomes

- **Exception handling**: If one subscriber's handler throws an exception, it might prevent other handlers from executing

To mitigate these challenges, follow these guidelines:

- Always unsubscribe from events when they're no longer needed

- Use thread-safe methods to invoke events

- Wrap individual event invocations in `try-catch` blocks to ensure one handler's exception doesn't block others

As we wrap up our segment on delegates, events, and lambda expressions, where we immersed ourselves in the exploration of event-driven programming and the concise syntax of lambda expressions, we are about to venture into another cornerstone of C# programming – using generic classes, methods, and interfaces to create reusable code.

The upcoming section will be your gateway to mastering the art of crafting versatile and reusable code structures in C#, promoting code reusability and type safety. Brace yourself to delve into the world of generics, where we will learn to create flexible yet type-safe code, a step toward becoming proficient in sophisticated programming with C#.

How to use generic classes, methods, and interfaces to create reusable code

At the heart of efficient and robust programming lies the ability to write code that stands the test of time, adapts to diverse scenarios, and minimizes redundancy. **Generics**, introduced in C#, represent a quantum leap toward this ideal. This section introduces the powerful world of generics, enabling developers to define **classes**, **methods**, and **interfaces** with a type-safe, scalable, and reusable approach. Rather than committing to a specific data type, generics allow for a more abstract and versatile coding style, ensuring that you can cater to a wide array of requirements without the burden of excessive code repetition. Through a deep dive into generic classes, methods, and interfaces, you will gain insights into creating code structures that not only meet the demands of the present but are also well equipped to evolve with future needs. Embrace generics and unlock a world where flexibility and type safety coexist harmoniously, paving the way for truly adaptable solutions.

What is the purpose of generics in C#, and what advantages do they offer over using the "object" base type?

Generics in C# provide a way to define classes, interfaces, and methods that operate on typed parameters while maintaining type safety and performance. Compared to using the `object` type, generics offer the following advantages:

- **Type safety**: Generics ensure that you are working with the correct data type, eliminating the risk of runtime type errors

- **Performance**: With generics, there's no need for boxing or unboxing when dealing with value types, leading to more efficient operations

- **Code reusability**: Generics allow you to write a piece of code that works with different data types, reducing code duplication

- **Elimination of type casting**: With generics, explicit type casting is reduced, making the code cleaner and more readable

How do you define a generic class, and how does it differ from a standard class? How can you set constraints on generic type parameters?

A generic class is defined using type parameters, typically denoted by angle brackets (`<T>`). While a standard class works with specific data types, a generic class can work with any data type, based on the type parameter provided at the time of instantiation. For instance, `List<int>` and `List<string>` are instances of the generic `List<T>` class but work with `int` and `string` types, respectively.

Constraints on generic type parameters can be set using the `where` keyword. This allows you to limit the types that can be used as arguments for generics based on inheritance hierarchy, interfaces, or constructors. For example, `class MyGenericClass<T> where T : MyClass, new()`, ensures that `T` is or inherits from `MyClass` and has a parameterless constructor.

Can generics integrate with other key features of C# such as delegates or attributes?

Yes – generics can be combined with various features in C#, such as the following:

- **Delegates**: You can define generic delegates, which can point to methods of various types

- **Events**: Events can be based on generic delegates

- **Attributes**: While you can't create a generic attribute class, you can apply attributes to generic constructs

How are covariance and contravariance applied to generic interfaces and delegates in C#?

In C#, **covariance** and **contravariance** provide flexibility in assigning and using generic types with interfaces and delegates in the following ways:

- **Covariance** (`out` keyword): Enables you to use a more derived type than originally specified. For example, you can assign an object of `IEnumerable<Derived>` to a variable of `IEnumerable<Base>`.

- **Contravariance** (`in` keyword): Allows for a less derived type. This is commonly seen with delegates.

For instance, an interface can be defined as `IInterface<out T>` for covariance or `IInterface<in T>` for contravariance.

What are the characteristics of static fields and methods in generic classes compared to standard classes?

In generic classes, static fields and methods are unique. For each type specialization of a generic class, there's a separate set of static fields. This means that `MyClass<int>` and `MyClass<string>` will each have their own distinct instances of static fields. This behavior differs from non-generic classes, where there's only one set of static fields shared across all instances of the class.

What does a "generic type extension method" mean, and how is it applied?

A **generic type extension method** allows developers to *add* methods to existing types (both built-in and user-defined) without modifying them or creating new derived types. These are static methods defined in static classes but can be called as if they were instance methods on the extended type. They use the `this` keyword before the generic type parameter in the method signature, as in the following example:

```
public static class ExtensionMethods
{
```

```
public static void MyMethod<T>(this T obj)
{
    // Implementation here
}
}
```

By using such extension methods, developers can enhance the functionality of existing types in a clean and modular way, benefiting from the flexibility and type safety provided by generics.

Can we inherit from generic type classes? What are the nuances of this process?

Yes – you can inherit from generic type classes. When inheriting, you can do the following:

- You can specify a concrete type for the base generic class; for example, `class Derived : Base<int> { }`

- Alternatively, you can maintain the generic nature in the derived class: `class Derived<T> : Base<T> { }`

It's important to be aware of any type constraints placed on the base generic class, as these will also apply to the derived class.

What compilation mechanism is used for generic types? Is separate machine code generated for each specialized type?

In .NET, generic types are compiled into a single template in **Intermediate Language** (IL). When a specific type instance is required at runtime, the **Just-In-Time** (JIT) compiler generates the specialized code. For value types (for example, `int`, `double`), separate code is generated for each type to ensure optimized performance. However, for reference types, the same code is shared, making the process more memory-efficient.

As we conclude our exploration of generics classes, methods, and interfaces, where we harnessed the power of adaptable and type-safe code structures, we are gearing up to delve into the sophisticated realm of multithreading, creating and managing threads, synchronization primitives, and handling thread synchronization and communication.

In the forthcoming section, brace yourself to uncover the intricacies of multithreading in C#, a pivotal skill in developing robust and efficient applications. Anticipate gaining hands-on experience in creating and coordinating threads adeptly, embracing synchronization primitives, and navigating the complexities of thread synchronization and communication. Let's forge ahead, equipped to tackle the challenges and opportunities that multithreaded programming in C# presents!

Multithreading – Creating and managing threads, synchronization primitives, and handling thread synchronization and communication

In today's world of multi-core processors and demands for seamless user experiences, the art of multithreading has become an indispensable part of a developer's toolkit. This section ventures into the intricate realm of multithreading, offering a comprehensive guide to creating, managing, and coordinating threads in C#. Beyond the simple creation of threads, you'll delve into the nuances of synchronization primitives, ensuring that your multithreaded applications operate without glitches or data inconsistencies.

But threading isn't just about execution; it's also about communication. We'll explore how threads can communicate effectively, ensuring smooth data transfer and task coordination. As you navigate through this section, you'll discover the balance between maximizing performance through concurrent operations and maintaining the integrity and reliability of your applications. Welcome to the world of multithreading, where speed and coordination come together to supercharge your applications.

How can one create a thread in C#, and what are the primary methods for its initiation?

In C#, threads can be created using the `Thread` class from the `System.Threading` namespace. Once you've instantiated a thread, you can initiate it using the `Start()` method. Here's an example:

```
Thread myThread = new Thread(new ThreadStart(MyFunction));
myThread.Start();
```

Here, `MyFunction` is the method you want to run on a separate thread. It's worth noting that while creating threads this way provides granular control, for many scenarios, TPL offers a higher-level and more efficient approach to parallel execution.

What synchronization primitives are available in C# for managing resource access?

C# provides various synchronization primitives to control access to shared resources and ensure data safety in a multithreaded environment. These include the following:

- `Monitor`: Often used implicitly with the `lock` keyword to acquire a lock on an object
- `Mutex`: Similar to `Monitor` but can be used across multiple processes, ensuring inter-process synchronization
- `Semaphore`: Controls access to a resource by multiple threads by limiting the number of simultaneous accesses

- `ReaderWriterLock` and `ReaderWriterLockSlim`: Allow multiple threads to read shared data, but only one to write, optimizing scenarios with frequent reads and occasional writes

- `lock` statement: A shorthand for `Monitor.Enter` and `Monitor.Exit`, providing a block-based scope for acquiring and releasing a lock

What's the difference between Monitor, Mutex, and Semaphore when it comes to thread synchronization?

Let's see the differences between these mechanisms:

- `Monitor`: It allows a thread to acquire a lock on an object and is typically used via a `lock` statement in C#. It's the fastest synchronization mechanism but operates only within a single process. It's best suited for short-lived locks where contention is low.

- `Mutex`: Functions similar to `Monitor` but can be used across multiple processes. This means if you have several applications that need to synchronize access to a shared resource, a `Mutex` mechanism can be employed. It's more heavyweight than a `Monitor` mechanism and has a performance overhead due to its cross-process capabilities.

- `Semaphore`: It's a signaling mechanism that controls access by multiple threads to a shared resource. Unlike `Monitor` and `Mutex`, which are binary locks (locked/unlocked), a `Semaphore` mechanism has a count, limiting the number of threads that can access a resource or group of resources concurrently. It's useful when you have a pool of resources and you want to limit the number of simultaneous accesses – for instance, in scenarios such as limiting concurrent database connections.

What is a "deadlock" in multithreading, and how can it be avoided?

A **deadlock** in multithreading occurs when two or more threads are locked in a state where each thread is waiting for another to release a resource, creating a standstill where no thread can proceed. This effectively halts the execution of the threads involved. To avoid deadlocks, consider the following strategies:

- **Lock ordering**: Always acquire locks in a consistent, predetermined order. If all threads follow the same order when acquiring locks, circular waiting (a key condition for deadlocks) can be avoided.

- **Lock timeouts**: Use timeouts when attempting to acquire a lock. If a thread cannot obtain all the necessary locks within a certain time frame, it can release any locks it has acquired and retry.

- **Deadlock detection**: Have mechanisms in place to detect deadlocks. This can be complex and may not be suitable for all scenarios, but in systems where deadlocks can have significant impacts, detection and recovery mechanisms are essential.

How can "ThreadPool" help manage threads more efficiently than manually creating threads?

`ThreadPool` manages a pool of worker threads, providing an efficient mechanism for executing short-lived tasks in the background. Benefits include the following:

- **Reduced overhead**: `ThreadPool` minimizes the overhead associated with thread creation and destruction by reusing threads

- **Optimized resource utilization**: `ThreadPool` dynamically adjusts the number of threads in the pool based on the workload, ensuring optimal utilization of system resources

- **Ease of use**: `ThreadPool` simplifies parallel execution by abstracting away thread management details, allowing developers to focus on task execution logic

What does "Task" represent in C#, and how does it differ from a regular thread?

`Task` in C# represents an asynchronous operation. It provides a higher-level abstraction over threads and offers several benefits:

- **Asynchronous programming**: With the use of `async` and `await` keywords, `Task` makes it simpler to write asynchronous code

- **Resource management**: A `Task` instance may run on a thread from the `ThreadPool`, optimizing thread utilization and management

- **Composability**: Tasks can be easily composed, allowing for the creation of chains of asynchronous operations

- **Exception handling**: `Task` provides a centralized way to handle exceptions in asynchronous code

The primary difference from a regular thread is that a `Task` instance abstracts the underlying threading details and provides a richer API for representing asynchronous computations, while a thread represents a single execution path in a program.

How can you ensure safe data exchange between threads?

Ensuring safe data exchange between threads is crucial for data consistency and system stability. Here's how it can be achieved:

- **Synchronization primitives**: Use synchronization mechanisms such as `lock`, `Mutex`, `Semaphore`, and `ReaderWriterLock` to ensure that only one thread accesses shared resources at a time.

- **Concurrent collections**: Utilize thread-safe collections, such as `ConcurrentDictionary`, `BlockingCollection`, or `ConcurrentQueue`, which are designed to handle concurrent access without the need for additional synchronization.

- **Immutable data structures**: Use immutable objects that can't be modified after they're created. Since they can't change state, they can be shared safely among multiple threads.

- **volatile keyword**: In scenarios where you need to ensure that a particular field is always read from the main memory location (and not cached), you can use the `volatile` keyword.

How do "async" and "await" help create asynchronous code without directly managing threads?

`async` and `await` provide a means to write asynchronous code that appears synchronous in structure. When you use `await`, the method's execution is paused, freeing up the executing thread to return to the thread pool until the awaited asynchronous operation completes. This approach allows for efficient resource utilization without the intricacies of direct thread management. Essentially, they abstract the complexities of asynchronous programming, enabling developers to focus on logic rather than concurrency mechanisms.

What is "thread-local storage" in C#, and how is it used?

Thread-local storage (TLS) in C# provides a mechanism to store data that is unique to each individual thread. This ensures that each thread has its own private copy of a variable, isolated from other threads. In C#, this can be achieved using the `ThreadStatic` attribute or the `ThreadLocal<T>` class. TLS is particularly useful for scenarios where thread-specific contextual information or state needs to be stored without interference from other threads.

What are the main approaches and best practices recommended when working with multithreading in C#?

Some recommended approaches and best practices include the following:

- **Use synchronization primitives**: Always use synchronization mechanisms such as `lock`, `Mutex`, `Semaphore`, and `ReaderWriterLock` when accessing shared resources to prevent race conditions

- **Minimize lock contention**: Avoid holding locks for extended periods, especially when performing I/O operations or other blocking tasks

- **Leverage built-in libraries**: Utilize `ThreadPool` or `Task` for asynchronous operations instead of manually creating and managing threads

- **Beware of race conditions and deadlocks**: Understand common pitfalls and scenarios that lead to these issues and actively work to prevent them

- **Embrace asynchronicity**: Use the `async`/`await` paradigm for operations that might block a thread, such as I/O or network requests

- **Testing**: Regularly test multithreaded code under various conditions, including stress and load tests, to uncover potential concurrency issues

What is the role of "memory barriers" or "fences" in multithreaded C# code?

Memory barriers or **fences** are mechanisms that ensure a specific order of memory operations in a multithreaded environment. They prevent certain operations from being reordered by the compiler or the processor. This ensures that specific operations are executed before or after the barrier as intended, maintaining the integrity and consistency of data across threads. They play a crucial role in scenarios where the order of operations is critical for correct program behavior.

When is it most effective to apply "SpinLock"?

SpinLock is a lock primitive that actively *spins* or busy-waits, rather than putting the thread to sleep, when waiting for a lock to be released. It is most effective in scenarios where the lock hold times are expected to be very short, and the overhead of suspending and resuming a thread (context switching) would be more expensive than the short busy-wait. It's particularly useful in high-performance scenarios, where threads are expected to acquire locks almost immediately.

What is the purpose of the "volatile" keyword in multithreaded C# code, and how does it interact with compiler optimization?

The volatile keyword in C# indicates to the compiler that a field can be accessed simultaneously by multiple threads. This prevents certain compiler optimizations on that field to ensure proper visibility and ordering of reads and writes. Essentially, it guarantees that any read or write operation to a volatile variable will always interact directly with main memory, rather than using cached data. This ensures that all threads will observe the most recent value of the variable, providing a memory barrier-like behavior to prevent unexpected results due to compiler or hardware optimizations.

What are the primary distinctions between the "BlockingCollection", "ConcurrentBag", "ConcurrentQueue", and "ConcurrentStack"collections?

Let's take a look at the different collections:

- BlockingCollection: This is a wrapper around other collections, providing blocking and bounding capabilities. It's useful for scenarios where you want to control the rate of data flow between producer and consumer threads.

- ConcurrentBag: A thread-safe, unordered collection optimized for scenarios where each thread frequently adds and removes items.

- ConcurrentQueue: A thread-safe FIFO collection.

- ConcurrentStack: A thread-safe LIFO collection.

What is the purpose of "ThreadLocal<T>", and what are its advantages and drawbacks?

ThreadLocal<T> provides a way to create data that is local to the thread it's accessed from, ensuring each thread has its own unique value.

Its advantages include the following:

- **Data isolation**: Ensures that data is isolated between threads, reducing the need for synchronization
- **Performance**: Access to thread-local data is generally faster than shared data with locks

Its drawbacks include the following:

- **Increased memory usage**: Each thread having its own instance can lead to higher memory consumption
- **Potential memory leaks**: If threads are not terminated correctly or if ThreadLocal instances are not disposed of properly, it can lead to memory leaks

What does "starvation" mean in the context of multithreaded programming?

Starvation in multithreading refers to a situation where one or more threads are perpetually unable to access a resource or execute because other threads are continuously monopolizing the resource or CPU. This can lead to reduced system throughput, unresponsiveness, or even total application stall. Starvation often arises in systems where thread prioritization is mishandled or where certain threads are deprioritized to the extent that they rarely or never get to execute.

How does "CancellationToken" assist in managing the execution of threads and tasks?

CancellationToken provides a mechanism to request the cancellation of threads, tasks, or asynchronous operations. It enables the following:

- **Cooperative cancellation**: Tasks and threads can periodically check the token to see if a cancellation has been requested, allowing them to exit gracefully
- **Safe termination**: Ensures that long-running operations can be terminated in a controlled manner without causing data corruption or other issues
- **Reactivity**: Enables applications to be more responsive by canceling tasks in response to external events or changes in state, such as user requests or timeouts

How do atomic operations, such as the methods in the "Interlocked class", facilitate synchronization in multithreaded code?

The methods in the `Interlocked` class provide atomic operations for variables, ensuring that the operations are completed without being interrupted by other threads. This offers the following benefits:

- **Safety**: Interlocked methods allow for safe updates to variables in a multithreaded environment without the need for locks

- **Performance**: Atomic operations are often faster than using locks, especially when contention is low

- **Consistency**: Interlocked methods guarantee that the data remains consistent even when accessed by multiple threads concurrently

Interlocked classes are commonly used for operations such as incrementing counters, swapping values, or updating shared data in a thread-safe manner.

What is meant by non-blocking calls in multithreaded programming, and why are they considered advantageous compared to blocking calls?

Non-blocking calls do not halt the execution of a thread while waiting for a resource or a response. This means the thread can continue performing other tasks or operations concurrently. Their advantages include the following:

- **Resource efficiency**: Non-blocking calls enable optimal system resource utilization since the thread can perform other tasks while waiting

- **Responsiveness**: Applications remain responsive, especially in I/O-bound operations or network calls, as they don't get stuck waiting

- **Scalability**: Non-blocking operations often lead to more scalable systems, especially when dealing with high concurrency, as threads aren't left idle

In contrast, **blocking calls** pause the execution of a thread until it obtains the required resource or response, potentially leading to inefficient resource use and reduced application responsiveness.

Why does the traditional "lock" mechanism not work for asynchronous operations?

The traditional `lock` mechanism blocks the executing thread while it waits for the lock to be released. In the context of asynchronous operations, using such a blocking mechanism can lead to deadlocks, especially if the locked resource is accessed later by the same logical flow but on a different thread.

Additionally, using `lock` in asynchronous code can increase the strain on the thread scheduler since threads might be blocked asynchronously. Instead of efficiently freeing up the thread to handle other tasks, it remains blocked, diminishing the benefits of asynchronicity.

How can synchronization be ensured in asynchronous methods? What primitives can be used for this purpose?

Synchronization in asynchronous methods can be achieved using certain synchronization primitives designed for asynchronous operations. These include the following:

- `SemaphoreSlim`: Supports both synchronous and asynchronous locking, making it useful for scenarios where you might have mixed synchronous and asynchronous code

- `AsyncLock`: While not part of the .NET Framework itself, patterns such as `AsyncLock` (often implemented using `SemaphoreSlim`) can provide a lock-like mechanism for asynchronous code

- `Mutex` and `ReaderWriterLockSlim`: While these synchronization primitives are traditionally associated with thread synchronization, they can also be judiciously employed in specific asynchronous scenarios to ensure safe and correct program execution

Using these primitives allows for mutual exclusion in asynchronous code without blocking threads, ensuring resources are accessed safely and efficiently.

How does "Task.Yield()" interact with the task scheduler, and what is its use?

`Task.Yield()` is an asynchronous method that immediately yields control back to the task scheduler. This allows the scheduler to process other waiting tasks before resuming the current one. Its primary uses include the following:

- **Fairness**: Ensures that long-running or tightly looping tasks don't monopolize a thread, giving other tasks a chance to execute

- **Responsiveness**: Can be used to keep the UI responsive by allowing rendering or other UI tasks to run

- **Advanced scenarios**: Useful in specific scenarios where fine-grained control over task execution order is required

This method introduces a scheduled point of asynchrony in the code, momentarily yielding the current task's execution and allowing other pending tasks to proceed, thereby promoting a more responsive and interleaved execution of operations.

How does C#'s memory model impact multithreading, and what key features of this model are important to understand?

C#'s memory model defines the order and visibility guarantees of memory operations across multiple threads. Key features to understand include the following:

- **Order guarantees**: Within a single thread, C# guarantees a consistent order of execution, known as sequential consistency. However, when observed from multiple threads, operations might appear out of order unless proper synchronization is used.

- **Memory barriers**: These are implicit or explicit operations that prevent reordering and ensure memory visibility across threads. For instance, the `volatile` keyword and operations such as `Thread.MemoryBarrier()` introduce barriers.

- **Volatile reads/writes**: The `volatile` keyword ensures that reads and writes to a field occur directly and are not cached, ensuring real-time visibility across threads.

- **Atomicity**: Some operations in C# are atomic (such as reading/writing a reference or most built-in numeric types), but compound operations (for example, increment) are not atomic unless specifically synchronized.

As we draw a close to our intensive journey through this section, where we mastered the intricate landscape of concurrent programming in C#, we are poised to venture into the vital sphere of *garbage collection*. In this upcoming section, we will demystify the mechanisms of memory management in C#, focusing on the automated process of garbage collection that helps to reclaim memory occupied by objects that are no longer in use. Prepare to delve into the nuances of this essential system component, gaining insights that will empower you to develop applications with optimized memory usage and enhanced performance. Let's continue to deepen our understanding of the sophisticated world of C# programming!

Garbage collection

As developers, we allocate memory for objects, data structures, and various other components, but what happens to this memory when it's no longer in use? Enter the realm of the **garbage collector** **(GC)** – a silent guardian of memory management in the .NET ecosystem. This section will introduce you to the intricacies of the garbage collection process, elucidating how C# and .NET ensure efficient utilization and reclamation of memory resources. Delving deeper, you'll learn about the inner workings of the GC, its generations, and how it identifies and cleans up unreferenced objects. While the GC operates mostly behind the scenes, understanding its behavior and mechanisms can be crucial for optimizing application performance, especially for resource-intensive applications. Journey with us as we demystify the GC, providing you with tools and knowledge to keep your applications running smoothly and efficiently.

What is the primary difference between the stack and heap in the context of memory management and garbage collection in C#?

The stack is used for storing local variables, method execution details, and controlling program flow. It operates in a LIFO manner, and memory is automatically reclaimed when the method or block of code exits. The heap, on the other hand, is used for storing dynamically allocated memory such as objects. Memory on the heap is managed by the GC in C#. Objects in the heap exist until the GC determines that they are no longer reachable and reclaims the memory.

How does .NET recognize that an object has no active references and is ready for garbage collection?

.NET uses a mark-and-sweep algorithm for garbage collection. Initially, all objects on the heap are considered *unreachable*. Starting with root objects (for example, global and static objects, local variables on the stack, and CPU registers), the GC traces and marks each object that is accessible. After the marking phase, any object that remains unmarked is considered **garbage** and is a candidate for collection. These unreachable objects are then swept or collected, freeing up the memory they occupied.

Why are generations in garbage collection important, and how do they function?

Generations in garbage collection optimize the collection process. The .NET GC uses a generational approach, dividing the heap into three generations: 0, 1, and 2. Let's take a closer look at these:

- **Generation 0 (Gen 0)**: Contains short-lived objects, such as temporary variables. Collecting this generation is fast and occurs frequently.

- **Generation 1 (Gen 1)**: Acts as a buffer between short-lived objects and long-lived objects.

- **Generation 2 (Gen 2)**: Contains long-lived objects.

The idea behind this approach is that most objects are short-lived. By collecting Gen 0 frequently, the GC can efficiently reclaim memory from short-lived objects without having to scan older generations. Objects that survive a collection are promoted to the next generation, and the GC checks older generations less frequently.

What is the difference between the "Finalize" and "Dispose" methods in memory management?

Both `Finalize` and `Dispose` methods are mechanisms to release unmanaged resources, but they serve different purposes and are used in different contexts:

- `Finalize`: The `Finalize` method is called by the GC before it reclaims the memory occupied by an object. It's defined in the object's destructor and is intended to release unmanaged resources that the object might be holding. However, relying on finalization has its pitfalls as you can't predict when the GC will run, making it non-deterministic.

- `Dispose`: The `Dispose` method is a part of the `IDisposable` interface. When implemented, it provides a deterministic way to release both managed and unmanaged resources. Typically, you'd call the `Dispose` method explicitly or use the object inside a `using` statement in C#, ensuring that `Dispose` gets called when the object goes out of scope. Using `Dispose` allows for timely resource cleanup, ensuring that resources such as file handles, database connections, and so on are released as soon as they are no longer needed.

How can you signal to the GC about the need for a garbage collection?

You can explicitly request the GC to perform a collection using the `GC.Collect()` method. However, it's important to note that manually invoking garbage collection is usually discouraged. The GC is optimized to run at optimal times based on the application's memory consumption patterns. Forcing a collection can disrupt these optimizations and potentially degrade performance.

What does "memory leak" mean in .NET, and how can garbage collection assist in detecting it?

A **memory leak** in .NET refers to situations where objects remain in memory even though they are no longer needed or accessible. While the GC is designed to automatically reclaim memory occupied by unreachable objects, it can't free objects that still have active references. Therefore, even if an object is no longer in use but still has references pointing to it (for example, due to event handlers or static collections), it will not be collected, leading to memory leaks.

How can weak references help prevent objects from being locked by the GC?

Weak references allow you to hold a reference to an object without preventing that object from being collected by the GC. This can be useful when you want to maintain a cache or temporary reference to an object but don't want that reference to be the sole reason the object remains in memory. When the only existing references to an object are weak references, the object becomes eligible for garbage collection. By using the `WeakReference` class in .NET, you can access the target object if it's still in memory, but you don't prevent the GC from collecting it when necessary.

What is the purpose of the "GC.KeepAlive()"method, and when should it be used?

The `GC.KeepAlive()` method ensures that a specified object remains *alive* and is not collected by the GC until the method call. This can be useful for preventing premature garbage collection, especially for objects with significant finalization logic. For example, if an object holds a resource such as a file handle or network connection and its finalizer releases that resource, using `GC.KeepAlive()` can prevent the finalizer from running prematurely.

How do GC modes of operation (for example, workstation and server) influence its activity?

The GC in .NET operates in different modes to optimize for different scenarios:

- **Workstation mode**: Typically used for single-threaded applications or applications running on a single-core machine. It does not utilize parallelism for garbage collection and is designed to be less intrusive, prioritizing application responsiveness.

- **Server mode**: Optimized for multi-core systems and uses parallel garbage collection to maximize throughput. It's suitable for server applications where performance and scalability are essential.

These modes adjust the GC's behavior to better match the expected application workload and hardware.

What's the difference between the Large Object Heap and the regular heap, and how does it impact garbage collection?

The **Large Object Heap (LOH)** is a special heap in .NET's memory management used to store objects that are 85,000 bytes or larger. The primary differences between LOH and a regular heap are set out here:

- LOH is not compacted as frequently as regular heaps. Compacting large objects can be performance-intensive.

- Objects in LOH are collected during a Gen 2 garbage collection.

Because of these characteristics, it's essential to be cautious when allocating large objects frequently, as it can lead to memory fragmentation and increased Gen 2 collections.

What impact do pinned objects have on the operation of the GC, and what is the Pinned Object Heap?

Pinned objects are objects that the GC is instructed not to move during a memory compaction phase. This is essential when the memory address of an object needs to remain constant, typically when interfacing with native code. Pinned objects can disrupt the efficient compaction of memory and lead to fragmentation. The **Pinned Object Heap** (**POH**), introduced in .NET 5, is a dedicated segment for storing pinned objects, ensuring that they don't interfere with regular heaps and providing more efficient management of pinned objects.

How does the presence of finalizers in objects impact the garbage collection process?

Objects with finalizers complicate the garbage collection process because they require two garbage collection cycles for their complete cleanup. In the first cycle, when the object is detected as unreachable, its finalizer is called. The object is then moved to a list of finalized objects. Only in a subsequent garbage collection cycle is the object actually reclaimed. This means objects with finalizers stay in memory longer, which can potentially lead to increased memory usage if not managed correctly.

How does the GC handle objects that are frequently created and destroyed (for instance, in a loop)?

The GC employs generational collection. Objects that are frequently created and likely to be short-lived are placed in the younger generation (Gen 0). The idea is that it's more efficient to collect from this generation (Gen 0) frequently, as many objects will become unreachable quickly. When garbage collection occurs for this generation, only a subset of the heap (the younger generation) is considered, making the process faster. Objects that survive multiple collections are promoted to older generations, which are collected less frequently.

How does the usage of unmanaged resources impact the GC, and how can one ensure their proper disposal?

Unmanaged resources, such as file handles, database connections, or native memory, are not managed by the .NET GC. If not handled properly, they can lead to resource leaks. To ensure their proper disposal, follow these guidelines:

- **Implement the IDisposable interface**: This allows you to provide a `Dispose` method where you can release unmanaged resources.

- **Use a using statement**: This ensures that the `Dispose` method is called automatically when the object goes out of scope.

- **Use finalizers**: In situations where developers might forget to call `Dispose`, a finalizer (`~ClassName` method) can be used to release resources. However, relying solely on finalizers can introduce delays in resource cleanup, so it's recommended to use them as a backup to the `Dispose` method.

Summary

In this chapter, we embarked on a detailed journey through the intricate realms of C# programming, initiating a deep dive into collections and LINQ to foster adept data structure management. This was closely followed by a study of robust error management through exception handling and debugging, setting the stage for the exploration of dynamic asynchronous programming with `async` and `await`.

The narrative further unfolded to reveal the essentials of event-driven programming through delegates, events, and lambda expressions, paving the way to the versatile world of generics for crafting reusable and type-safe code. As we navigated toward the latter sections, readers could immerse themselves in the complexities of multithreading, offering insights into concurrent programming and efficient memory management through garbage collection.

This chapter serves as a precursor to *Chapter 5, Fundamentals Governing Maintainable and Efficient C# Programming*, in which readers will further enhance their expertise, equipped with a deepened understanding and refined skill set acquired from the exploration of advanced concepts delineated in this chapter.

Additional reading

- *Parallel Programming and Concurrency with C# 10 and .NET 6*, by Alvin Ashcraft

  `https://www.packtpub.com/product/parallel-programming-and-concurrency-with-c-10-and-net-6/9781803243672`

- *50 Algorithms Every Programmer Should Know - Second Edition*, by Imran Ahmad

  `https://www.packtpub.com/product/50-algorithms-every-programmer-should-know-second-edition/9781803247762`

5

Fundamentals Governing Maintainable and Efficient C# Programming

In today's rapidly evolving technological landscape, programming skills are garnering exceptional value and becoming a prerequisite for numerous career paths. This chapter stands as a pivotal resource in enhancing your proficiency in C# coding, facilitating a deep and comprehensive exploration of the cardinal principles underlying the creation of clean, efficient, and maintainable code.

We are set to delve into the critical aspects that characterize successful programming in C#, encompassing the adept application of SOLID principles and the integration of popular design patterns within C# projects. Additionally, this section promises to furnish a well-rounded perspective on the diverse array of C# development tools at your disposal, alongside a foundational understanding of the intricacies of.NET Framework.

Embarking on this chapter not only equips you with vital knowledge requisite for acing interviews but also lays a robust foundation for carving out a flourishing career in the dynamic and rewarding world of C# programming.

By the end of this chapter, you'll be well versed in the following areas:

- Writing clean, maintainable C# code
- Implementing SOLID principles
- Using common design patterns in C# projects
- Utilizing popular C# development tools
- Understanding .NET and .NET Core frameworks
- Unit testing in C# projects

Let's start with how we can write clean, maintainable C# code.

Writing clean, maintainable C# code

In the realm of software development, writing clean and maintainable code is not just a desirable skill but a necessary one. As you delve into C#, it's pivotal to grasp the significance of crafting code that not only works but is also readable, reusable, and easy to modify. At the outset, focus on adhering to naming conventions, organizing your code with appropriate namespaces, and making judicious use of comments to document your code. Embrace the principle of writing code that *speaks* clearly, thereby facilitating a smoother development process in the long run.

In your opinion, what are the main principles of writing "clean" code, and why do you consider them the most important?

The fundamental principles of crafting *clean* code can be considered as follows:

- **Readability**: The code should be easy to read and comprehend, not only for the creator but also for other developers. This facilitates smoother collaboration and knowledge transfer.

- **Modularity**: The code should be divided into logical blocks or modules that can be tested and utilized independently. This approach aids in isolating issues and enhancing code reusability.

- **Don't Repeat Yourself** (**DRY**): Avoid code duplication by utilizing methods, functions, and classes that promote code reusability, which helps in maintaining code more easily and reduces the potential for errors.

- **Clear interfaces**: Functions and classes should have clear and understandable interfaces to promote better interaction and integration between different code components.

- **Simplicity**: Avoid complex and convoluted constructions that can make code maintenance more challenging. Strive for simplicity and clarity to make code more approachable and easier to modify.

How can one identify and avoid "code smells" during C# project development?

Identifying and avoiding *code smells* can be achieved through the following strategies:

- **Code review**: Regularly conduct code reviews with the team to detect and rectify potential issues early in the development process

- **Using code analyzers**: Tools such as **StyleCop** or **ReSharper** can assist in identifying *code smells* by analyzing code for potential issues and suggesting improvements

- **Refactoring**: Regularly refactor the code to avoid complexities and enhance its structure, making it more maintainable and scalable

How do you structure your code to facilitate its maintenance and scalability in the future?

To simplify maintenance and scalability of code, I usually adhere to the following practices:

- **Modular architecture**: Organize code into modules or components that can be easily adjusted or replaced, promoting better organization and **separation of concerns (SoC)**

- **SOLID principles**: Follow *SOLID principles* to create flexible and extensible code that can adapt to changing requirements without significant rework

- **Automated testing**: Employ automated testing to ensure code stability and quality, helping to identify and fix issues promptly

- **Utilizing functions and classes**: Create reusable functions and classes to avoid code duplication and promote code reuse, enhancing overall code quality

- **Design patterns**: Use design patterns to create flexible and reusable solutions, facilitating the development of more complex functionalities with simpler, well-established patterns

- **Refactoring**: Regularly undertake code refactoring to eliminate duplication and improve its structure, making the code more robust and maintainable

What is the importance of self-documenting code in C#, and which methods can be used to create it?

Self-documenting code in C# is significant as it simplifies the process of understanding and maintaining code in the long-term perspective. To create such code, the following methods can be employed:

- Using descriptive names for variables, methods, and classes that convey their purpose and functionality clearly

- Organizing code into logical blocks or sections, thereby facilitating easier navigation and understanding of the code structure

- Adhering to consistent coding standards and formatting, promoting a cohesive and professional code base

- Limiting the length of methods and classes to ensure they perform a specific task, adhering to the **Single Responsibility Principle (SRP)**, which aids in code maintenance and readability

Which exception-handling strategies do you consider to be the most effective for developing clean and easily maintainable code?

To develop clean and easily maintainable code, I consider the following exception-handling strategies to be the most effective:

- Utilizing specific exception types instead of generic ones to provide clear insights into the nature of the error

- Logging exception details to facilitate problem diagnostics and track potential issues more accurately

- Using `try-catch-finally` blocks for effective resource management and code organization, allowing for a structured approach to error handling

- Implementing centralized exception handling to avoid code duplication, promoting a cohesive and streamlined error management strategy

Which tools and methodologies do you recommend for ensuring high code quality in C# projects?

To ensure high code quality in C# projects, I recommend utilizing the following tools and methodologies:

- Static code analysis with tools such as ReSharper, SonarQube, or StyleCop to identify and rectify potential issues early in the development process

- Automated testing, including unit testing and integration tests, to validate code functionality and identify issues promptly

- Code reviews to facilitate knowledge sharing among developers and maintain code quality by encouraging peer feedback and collaboration

- **Continuous integration and continuous delivery/deployment** (CI/CD) to automate verification and deployment processes, ensuring a smooth and efficient development workflow

What strategies do you use to create code that can be easily tested?

To create easily testable code, I employ the following strategies:

- Adopting **test-driven development** (TDD), a methodology that emphasizes writing tests before code needs to be tested.

- Utilizing **dependency injection** (DI) to simplify mocking, thereby facilitating the testing of individual components in isolation.

- Creating small, single-responsibility functions and methods that promote testability by reducing complexity and potential points of failure.

- Using interfaces and abstractions to simplify component substitution during testing, enabling more focused and efficient testing processes.

- Incorporating **domain-driven design** (DDD). This approach, while primarily focused on modeling complex domains, indirectly enhances testability. By clearly defining the domain model, DDD naturally leads to high unit test coverage, making code more robust and easier to test.

How do you ensure that comments in your code are helpful and do not hinder reading and maintaining the code?

To ensure that comments in code are beneficial and do not obstruct code readability and maintenance, I adhere to the following guidelines:

- Using comments to explain complex or non-obvious parts of code, providing clarity and aiding in code comprehension

- Avoiding duplicating information that is already conveyed clearly through the code itself, to prevent redundancy and potential discrepancies

- Regularly updating comments to ensure they remain accurate and reflect the current state of the code, fostering clear and effective documentation

- Utilizing XML documentation to provide detailed information about the API, which can be used by other developers to understand and utilize the code effectively

Could you name a few code quality metrics that you use for monitoring and improving the code base in C# projects?

Some code quality metrics I utilize include the following:

- Cyclomatic complexity, which helps in understanding the code's complexity and identifying areas that might require simplification or refactoring

- Code coverage by tests, which provides insights into the proportion of code that is covered by automated tests, helping to pinpoint areas that might be at risk of containing undetected issues

- Number of bugs per thousand lines of code, a metric that helps in tracking the overall health and stability of the code base

- Feedback and ratings from users, which can offer valuable insights into potential areas for improvement from an end-user perspective

These metrics aid in monitoring and enhancing code quality over time, supporting a proactive approach to code maintenance and improvement.

How do you structure branches in your Git projects, and what best practices do you adhere to when working with them?

In my projects, I typically organize branches using Git Flow or GitHub Flow, depending on the specific requirements of the project. I adhere to best practices such as utilizing separate branches for features, adhering to meaningful branch naming conventions, and regularly merging with the main branch to prevent conflicts.

For instance, when creating a new feature, I initiate a separate branch with a name that clearly reflects its purpose, such as `feature/user-authentication`. Upon completion of the development, I conduct a code review and merge that branch with the main branch, ensuring stability and organized code management.

Which books have you read to learn about maintainable code?

To grasp the essence of maintainable code, I have studied several significant publications in the field of programming, including the following:

- *Clean Code: A Handbook of Agile Software Craftsmanship* by Robert C. Martin, which discusses principles of writing clean and efficient code

- *Refactoring: Improving the Design of Existing Code* by Martin Fowler, a book offering valuable advice on optimizing and enhancing existing code

- *Design Patterns: Elements of Reusable Object-Oriented Software* by Erich Gamma and others, which provides an in-depth introduction to design patterns that foster the creation of scalable and maintainable code

- *Mastering C# and .NET Framework* by Federico Colasante, which offers a deep dive into C# and .NET Framework, exploring best practices and design patterns that promote the creation of maintainable code

- *Hands-On Design Patterns with C#* by Eric Fernandes, a book with a detailed exploration of various design patterns that can assist in writing more organized and easily maintainable code

- *C# 9 and .NET 5 – Modern Cross-Platform Development* by Mark Price, which offers a good introduction to modern C# development practices and helps understand how to write clean and maintainable code

- *C# 8.0 and .NET Core 3.0 – Modern Cross-Platform Development*, also by Mark Price, a good continuation of the first book, incorporating updated practices and technologies for writing modern and maintainable C# code

These books have helped me develop a deep understanding of how to write maintainable, efficient, and clean code that serves as a reliable foundation for any project.

As we draw this section to a close, remember that the journey toward mastering clean, maintainable C# code is a continuous one. It's more than just following guidelines; it's about fostering a mindset of quality, efficiency, and collaboration. Remember to review your code regularly, refactoring when necessary to enhance its clarity and maintainability. Moreover, don't hesitate to learn from the community, continually incorporating best practices and innovations into your coding style. By doing so, you pave the way for not only successful projects but also a rewarding career in C# development.

Having delved into the foundational concepts, our next step is to explore SOLID principles, a crucial set of design principles in **object-oriented** (**OO**) software development. These principles are paramount for writing code that is easy to maintain, understand, and extend. Understanding these principles will equip us with the knowledge to design robust and efficient systems.

Implementing SOLID principles

In this section, we delve into the essence of implementing SOLID principles, the cornerstone of **OO programming** (**OOP**). These guidelines, conceptualized by Robert C. Martin, serve as a golden standard in crafting maintainable, scalable, and robust software. As we navigate through each principle – **Single Responsibility Principle** (**SRP**), **Open/Closed Principle** (**OCP**), **Liskov Substitution Principle** (**LSP**), **Interface Segregation Principle** (**ISP**), and **Dependency Inversion Principle** (**DIP**) – we will unravel the techniques to imbue your C# programming projects with coherence and versatility.

Could you explain each of the SOLID principles in detail and provide specific examples of their application in C# programming?

The SOLID principles are as follows:

- **SRP**: Picture a bakery; each worker has a specific job, and they do that one job really well. Similarly, in programming, every class should have just one job or responsibility. If a class starts doing too many things, it may be time to split it into separate classes, just as how in a bakery you'd hire more people for different roles. This keeps your code tidy and makes it easier to understand and manage.

- **OCP**: Imagine a LEGO building; you can add more blocks, but you don't modify the ones that are already there. Likewise, in coding, a class should be like that LEGO building: open for extending (adding more blocks) but closed for modifying (not changing existing blocks). This way, you can introduce new functionalities without breaking or changing existing code. Just as you use different LEGO blocks, use abstract classes and interfaces in C# to extend your class functionality.

- **LSP**: Consider a generic screwdriver, specifically a cross-head screwdriver of size 2 inches. It's like saying, whether this screwdriver is green or has a chevron pattern, it's still a 2-inch cross-head screwdriver. In C#, this means your subclass must be interchangeable with its base class without causing any issues in the program. By properly utilizing inheritance and polymorphism in C#, we can introduce various "2-inch cross-head screwdrivers" (subclasses) with different appearances without altering the fundamental role of a "screwdriver" (base class).

- **ISP**: Think about a restaurant menu; you wouldn't want to look through the entire menu if you were only interested in desserts, right? This principle suggests that classes shouldn't be forced to implement interfaces they don't use. In C#, this means we should break our interfaces into smaller, more specific ones so that any class *ordering from the menu* only needs to *look at* the parts that matter to it.

- **DIP**: Imagine a car assembly line where the order of assembly doesn't govern the design of the car parts. Just like that, higher-level parts of your code (classes) shouldn't be dependent on lower-level ones; rather, they should both rely on the same set of rules or contracts (abstractions). You can achieve this in C# by using DI, which helps in keeping your code flexible and easily testable, like car parts ready to be installed in any car model.

How can applying the SRP contribute to developing code that is easier to maintain and adapt?

Applying the SRP aids in creating code that is easier to maintain and adapt since each class or module focuses only on one functional area. This simplifies the process of making changes, as modifications in one part of the system have a lesser impact on other parts, promoting greater flexibility and reducing the risk of introducing errors when making changes.

Could you describe how you implement the OCP in your projects to avoid issues related to modifying existing code?

I implement the OCP in my projects through the use of abstract classes and interfaces, which allow for the extension of functionality without changing existing code. This helps to avoid regression errors and ensures the system's flexibility for future expansions. By adhering to this principle, I can add new features or modify existing ones without affecting the stability of the existing system, promoting a more robust and adaptable code base.

How do you utilize the LSP in your projects to build systems that are easily scalable and adaptable to changes?

I utilize the LSP in my projects by carefully planning the class hierarchy and ensuring that subclasses can be substituted for base classes without losing functionality or causing unpredictable behavior. This aids in creating a system that is easily scalable and adaptable to changes since new features can be added through inheritance and polymorphism, fostering a more flexible and robust architecture.

How do you implement the ISP in your projects to avoid the creation of "fat" interfaces that contain too many methods?

I implement the ISP in my projects by creating small, specific interfaces that focus on particular functionalities, instead of creating *fat* interfaces with numerous methods. This allows for a more flexible and adaptable system, as clients can depend only on the interfaces they require, instead of being forced to implement unnecessary methods. This approach promotes cleaner and more manageable code, making the system more modular and easier to maintain.

How can the SRP be implemented within a class in C#? Could you provide a specific example?

Certainly – to implement the SRP in C#, it's important to design a class in such a way that it performs only one function or holds one responsibility. Let's consider an `OrderProcessing` class that has the responsibility of handling orders:

```csharp
public class Order
{
    public int Id { get; set; }
    public string[] Items { get; set; }
    public double Price { get; set; }
    public double Email { get; set; }
}

public class OrderProcessing
{
    public void ProcessOrder(Order order)
    {
        ValidateOrder(order.Items);
        SaveOrder(order);
        SendConfirmationEmail(order.Id, order.Email);
    }

    private void ValidateItems(string[] items)
    {
        // Items validation logic
    }

    private void SaveOrder(Order order)
    {
        // Logic to save the order in the database
    }

    private void SendConfirmationEmail(string orderId, string email)
    {
        // Logic to send confirmation email
    }
}
```

In the preceding example, although the `OrderProcessing` class performs several tasks, all these tasks are unified under a single responsibility – order processing. Each method handles a separate aspect of this process, adhering to the SRP, which facilitates easier maintenance and enhances the class's adaptability to changes without affecting other functionalities.

Can you discuss a scenario in C# where a violation of the LSP led to problems in the software system?

Yes – a violation of this principle can occur when a subclass alters the behavior of one of the methods of the base class in such a way that it no longer meets the expectations defined by the base class. For instance, if in the base class you have an `int Add(int a, int b)` method that returns the sum of two elements, and in the subclass you override this method to now return the difference of the elements multiplied by 2, it can lead to unexpected errors or bugs in the software code. This deviation can create unpredictability and complexity, making the system more prone to errors and harder to manage and maintain.

How would you employ the ISP in C# to avoid the obligation of implementing unnecessary methods in a specific class?

I would adhere to this principle by creating small, specialized interfaces instead of one large interface that encompasses all possible methods. In this way, classes can implement only the interfaces that are necessary for them, avoiding unnecessary overhead. This not only prevents classes from being burdened with unnecessary methods but also promotes a clean and organized code structure, enhancing the maintainability and scalability of the system.

Could you provide an example of the implementation of the DIP in C# through DI or the use of service containers?

One way to implement this principle in C# is to utilize the DI pattern or constructor injection. This can be achieved using service containers, which allow us to dynamically inject dependencies, providing flexibility and testability.

In this application, we have different audio formats such as MP3, WAV, and so on. Each of these formats requires a specific decoder to be played.

First, we define an interface, `IAudioDecoder`:

```
public interface IAudioDecoder
{
    void Decode();
}
```

Next, we implement this interface for each of the audio formats (MP3 and WAV, in this case):

```
public class MP3Decoder : IAudioDecoder
{
    public void Decode()
    {
        // Logic to decode MP3 files
    }
}

public class WAVDecoder : IAudioDecoder
{
    public void Decode()
    {
        // Logic to decode WAV files
    }
}
```

The `MusicPlayer` class, which is a higher-level module, depends on `IAudioDecoder`, an abstraction of the audio decoder, rather than depending on low-level modules such as `MP3Decoder` or `WAVDecoder` directly. This way, we follow the *DIP*.

Here's how the `MusicPlayer` class looks:

```
public class MusicPlayer
{
    private readonly IAudioDecoder _decoder;

    // The constructor receives a dependency on the IAudioDecoder
    abstraction.
    public MusicPlayer(IAudioDecoder decoder)
    {
        _decoder = decoder;
    }

    public void PlayMusic()
    {
        _decoder.Decode();
        // Additional logic to play the music
    }
}
```

Now, the `MusicPlayer` class doesn't need to know what specific type of decoder it is using, making it possible to play different types of audio files, as long as they use an implementation of `IAudioDecoder`:

```
public class Program
{
    static void Main(string[] args)
    {
        // Using the MusicPlayer with an MP3 decoder
        var mp3Player = new MusicPlayer(new MP3Decoder());
        mp3Player.PlayMusic();

        // Using the MusicPlayer with a WAV decoder
        var wavPlayer = new MusicPlayer(new WAVDecoder());
        wavPlayer.PlayMusic();
    }
}
```

This example separates the responsibility of audio decoding from the actual music player and allows us to easily add support for more audio formats in the future, without modifying the `MusicPlayer` class.

Could you describe the use of delegates and events in C# to support the OCP?

Yes – by using delegates and events, you can create a system that is open for extension but closed for modification. This means that you can add new functionalities through events without modifying the main class. Here is an example:

```
public class OrderProcessor
{
    public delegate void OrderProcessedEventHandler(Order order);
    public event OrderProcessedEventHandler OrderProcessed;

    public void ProcessOrder(Order order)
    {
        // Order processing logic

        OrderProcessed?.Invoke(order);
    }
}

public class OrderNotification
{
```

```
        public void OnOrderProcessed(Order order)
        {
            // Notification logic for order processing
        }
    }
```

In the preceding example, the `OrderProcessor` class leverages delegates and events to notify other components of the order processing, without directly coupling to them. This approach allows for a more flexible and extensible system where new functionalities can be added by subscribing to events, adhering to the OCP, and promoting a clean and modular code structure.

Can you provide examples of classes or interfaces in C# that effectively demonstrate the ISP?

Yes – here is an example of how interfaces can be segregated for different roles within a system:

```csharp
public interface IOrderProcessor
{
    void ProcessOrder(Order order);
}

public interface IOrderValidator
{
    bool ValidateOrder(Order order);
}

public interface IOrderSaver
{
    void SaveOrder(Order order);
}

public class OrderManager : IOrderProcessor, IOrderValidator,
IOrderSaver
{
    // Interface methods implementation here
}
```

In this example, the interfaces are segregated into specific roles, such as processing, validating, and saving orders. This allows the `OrderManager` class to implement only the methods it requires, promoting a cleaner and more modular design in adherence to the ISP.

Could you discuss a few examples of "code smells" or anti-patterns in C# that often indicate a violation of SOLID principles?

Certainly – here are a few common *code smells* that might indicate a breach of SOLID principles:

- **Gigantic classes or methods**: This may signal a violation of the SRP, as the classes or methods are undertaking too many tasks

- **Global variables**: These can complicate code tracking and modification, potentially violating the OCP

- **Tight coupling between components**: This might indicate a breach of the DIP, as components are difficult to change or replace independently of each other

- **The logic of a single physical process dispersed among various classes that call each other**: This could signal a lack of clear responsibility segregation

- **A large number of classes and abstractions that do nothing but pass control to another class**: This might indicate an over-engineered or unnecessarily complex system

- **Unclear class wrappers and method names**: This could represent a lack of clarity, making code less readable and maintainable

Avoiding these anti-patterns and code smells will help in crafting more robust, scalable, and maintainable code.

How can utilizing the DIP facilitate the development of scalable and independent modules?

The DIP encourages us to design our systems so that they depend on abstractions, not concrete implementations. This means that instead of high-level modules depending on low-level modules, both types of modules depend on abstractions. This ensures flexibility, allowing for changes in internal implementation without affecting external modules and aiding in the creation of scalable and independent systems.

Could you discuss some typical situations where adhering to certain SOLID principles can be particularly challenging, and how do you find a balance in such cases?

One typical scenario is when adhering to the SRP leads to excessive fragmentation of code into smaller parts, complicating the understanding of the system. In such situations, I seek a balance by trying to identify *logical* responsibilities.

Another case is when adhering to the OCP results in too much generalization, making code less efficient. Here, it's important to understand which parts of the system are most prone to changes and to focus on them. Finding a balance involves a thoughtful approach to code design, considering both the potential benefits of adherence to SOLID principles and the practical implications of doing so.

As we wrap up this section, it's evident that SOLID principles are not just theoretical concepts but powerful tools in the hands of a skilled developer. Implementing these principles in your C# programming journey is akin to building a strong foundation for a house; it promises stability, durability, and resilience. We encourage you to assimilate these principles profoundly, as they are bound to become your trusted allies in crafting software solutions that stand the test of time.

Next, we will explore common design patterns in C# projects: essential tools for solving recurring design problems and writing maintainable, scalable code. Understanding these patterns will allow us to enhance our coding practices and facilitate efficient problem-solving within our projects.

Using common design patterns in C# projects

In the forthcoming section, we set our sights on common design patterns prevalent in C# projects, an essential topic for developers striving for proficiency and expertise. These patterns, often regarded as time-tested solutions to common problems, facilitate the creation of software architectures that are both robust and adaptable. From the Singleton to the Factory Method, each pattern offers unique approaches to tackle specific issues, streamlining the development process and fostering code reusability. Let's embark on a journey to decode the intricacies of these patterns and understand how they can be leveraged to enhance your C# project developments.

Why is it important to adhere to design patterns during the development of software solutions in C#?

Utilizing design patterns in C# programming is crucial as they offer time-tested and efficient solutions for common design problems. These patterns promote the creation of clean, scalable, and maintainable code, effectively serving as *best practices* for software development. They help in structuring code in a way that facilitates ease of understanding, modification, and testing, thereby enhancing the overall quality and robustness of the software solution.

How can design patterns facilitate the ease of maintenance and scalability of projects in C#?

Design patterns can ease the maintenance and scalability of C# projects by offering structured and organized solutions to commonly encountered design challenges. They help in keeping code organized, transparent, and adaptable to changes or expansions, reducing the time and effort required. Through their implementation, developers can establish a solid foundation, promoting code reusability and modular design, which in turn enhances the project's longevity and adaptability.

Is there a risk of complicating the software or encountering other problems due to the use of design patterns, and how can this be prevented?

Yes – sometimes, the use of design patterns can induce excessive complexity, especially if they are applied incorrectly or unnecessarily. To prevent this, developers should critically assess the problem they are attempting to solve and determine whether the design pattern is truly the optimal solution. Additionally, it is important to maintain proper documentation and adhere to principles of clean coding to ensure that the software remains manageable and maintainable.

How can design patterns influence the efficiency of software developed in C#?

Design patterns can enhance the efficiency of software developed in C# by fostering modularity and facilitating easier testing and maintenance. However, incorrect or excessive use of patterns can increase complexity and reduce efficiency. Therefore, it is vital to approach them judiciously, selecting only those patterns that genuinely align with the specific needs of the project. This thoughtful application helps in creating a balanced architecture that supports smooth functionality and future expansions.

Can you explain how the Singleton pattern works in C# and scenarios where it is best applied? How will you implement it?

The **Singleton** pattern in C# is utilized to ensure that a class has only one instance throughout the application and provides a global point of access to that instance. This can be achieved by creating a private constructor and a static property or method to access the single instance. This pattern is often used in situations where there is a need to coordinate actions across different parts of the system or to maintain some shared state. It is particularly useful when an operation needs to be controlled centrally, such as managing connections or a configuration setting in an application.

```
public class Singleton
{
    // Lazy instance of the Singleton, instantiated only when needed
    private static readonly Lazy<Singleton> lazyInstance = new (() =>
new Singleton());

    // Private constructor so that other classes cannot instantiate it
    private Singleton() { }

    // Public static property to get the instance of the class
    public static Singleton Instance => lazyInstance.Value;
}
```

How can you apply the Factory pattern in C# to initialize objects belonging to the same class hierarchy?

The **Factory** pattern in C# facilitates the initialization of objects belonging to the same class hierarchy by choosing a specific class to create an object at runtime based on input parameters or logic. This makes the system more flexible, as it allows for the introduction of new types of objects without altering existing code. This design pattern promotes loose coupling and enables extending the application with new functionalities with ease.

Could you provide an example of implementing the Observer pattern in C#, possibly using delegates and events?

The **Observer** pattern in C# can be implemented using delegates and events. In this approach, a class known as the *subject* contains an event to which observers can subscribe. When the state of the subject changes, it triggers the event, notifying all subscribers about the change. The observers can then respond to this change accordingly. This allows for a dynamic relationship between objects, where specific actions can be taken in response to changes, facilitating a more interactive and responsive system.

How can the Strategy pattern contribute to flexibility and ease of maintenance in C# projects?

The **Strategy** pattern in C# facilitates flexibility and eases maintenance by allowing you to define a family of algorithms, encapsulating each one within a separate class. This permits the dynamic interchange of algorithms at runtime. The selection of a specific strategy can be based on various conditions, making the system more adaptable to changes and enhancing its ability to evolve without undergoing major alterations.

Could you describe how to implement the Decorator pattern in C# and its advantages compared to traditional inheritance?

The **Decorator** pattern in C# enables the addition of new functionalities to objects dynamically by creating a series of decorator classes that wrap specific objects. This offers more flexibility compared to inheritance, as it allows for the dynamic and selective alteration of an object's behavior without changing its class or creating new subclasses. This pattern is particularly beneficial when you want to add responsibilities to objects dynamically and transparently – that is, without affecting other objects.

How can the Composite pattern assist in developing hierarchical object structures in projects implemented in C#?

The **Composite** pattern in C# assists in creating hierarchical structures of objects by treating both individual and complex objects uniformly. This allows client code to handle individual and composite objects similarly, simplifying the architecture and development of the software. It is especially useful when developing systems with nested structures, such as menu trees or filesystems, facilitating the management and operation of complex structures in a more efficient manner.

Can you describe the utilization of the Proxy pattern in C# for controlling access to an object or for tracking (logging) operations?

The **Proxy** pattern in C# facilitates the creation of a substitute (proxy) for a real object to control access to it. A proxy can be employed for logging operations, restricting access to the real object, or performing certain actions before and/or after calling the methods of the real object. This simplifies the addition of new functionalities without altering the code of the real object, promoting a more manageable and adaptable code structure.

Could you provide an example of how the Adapter pattern can be used in C# to integrate two incompatible interfaces?

The **Adapter** pattern in C# aids in merging two incompatible interfaces by creating an adapter that implements one interface and encapsulates an object of the other interface. The adapter translates method calls from one interface to the corresponding method calls of the other interface, allowing the combination of two incompatible interfaces without modifying their original code. This facilitates smoother interactions between systems, streamlining the integration process and enhancing code reusability.

Could you discuss how the MVC pattern is integrated and utilized within the framework of ASP.NET Core?

The **Model View Controller** (MVC) pattern is a pivotal component of ASP.NET Core, organizing code into three primary components: model, view, and controller. The *model* is responsible for business logic and data management, the *view* handles data presentation, and the *controller* acts as an intermediary between the model and the view, handling input requests and managing data flow. This structure fosters clean and organized code, facilitating easier maintenance and scalability, thereby enhancing the robustness and efficiency of web application development.

How can the Repository pattern simplify the process of testing and maintaining databases in C# projects?

The **Repository** pattern can streamline the process of testing and maintaining databases in C# projects by abstracting the interaction with the database from the application's business logic. This allows developers to create mock repositories for unit testing and isolates changes in the database structure from the main application code, thereby simplifying maintenance and update processes. By promoting a clear SoC, it enhances the modularity and testability of the system.

Can you describe how the Unit of Work pattern interacts with the Repository pattern in the context of C# projects?

In C# projects, the **Unit of Work** pattern complements the Repository pattern, coordinating operations among several repositories and ensuring transaction consistency. It allows for grouping several operations into a single transaction, fostering greater data reliability and integrity. Moreover, it facilitates transaction management and error handling at a more general level, thereby promoting a cohesive and robust system architecture.

How can the Mediator pattern assist in creating decentralized systems in C# programming?

The **Mediator** pattern facilitates the creation of decentralized systems in C# by mediating communication between objects, instead of allowing them to interact with each other directly. This reduces dependencies between classes and encourages the development of more modular and flexible systems, where components can be easily substituted or scaled independently of one another. By centralizing external communications, this pattern promotes a cleaner and more maintainable code base, enhancing the system's adaptability to evolving requirements.

Can you explain the differences between the Bridge and Adapter patterns and when it is optimal to use each of them in C# projects?

The **Bridge** pattern is used to separate an abstraction from its implementation, allowing both to vary independently. This is beneficial when you aim to segregate system components into separate hierarchies, fostering scalability and flexibility. On the other hand, the Adapter pattern is utilized to ensure compatibility between two incompatible interfaces, transforming the interface of one class into another expected by the client. In C# projects, the Bridge pattern is more suitable when you need to build a flexible and scalable system with extendable abstractions and implementations. The Adapter pattern is ideal for integrating new features or libraries with existing code without altering the original interface, facilitating smoother transitions and system expansions.

How is the flexibility of a request-handling system characterized, which can be achieved through the use of the Chain of Responsibility pattern?

The **Chain of Responsibility** pattern facilitates the creation of a flexible request-handling system by forming a chain of handler objects, where each handler contains a reference to the next handler in the chain. A request is passed from one handler to another until it is processed or the chain ends. This structure allows for dynamic modification of handlers and provides flexibility when adding or removing handlers, enhancing the adaptability of the system to different types of requests and changing requirements.

How have you utilized the Builder pattern in C# to simplify the process of creating objects with numerous attributes or complex constructors?

The **Builder** pattern can be utilized to encapsulate the complex process of object creation, providing a smooth and step-by-step method to construct its various components. This not only makes the code more readable but also facilitates easier management of the object's construction parameters. It helps in avoiding constructor pollution with numerous parameters and allows for constructing an object with a clear set of operations, enhancing code maintainability and readability.

In which scenarios can the use of the Prototype pattern be beneficial for enhancing system performance through object cloning instead of creating new instances?

The **Prototype** pattern can be beneficial in systems where creating a new instance from scratch is time-consuming or resource-intensive. Utilizing this pattern allows for the cloning of an existing object, which can be significantly faster and more efficient, especially if most of the object's attributes remain unchanged. This approach is particularly useful when the cost of creating an object is more complex or involves more resources than copying an existing instance, thereby optimizing system performance.

Can you describe a scenario where you successfully implemented the Visitor pattern in C# to extend the functionality of existing classes without modifying them?

The **Visitor** pattern can be employed to add new operations to existing object classes without the necessity to modify those classes directly. This helps preserve the SRP and the OCP, thereby ensuring the system's stability and flexibility. In a specific scenario, for instance, the Visitor pattern can allow you to add reporting features or complex data manipulation operations to a set of objects without altering their existing class structures, promoting a cleaner and more maintainable code architecture.

How can one implement the Saga and CQRS design patterns in a microservices architecture on the .NET platform, and what potential challenges and solutions might arise during this process?

Integrating the Saga and **Command Query Responsibility Segregation** (**CQRS**) design patterns into a microservices architecture can be quite effective in ensuring system consistency and responsive performance for the following reasons:

- **Saga pattern**: It can be employed to orchestrate long transactions across microservices through a sequence of local transactions, each capable of being compensated in case of failure. The transactions can be tracked through a correlation ID, and compensating transactions can be utilized to handle adverse scenarios, thereby ensuring data consistency and reliability.

- **CQRS pattern**: This pattern allows you to segregate the read and write models, which can enhance system performance and scalability. However, it can increase the system's complexity since you will have to manage two separate models, necessitating careful planning and coordination.

Potential challenges might encompass the complexity of managing transactions in Saga and maintaining consistency in CQRS. Solutions might include leveraging an **event-driven architecture** (**EDA**) and implementing a well-planned strategy for error handling, thus fostering a more robust and adaptable system structure.

Can you provide an example of a situation where applying a design pattern wasn't the best choice and how you adapted your approach to address this challenge?

Sometimes, utilizing a design pattern can turn out to be excessive and introduce unnecessary complexity in simple projects. For instance, in a small project, implementing the MVC pattern might be overly complex and time-consuming. In such cases, the optimal solution might be to reassess the approach and opt for a simpler and more direct method to implement the functionality. This could involve refactoring the code or selecting a less complicated pattern, aiming to maintain a balance between the project's scope and the complexity introduced by the pattern.

Have you encountered situations where standard design patterns were insufficient and you had to create customized patterns to address specific issues in your C# project? Please share your experience with examples.

Yes – there are instances where standard design patterns might not offer the flexibility required to address specific challenges in a project. In such situations, it becomes necessary to develop customized patterns or adapt existing patterns to meet the particular needs of your project.

An example could be developing a customized pattern to manage specific performance or security requirements in your project. This could entail creating application-specific patterns for managing caching, logging, or error handling, which are specially designed to meet your particular requirements and circumstances.

The critical aspect here is to ensure that your customized patterns are well documented and easily maintainable, enabling them to serve your project effectively in the long run, without adding unnecessary complexity or maintenance challenges.

As we conclude this insightful journey through the landscape of common design patterns in C# projects, it's clear that these patterns are more than mere templates; they are the blueprint for constructing efficient, scalable, and maintainable software. Implementing these patterns effectively can transform the very essence of your programming endeavors, guiding you to craft code that is not only robust but also adaptable to changing requirements. We hope that you'll carry the knowledge gained in this chapter forward, utilizing these patterns as powerful tools in your future C# development ventures.

Now, let's shift our focus to an overview of popular C# development tools, essential components for any developer working with this versatile language. Exploring these tools will provide insights into optimizing our development processes and enhancing productivity in C# project implementation.

Utilizing popular C# development tools

As we delve into this critical section, we turn our attention to the myriad of popular development tools that have positioned C# as a powerhouse in the programming world. These tools, ranging from robust **integrated development environments (IDEs)** such as Visual Studio to **version control systems (VCS)** such as Git, are designed to augment the productivity and efficiency of developers. In this section, we will navigate through the functionalities and features of these tools, offering you a comprehensive perspective that aims to enhance your C# development experience. Let's embark on this enlightening exploration to equip you with the knowledge to select and utilize the most suitable tools for your projects.

What do you see as the key advantages of using Visual Studio while programming in C#?

Utilizing Visual Studio for C# development offers several advantages, including the following:

- **IDE**: Visual Studio provides a comprehensive IDE that simplifies the development process by consolidating all necessary tools in one place

- **Support for various project types**: Visual Studio supports a broad spectrum of project types, ranging from console applications to web services and mobile applications

- **Extensibility**: Through extensions and plugins, Visual Studio can be adapted to meet the specific needs of developers, enhancing its functionality and versatility

- **Powerful debugging tools**: Visual Studio comes equipped with robust debugging tools that facilitate the identification and rectification of errors, streamlining the development process

- **Integration with VCS**: Visual Studio integrates seamlessly with popular VCS such as Git, making code version management more straightforward and efficient

Have you utilized tools such as ReSharper for optimizing C# code? If so, what are the primary advantages of these tools that you would highlight?

Yes – I have used tools such as ReSharper for optimizing C# code. The primary advantages of these tools include the following:

- **Clean code support**: These tools assist in maintaining high code quality by offering recommendations and automatic corrections for common coding issues, promoting cleaner and more maintainable code

- **Productivity enhancement**: They help enhance productivity by facilitating quicker and more efficient code development, offering features such as automatic code completion, navigation, and others

- **Refactoring**: Tools such as ReSharper provide powerful refactoring capabilities, allowing developers to easily make structural changes to the code without introducing errors, thus ensuring code integrity and organization

Which VCS would you recommend for use during the development of C# programs?

For C# development, I would recommend using VCS such as Git, which is widely popular and offers great flexibility and integration with many platforms and tools. It facilitates efficient code management and collaboration, ensuring project consistency and streamlined workflows.

Could you please compare the experience of developing programs in C# using Visual Studio and Visual Studio Code?

Visual Studio and Visual Studio Code are both powerful tools for C# development, but they exhibit some distinct differences:

- **Visual Studio**: This is a fully featured IDE offering a vast array of tools and capabilities for developing complex projects. It integrates deeply with various Microsoft services and offers extensive support for C# development.

- **Visual Studio Code**: This is a lighter and more flexible code editor, which can be adapted for C# development through extensions. It offers fast operation and ease of use, especially for smaller projects or for developers who prefer working with a text editor over a full-fledged IDE. The choice between the two would depend on the specific needs of your project and personal preferences in working style.

What has been your experience using .NET Core for creating cross-platform applications?

Utilizing .NET Core, I have had the opportunity to create applications that function well on Windows, macOS, and Linux. The main advantages include the following:

- **Cross-platform capability**: .NET Core applications can be deployed on various operating systems, enhancing the reach and versatility of your applications

- **Performance**: .NET Core is optimized for high performance, ensuring smooth and responsive application operations

- **Modularity**: .NET allows the inclusion of only the necessary libraries for your project, promoting lean and efficient development processes

Which profiling tools do you use for analyzing and optimizing the performance of C# programs?

I employ profiling tools such as Visual Studio Diagnostic Tools and JetBrains dotTrace to identify bottlenecks in code. These tools facilitate the analysis of code execution in terms of time and resource usage, aiding in pinpointing and optimizing the most resource-intensive sections of code, thereby enhancing overall performance.

Do you use automation tools for build and deployment, such as GitHub Actions, GitLab CI/CD, Jenkins, or Azure DevOps, for your C# projects?

Yes – I utilize various automation tools depending on the project. For instance, Azure DevOps offers integrated solutions for building and deploying .NET applications, while GitHub Actions and Jenkins provide the flexibility to create adaptable CI/CD pipelines. These tools facilitate streamlined, reliable, and efficient deployment workflows, helping to maintain a consistent and high-quality development process.

Which frameworks and libraries for unit testing have you utilized in your C# development practice?

In my C# development practice, I frequently use NUnit and xUnit for unit testing. Additionally, I utilize Moq to create mock and fake objects during testing. These tools assist in establishing a robust testing environment, facilitating more reliable and maintainable code.

Could you share your experience in integrating databases with C# applications? What technologies and tools have you used?

I have integrated a variety of databases with C# applications. For relational databases, I often employ **Entity Framework** (**EF**) or Dapper. Regarding NoSQL databases, I have experience working with MongoDB and Azure Cosmos DB. EF facilitates working with databases at a higher level of abstraction through **object-relational mapping** (**ORM**), while Dapper provides speed and flexibility when working with SQL queries, ensuring an optimized and efficient data-handling process.

Please share your experience using the Git VCS and the GitHub platform for managing C# projects.

In my C# projects, I actively use Git and GitHub for version control and collaboration with other developers. Git allows tracking of changes, creating branches for individual features, and easily merging changes. GitHub offers a platform for collaborative work on projects, including features such as pull requests, code reviews, and integration with CI/CD systems, promoting a cohesive and streamlined development process.

Which tools for static code analysis have you used in C# projects, and what specific issues have they helped you identify?

In my C# projects, I have used static code analysis tools such as SonarQube and StyleCop. These tools assist in identifying various issues, including coding style violations, potential errors, and security vulnerabilities. For instance, these tools can pinpoint places where `null` reference exceptions might occur or where APIs are used incorrectly, helping to maintain code quality and prevent potential bugs.

Could you discuss the tools you have used for measuring code coverage in your C# projects and why this aspect is important?

I have used tools such as Coverlet and Visual Studio Code Coverage to measure code coverage in my C# projects. Measuring code coverage is vital as it helps to identify areas of code that have not been tested, thereby reducing the risk of bugs in production. It facilitates the creation of a more reliable and robust application by ensuring that critical code paths are adequately tested.

Have you utilized log analysis systems in your C# projects, and if so, how have they contributed to identifying and resolving issues?

Yes – I have utilized log analysis systems such as the ELK Stack (Elasticsearch, Logstash, and Kibana) and Serilog in my C# projects. These systems aid in the collection and analysis of logs, significantly simplifying the process of detecting and resolving issues, especially in large and complex systems. These systems provide invaluable insights into application behavior, facilitating rapid issue detection and resolution.

Do you have experience implementing CI/CD systems during C# development, and if so, how are they integrated into your workflow?

Yes – in my C# projects, I actively utilize CI/CD systems such as Jenkins, Azure DevOps, and GitLab CI. These systems facilitate the automation of the testing and deployment process, promoting rapid error detection and correction and contributing to a smooth and efficient product delivery. These systems are integrated into my workflow in a way that streamlines the development process, ensuring that code is continuously tested and ready for deployment, which helps maintain a high pace of development while ensuring product quality.

hat strategies and tools have you applied to optimize database performance in your C# applications?

To optimize database performance in my C# applications, I have employed various approaches, including utilizing indexes to enhance database queries, optimizing queries using database profilers, and employing caching to reduce database load. The tools I have used encompass **SQL Server Management Studio (SSMS)** and EF. These strategies help ensure that database operations are efficient and do not become a bottleneck in the application, thereby ensuring smooth and responsive application performance.

Have you used tools for automatic code documentation generation in your C# projects, and if so, which ones would you recommend?

Yes – I have used tools such as Doxygen and Sandcastle for automatic code documentation generation in my C# projects. These tools analyze the source code and comments to generate comprehensive documentation, facilitating better understanding and maintenance of code. I would recommend these tools as they can significantly aid in maintaining code quality and facilitating collaboration and knowledge sharing among development teams.

Do you have experience implementing monitoring systems to track the performance and stability of your C# applications?

Yes – I have utilized monitoring systems such as Grafana, Prometheus, and OpenTelemetry to track the performance and stability of my C# applications. These systems help monitor various parameters such as server response time and memory usage, among others, allowing for timely identification and resolution of issues. Implementing such systems is vital in maintaining the stability and reliability of applications, as they provide insights into the applications' behavior and help in proactive issue detection and resolution.

Could you describe your experience with utilizing external libraries and APIs in your C# projects, as well as using the NuGet package manager?

Yes – in my C# projects, I frequently make use of external libraries and APIs to extend functionality and enhance productivity. These tools often provide ready-to-use solutions and capabilities that can significantly accelerate the development process, allowing me to focus on building unique features rather than reinventing the wheel.

Regarding the NuGet package manager, it is an indispensable tool for managing dependencies in C# projects. It greatly simplifies the process of adding, updating, and managing external libraries and packages. By using NuGet, I can easily integrate a wide variety of libraries, which not only saves time but also ensures that I am using well-tested and community-supported components. This, in turn, contributes to the stability and maintainability of the projects I work on.

As we wrap up this section, it's evident that the rich ecosystem of C# development tools is a testament to the language's versatility and robustness. These tools, with their unique capabilities, serve as the backbone for successful, streamlined, and efficient project development. The insights shared in this segment should serve as a cornerstone, assisting you in making informed decisions when it comes to choosing the right toolset for your development endeavors. We trust that with this knowledge, you are better prepared to embark on your journey of crafting outstanding C# projects with ease and proficiency.

Next, we will delve into the .NET and .NET Core frameworks, foundational elements for developing applications in C#. Grasping these frameworks is crucial as it will allow us to comprehend the environment in which our C# applications operate and how to harness the frameworks' capabilities to develop efficient and scalable applications.

Understanding .NET and .NET Core frameworks

In this section, we venture into the heart of C# development – the **.NET** and **.NET Core** frameworks. These frameworks lay the foundation for a wide variety of applications, ranging from web to desktop to mobile solutions. As we navigate through this section, we will demystify the core components, their functionalities, and the primary distinctions between the two frameworks. This exploration aims to offer you a clear understanding and insight into how these frameworks empower developers to build scalable, secure, and high-performance applications. Let's dive in to unravel the essence of .NET ecosystems and how they can be the cornerstone of your development journey.

Could you elucidate the differences between .NET Framework, .NET Core, and .NET 7 and discuss the motivations for their implementations?

.NET Framework is a traditional framework that has been available for many years, predominantly used for developing Windows applications. In contrast, .NET Core is a cross-platform, open source version of .NET, designed to support modern applications, including cloud-based and containerized solutions. .NET 7 represents the next step in unifying the .NET platform, merging the capabilities of both .NET Framework and .NET Core and offering developers a singular platform to create applications of any kind. These developments were necessitated to adapt to modern technological trends and demands for improved performance and scalability.

Could you highlight the main advantages of transitioning from .NET Framework to .NET Core?

Transitioning from .NET Framework to .NET Core can offer a number of benefits, including enhanced performance, cross-platform capabilities, support for containerization and cloud solutions, as well as an improved security model. Moreover, .NET Core is open source, fostering a broader community and flexibility in development, which encourages community contributions and collaborative problem-solving, thus constantly evolving and adapting to the modern software development landscape.

Could you discuss how the .NET and .NET Core frameworks interact with databases?

Both .NET and .NET Core interact with databases through various libraries and APIs such as ADO.NET, EF, and **Language Integrated Query (LINQ)**. These tools provide powerful mechanisms for interacting with databases, including ORM support, query execution, and transaction management. EF Core, which is a part of .NET Core, offers additional features and optimizations for working with contemporary databases, enabling developers to efficiently build data-driven applications with enhanced capabilities and performance.

Could you describe the typical process of migrating a project from .NET Framework to .NET Core?

The process of migrating a project from .NET Framework to .NET Core generally involves several steps:

1. Analyzing the current project and its dependencies
2. Updating or replacing libraries that are incompatible with .NET Core
3. Adapting code to the new APIs and features of .NET Core
4. Testing and tuning the project to ensure its stability and performance on the new platform

Could you mention a few new features or improvements that were introduced in .NET Core?

.NET Core introduced a series of new features and improvements, including the following:

- Cross-platform capabilities that allow developers to create applications that can run on various operating systems, including Windows, Linux, and macOS
- Enhanced performance due to optimizations in memory management and better resource handling
- Support for containerization, which simplifies deployment and management of applications
- A more flexible and modular structure that allows developers to choose only the components necessary for their project
- An open source nature, fostering a large community and active project development

How do you evaluate the community and support for .NET and .NET Core, and how does this influence your choice of framework for projects?

The community and support for .NET are quite strong, with the open source code being accessible on GitHub. The community actively collaborates on enhancing the frameworks, and there is a vast amount of resources available for learning and support. This influences my choice of framework, as an active community and robust support can significantly facilitate the development process and problem-solving.

How is memory management implemented in .NET Core, and how does it differ from memory management approaches in other frameworks?

In .NET Core, memory management is based on a **garbage collection system**, which automatically identifies objects that are no longer in use and frees the memory they occupy. This process differs from some other frameworks, where developers might be required to explicitly manage memory. Additionally, .NET Core includes a series of optimizations aimed at reducing memory overhead and enhancing performance, such as Span<T> and Memory<T> for efficient memory operations without additional allocations.

How does .NET Core support the development of microservices architecture and what are the primary tools and components it offers for this?

.NET Core facilitates the development of microservice architectures through a variety of tools and features, including the following:

- Support for Docker and Kubernetes, simplifying the deployment and management of microservices

- Built-in support for RESTful APIs through ASP.NET Core, making the creation and maintenance of microservices more straightforward

- Tools for monitoring and logging, which assist in obtaining detailed information about the status and performance of microservices

Could you describe how security is ensured in .NET Core, including protection against common web threats?

In .NET Core, security is ensured through a series of mechanisms, such as the following:

- Built-in features to protect against SQL injections, **cross-site scripting** (**XSS**), and other common web threats

- Support for secure protocols and standards for encryption and authentication

- Access and role management features for implementing **role-based access control** (**RBAC**)

Can we discuss the structure of a .NET Core project and its key differences compared to projects based on the classic .NET Framework?

One of the distinctions is that .NET Core utilizes a new project file (`.csproj`), which is more modern and simplified compared to classic .NET projects. Additionally, .NET Core allows for easier organization and management of dependencies with the aid of the **NuGet** package manager. The project structure has also evolved, providing more flexibility and scalability for modern application types.

Can we discuss how .NET Core interfaces with Docker containers and what advantages this can bring to developers?

.NET Core is ideally suited for use with Docker containers as it facilitates the creation of lightweight, independent, and scalable applications. Docker provides an isolated environment for each application, simplifying deployment and management. Furthermore, .NET Core enables you to easily create Docker images for your applications, simplifying CI/CD processes and deployments in a cloud environment.

Can we explore the various tools and methodologies available for test automation in the .NET Core environment?

In the .NET Core environment, there are numerous tools and frameworks available for test automation, including xUnit, NUnit, and MSTest for unit testing and Selenium for UI test automation. These tools allow developers to create and execute automated tests, fostering high code-quality maintenance and streamlining CI/CD processes.

How can a distributed caching system be implemented in .NET Core to enhance the performance of web applications?

In .NET Core, various technologies such as Redis or Memcached can be utilized to implement a distributed caching system. These systems allow for the storage of frequently accessed data in memory for quick retrieval, significantly enhancing the performance of web applications. .NET Core offers built-in services and libraries for easy integration with these caching systems.

How does .NET 6 support development across various platforms, including desktop, mobile, and cloud environments?

.NET 6 forms a part of the unified .NET ecosystem, facilitating development for desktop (Windows, macOS, Linux), mobile (iOS, Android), and cloud platforms. This is achieved through technologies such as Blazor, **Multi-platform App UI** (**MAUI**), and ASP.NET Core, which enable the creation of cross-platform applications from a single code base. This comprehensive support promotes flexibility and efficiency, allowing developers to craft responsive applications for various platforms with ease.

What role does MAUI occupy in the .NET ecosystem, and what new opportunities does it bring to developers?

MAUI is a new framework in the .NET ecosystem that facilitates the creation of native cross-platform applications for Windows, macOS, iOS, and Android. As a successor to Xamarin.Forms, it offers a unified set of UI components and APIs for development. This allows developers to create applications from a single code base, ensuring a native user experience on each platform. This represents a significant step forward in streamlining the development process and enhancing user engagement across different platforms.

What are the key innovations introduced in ASP.NET Core aimed at enhancing the productivity of web application development?

ASP.NET Core continually receives updates that include improvements in performance, tools for microservices development, support for gRPC protocols, more efficient memory management, and new resources for authentication and security, among other features. These innovations empower developers to build highly productive, scalable, and secure web applications, fostering a development environment that is both dynamic and robust.

How does Blazor integrate into the .NET ecosystem, and what features does it offer to facilitate the creation of cross-platform web applications?

Blazor is a framework designed to create interactive web applications using C# instead of JavaScript. It enables developers to construct **single-page applications** (**SPAs**) utilizing .NET and Razor. Blazor can operate through WebAssembly to run .NET code directly in the browser or adopt a server-side approach where the application logic is executed on the server, and only UI updates are transmitted via SignalR. This grants developers the flexibility to employ the full .NET stack in crafting modern web applications, enhancing the efficiency and performance of the development process.

Can we explore new features and strategies for data handling that EF Core offers?

Certainly – **EF Core** introduces several new features and improvements, including support for new data types, enhanced mapping capabilities, and optimized database queries. Moreover, it facilitates more flexible model configuration and implements innovative approaches to transaction management and concurrency. These advancements contribute to a streamlined and efficient data-handling process, aiding developers in building robust and scalable applications.

How does the .NET Framework foster the development of IoT solutions, and what are its key advantages for developing such systems?

The .NET Framework promotes the development of IoT solutions through the provision of libraries and tools that simplify the integration and management of IoT devices. It offers mechanisms for secure data collection, processing, and transmission and supports the development of smart contracts and blockchain technologies. This can be particularly beneficial in creating reliable and secure IoT solutions, providing a solid foundation for developers to build intelligent and interconnected systems.

Can we discuss tools and technologies available for creating cloud solutions based on .NET and Azure?

Absolutely – .NET, in conjunction with Azure, provides a comprehensive set of tools for developing cloud solutions. This includes **Azure Functions** for building serverless applications, **Azure App Service** for web services, and **Azure Kubernetes Service** (**AKS**) for containerization and orchestration, among other services for data, **artificial intelligence** (**AI**), and **machine learning** (**ML**). All of these are integrated into the .NET Framework, simplifying the development, deployment, and management of cloud solutions and enabling the rapid and efficient creation of scalable cloud-based systems.

Can we discuss methods of optimizing application performance using the latest tools of the .NET Framework?

Absolutely – the latest tools and features in the .NET Framework allow developers to enhance application performance through the implementation of asynchronous programming, utilization of modern memory optimization techniques, improved thread management, and other technologies that enhance the speed and efficiency of software applications. These advancements facilitate a more streamlined and effective development process, contributing to the creation of high-performance applications.

How do micro-frameworks, such as the .NET Nano Framework and .NET MAUI, affect the efficiency and speed of development in the .NET ecosystem?

The .NET Nano Framework and .NET MAUI have been developed to enhance development productivity and provide more flexible solutions for various platforms and devices. The .NET Nano Framework is geared toward devices with limited resources, such as IoT devices, offering an efficient solution for developing applications in resource-constrained environments. On the other hand, .NET MAUI provides a unified platform for developing cross-platform applications, facilitating the rapid creation of UIs and business logic for various devices. These frameworks thus play a crucial role in expediting the development process and fostering innovation within the .NET ecosystem.

What role does ML.NET play in the development of AI and ML within the .NET Framework?

ML.NET serves as a significant tool for .NET developers looking to integrate ML capabilities into their applications without the necessity for deep expertise in the field of AI. This tool enables the creation and training of models and facilitates predictions directly within the .NET environment, ensuring a seamless integration with existing systems. This empowers developers to easily incorporate advanced AI functionalities into their applications, fostering the development of more intelligent and responsive systems.

How does Azure Functions collaborate with .NET to create serverless solutions, and what advantages does this integration offer to developers?

Azure Functions enables .NET developers to create functions that respond to events and run in a cloud environment without the need to manage infrastructure. This facilitates automatic scaling, payment only for the actual execution time, and deep integration with other Azure services. For .NET developers, this translates to quicker deployments, less coding, and reduced costs. The integration thus presents a highly efficient and cost-effective approach to developing scalable and robust serverless solutions, enhancing the development experience within the Azure and .NET ecosystem.

How does .NET integrate with AWS, and which specific AWS services work most effectively with .NET applications?

.NET integrates seamlessly with **Amazon Web Services** (**AWS**) through the AWS SDK for .NET. This enables developers to interact effortlessly with a wide array of AWS services, including Amazon **Simple Storage Service** (**S3**), AWS Lambda, Amazon DynamoDB, and many others. This integration facilitates the development of scalable, reliable, and secure applications on the AWS platform while utilizing the familiar .NET environment. It essentially enables developers to harness the robust capabilities of AWS services, enhancing the functionality and performance of .NET applications.

How is DevOps implemented in the .NET ecosystem, particularly through the use of tools such as Azure DevOps and AWS CodePipeline?

In the .NET ecosystem, DevOps can be implemented using tools such as Azure DevOps and AWS CodePipeline. These tools offer developers comprehensive solutions to automate the **software development life cycle (SDLC)**, from planning and coding to building, testing, and deployment. These instruments foster increased productivity and delivery speed while ensuring a high level of security and stability for applications. By streamlining the development process, they facilitate a collaborative and efficient approach to software delivery, promoting CI/CD.

What features and capabilities do MAUI/Xamarin offer for mobile application development within the .NET platform?

MAUI/Xamarin forms a vital part of the .NET ecosystem, enabling developers to create cross-platform mobile applications using C# and .NET. With MAUI/Xamarin, developers can utilize a single code base to develop applications that function on both Android and iOS platforms, significantly reducing development and implementation time. Furthermore, Xamarin provides tools for direct access to native APIs, allowing for the creation of high-performance and optimized applications with rich functionality. This unified approach ensures that developers can craft feature-rich, high-performing mobile applications while maintaining a streamlined development process.

Can we explore methods of utilizing .NET for the development of IoT applications, as well as the possibilities for integration with platforms such as Azure IoT Hub and AWS IoT Core?

Absolutely – .NET offers powerful tools for developing IoT applications, including support for microcontroller development and integration with platforms such as Azure IoT Hub and AWS IoT Core. These platforms facilitate centralized management and monitoring of IoT devices, allowing for easy integration with other cloud services and solutions for data processing and analysis. Leveraging these integrations, developers can create robust and scalable IoT solutions, enhancing the efficiency and capabilities of their IoT infrastructures.

How does .NET support big data processing and cloud computing through tools such as Azure Synapse or AWS Glue?

.NET provides seamless integration with cloud platforms equipped with tools for big data processing and cloud computing. Utilizing Azure Synapse, developers can craft and manage big data solutions, efficiently analyzing and processing large volumes of data. Concurrently, AWS Glue enables straightforward data preparation and loading for analytics and ML. .NET offers libraries and SDKs to work with these services, simplifying the integration and development of big data solutions, thus facilitating a smoother development process and empowering developers to create sophisticated data analytics systems.

How does .NET integrate with container technologies such as Docker and Kubernetes, especially in the context of cloud platforms such as Azure and AWS?

.NET offers deep integration with container technologies such as Docker and Kubernetes. Developers can easily containerize their .NET applications, enhancing their portability and scalability. Cloud platforms such as Azure and AWS provide services to manage and deploy these containers on a large scale, offering tools for automatic scaling, monitoring, and management. This ensures a flexible and efficient deployment process, allowing for optimized application performance and resource utilization in cloud environments.

What tools and methodologies are available for optimizing the performance of .NET applications in cloud environments, utilizing monitoring and management tools provided by Azure and AWS?

To optimize the performance of .NET applications in cloud environments, Azure and AWS offer a variety of monitoring and management tools. These tools allow developers to track system uptime, analyze performance, and detect and rectify performance issues in real time. This encompasses tools for logging, tracing, resource monitoring, and automatic scaling, all of which help to optimize application operations and maintain high performance and reliability. By utilizing these tools, developers can ensure a robust and efficient application life cycle, fostering improved user experiences and operational efficiencies.

As we conclude this insightful section, we hope that you now possess a deeper understanding of the pivotal role that the .NET and .NET Core frameworks play in the world of C# development. These frameworks, with their robust features and versatile capabilities, form the backbone of numerous contemporary software solutions. With the knowledge gleaned from this section, you are well positioned to make informed decisions in your future projects, leveraging the power and flexibility these frameworks offer. May this knowledge serve as a stepping stone toward your mastery in crafting remarkable, resilient, and innovative applications in the C# landscape.

Let's now turn our attention to unit testing in C# projects, a fundamental practice to ensure the reliability and correctness of our code. By mastering unit testing techniques, we can foster the development of robust, error-free applications and enhance the maintainability of our code base.

Unit testing in C# projects

As we embark on this segment of our journey, we turn our attention to a pivotal aspect of C# development – **unit testing**. This process, central to the SDLC, ensures that each individual unit of your code operates as intended, fostering reliability and maintainability. As we delve deeper into this section, we will illuminate methodologies, frameworks, and best practices that encapsulate effective unit testing in C#. Whether you're a novice or an experienced developer, mastering unit testing is a cornerstone in building robust, bug-free applications. Let's step forward, equipped with an eagerness to foster quality and excellence in every line of code we craft.

Can you discuss the various unit testing strategies in C# projects and how to determine the most optimal approach for a specific project?

Absolutely – unit testing is a crucial aspect of ensuring software quality. In C#, there are several approaches to unit testing, including **TDD** and **behavior-driven development** (BDD), among others. Choosing the best approach depends on the specifics of the project, the team, and its preferences. It's important to consider factors such as the complexity of the project, resource availability, and implementation timelines. Developing a comprehensive testing strategy that aligns with project goals and team expertise can facilitate a smoother development process and better outcomes.

Could you describe how to structure unit tests in C# projects to ensure optimal code coverage?

To ensure optimal code coverage, unit tests should be structured in such a way that each test verifies a specific functionality or unit of functionality. It is important to use appropriate naming conventions so that the tests are self-descriptive. Also, utilizing techniques such as test parameterization is essential to examine various scenarios and edge cases. It is vital to establish a well-organized testing hierarchy and to employ assertion methods effectively, ensuring that each unit of code is tested thoroughly and maintains a high standard of quality.

In your opinion, what are the most effective unit testing frameworks in the .NET ecosystem, and why?

In the .NET ecosystem, there are several popular unit testing frameworks, including **NUnit**, **xUnit**, and **MSTest**. The choice of the most effective framework often depends on specific requirements and team preferences. For instance, xUnit is often praised for its flexibility and extensibility, offering a range of advanced features and functionalities. On the other hand, MSTest is tightly integrated with Visual Studio, which can simplify the setup and execution of tests. When selecting a framework, considerations such as community support, documentation, and integration capabilities with other tools should be taken into account to ensure a seamless and productive testing process.

Can we discuss strategies for creating test scenarios that effectively detect and isolate issues in C# code?

Certainly – when creating test scenarios, it's vital to focus on detecting and isolating issues in code effectively. Strategies might include writing tests that scrutinize specific functionalities (unit tests), utilizing mocks and stubs to isolate components from external dependencies, and composing tests at various levels of abstraction (unit, integration, system tests) for a deeper analysis. These approaches facilitate pinpointing potential issues early in the development process, enhancing code reliability and maintainability.

How do you utilize mocking frameworks such as Moq or NSubstitute for developing flexible and efficient unit tests?

Mocking frameworks such as Moq or NSubstitute assist in developing flexible and efficient unit tests by enabling the easy creation of mocks and stubs to simulate the behavior of external dependencies. This promotes the creation of tests that are more isolated, reproducible, and reliable, as they are not dependent on external systems or services. Furthermore, it allows developers to easily simulate various conditions and responses, enhancing test coverage and code quality. Leveraging these tools can streamline the testing process and foster a more robust code base.

How do you integrate unit testing tools for automating code verification within CI/CD processes in your C# projects?

In CI/CD processes, unit testing plays a significant role in automating code verification. I typically integrate unit tests into the CI/CD pipeline using tools such as GitHub or Azure DevOps, facilitating the automatic execution of tests with each merge or release. This approach helps identify and rectify issues at early development stages, enhancing code quality and delivery speed. It fosters a culture of continuous improvement, with frequent testing cycles ensuring code stability and reliability.

Could you share strategies for integrating unit testing into agile development methodologies such as Scrum or Kanban?

Certainly – in agile methodologies such as Scrum or Kanban, unit testing can be seamlessly incorporated as a part of the sprint or development cycle. Developers can concurrently create unit tests with feature development, allowing for continuous monitoring of code quality. This approach promotes maintaining code-base stability and facilitates early detection and remediation of issues, fostering a robust and agile development environment.

How do you implement the TDD approach in your C# projects, and in your opinion, what are the primary advantages of this approach?

When implementing TDD in my projects, I begin by writing unit tests that delineate the expected behavior of new functionality. Following this, I write the minimum amount of code necessary to pass these tests. The main advantages of this approach include early error detection, facilitating refactoring, and maintaining a high level of code quality throughout the development process.

Can we discuss your experience working with code coverage analysis tools, such as Coverlet or dotCover, in the context of evaluating the effectiveness of unit tests?

Yes – code coverage analysis tools such as Coverlet and dotCover provide a means to assess the percentage of code that is being verified through unit tests. I use these tools to identify areas of code that might require additional testing and to ensure that critical paths in the application are thoroughly tested. This helps in maintaining a high level of code quality and reliability in the software product.

Can we explore different strategies for optimizing the performance of unit tests in C#, including parallel test execution and utilizing test management tools integrated within Visual Studio?

Absolutely – to optimize the performance of unit tests in C#, various strategies can be employed, including parallel test execution to reduce the overall runtime. Visual Studio offers a suite of test management tools that allow for easy organization, filtering, and execution of test suites. These tools can also assist in identifying and focusing on the most critical or frequently used tests, maximizing the efficiency of the testing process and ensuring a robust and reliable software development pipeline.

What main strategies would you suggest for ensuring consistency and reliability in unit tests within C# projects?

To ensure consistency and reliability in unit tests, I would suggest the following strategies:

- Writing atomic tests that focus on verifying only one specific aspect at a time
- Avoiding dependencies between unit tests to allow them to run in any order without affecting one another
- Utilizing mock objects to simulate external dependencies, facilitating isolation and focused testing
- Ensuring that tests run quickly to prevent slowing down the development process
- Adhering to defined naming conventions for easier understanding and tracking of test cases

What are the best practices for creating abstractions in C# to facilitate the mocking process during unit testing?

To facilitate easier mocking during unit testing, it is recommended to do the following:

- Use interfaces and abstract classes to define contract-based components that can easily be mocked
- Avoid the use of static methods or classes, as they pose challenges when it comes to mocking
- Implement DI to inject external dependencies, promoting code modularity and testability

How do you implement BDD for developing user scenarios, and how does this integrate with your approach to testing?

When implementing BDD, I utilize tools such as SpecFlow to define user scenarios in a **natural language (NL)** format. These scenarios are then translated into automated tests. This approach helps ensure that the developed functionality aligns well with user expectations and business requirements, fostering a user-centric development process.

What are your key strategies for conducting integration testing of services, especially those hosted in cloud environments?

For integration testing, I typically employ the following strategies:

- Utilizing testing environments that closely mirror the production environment to achieve realistic testing conditions

- Creating automated test suites that scrutinize the interaction between various components to ensure cohesive performance

- Leveraging cloud-based tools for monitoring and logging to effectively track issues during test executions, facilitating prompt issue resolution and optimization

Could you share your experience using Docker and Testcontainers for establishing isolated testing environments?

Absolutely – Docker and Testcontainers are instrumental in creating isolated testing environments that guarantee consistent conditions for each test run. This proves particularly beneficial for integration tests where specific databases or external services might be required. These tools facilitate the easy creation, management, and removal of such environments, enhancing the efficiency and reliability of the testing process.

How do you plan and implement the testing of services where API calls are constrained by costs or availability, such as in the case of OpenAI services or cloud services?

When testing services with limited or costly API calls, I adopt the following approaches:

- Developing mock objects to simulate API responses, thereby avoiding the need for actual API calls during testing

- Using stubs to create controlled testing conditions that allow for the assessment of system behavior under various scenarios without incurring additional costs

- Planning and limiting the frequency of API calls to prevent exceeding budgetary constraints and facing accessibility issues

- Implementing caching mechanisms to reduce the number of necessary API calls, thereby optimizing performance and minimizing costs

Can we discuss how you consider potential side effects in different parts of the system when developing test scenarios?

Certainly – when developing test scenarios, I endeavor to anticipate and account for potential side effects using strategies such as the following:

- Analyzing the dependencies between different parts of the system to understand the potential ripple effects of changes or failures

- Crafting integration tests capable of detecting unexpected side effects, ensuring comprehensive coverage and risk mitigation

- Utilizing transactions or rollbacks to ensure that test actions do not adversely affect other parts of the system, maintaining stability and integrity throughout the testing process

Can we discuss methods of organizing and structuring test scenarios in projects utilizing the BDD approach?

Certainly – when utilizing the BDD approach, I typically do the following:

- Identify user stories or scenarios for each functionality, providing a detailed representation of expected behaviors and outcomes

- Create test scenarios that mirror the specific behaviors outlined in the user stories, ensuring a comprehensive analysis of each functionality

- Use tools such as SpecFlow to transform behavior descriptions into automated tests, promoting efficiency and accuracy in testing procedures

- Focus on evaluating the interaction between different components of the system instead of testing them in isolation, which facilitates a more holistic understanding of the system's behavior

Could you highlight the features of using test frameworks such as xUnit and NUnit in the context of unit and integration testing?

When utilizing frameworks such as xUnit and NUnit, I pay attention to the following aspects:

- The use of attributes to denote test methods and datasets, which helps in organizing and structuring tests systematically

- Employing assertions to verify expected outcomes, ensuring that the system operates as intended under various conditions

- Utilizing SetUp and TearDown methodologies for initializing and cleaning up the test environment, promoting a controlled and consistent testing atmosphere

- Leveraging mocking frameworks such as Moq or NSubstitute to simulate external dependencies, facilitating more comprehensive and realistic testing scenarios

How do you plan and implement strategies to ensure maximum code coverage at various levels (unit, integration, system) of testing?

To achieve maximum code coverage through testing, I employ the following strategies:

- Defining criteria for different levels of testing to ensure that all aspects of the system are properly examined and validated

- Developing test plans that pinpoint areas requiring additional testing, enabling a more targeted and effective testing strategy

- Using tools for code coverage analysis to identify areas that necessitate further tests, ensuring comprehensive examination and validation of the system

- Reviewing and refactoring tests to enhance their effectiveness and coverage, fostering continuous improvement in the testing process

Could you describe how you utilize mocking frameworks to simulate interactions with external dependencies during unit testing?

Certainly – I utilize mocking frameworks such as Moq or NSubstitute to create virtual objects that mimic the behavior of external dependencies. This allows me to conduct testing in an isolated environment where I can control the behavior and state of virtual objects, ensuring precise and reproducible test scenarios.

What approaches do you employ for automating test suites in your CI/CD pipeline?

To automate test suites in the CI/CD pipeline, I implement the following strategies:

- Integration with automated testing tools, such as NUnit or xUnit, into CI systems to streamline the testing process

- Setting up triggers for automatic test initiation upon code repository changes, ensuring that code is consistently tested throughout its development life cycle

- Utilizing scripts for automatic creation, configuration, and dismantling of the test environment, fostering a more dynamic and efficient testing process

- Generating and analyzing code coverage reports to monitor code quality over time, aiding in maintaining high standards of code reliability and performance

Could you discuss methods of utilizing fixtures and object factories to enhance the unit testing process?

Certainly – fixtures and object factories can be extremely beneficial in optimizing the unit testing process. I use fixtures to initialize a common state or objects that are used across multiple tests, fostering consistency and efficiency. Object factories allow me to create objects with predefined characteristics, simplifying the test writing and maintenance process and ensuring more robust and reliable tests.

How do you approach testing code sections that interact with databases or other external resources?

When testing sections of code that interact with databases or other external resources, I employ the following strategies:

- Using mocking frameworks to simulate interactions with external resources, allowing for controlled and isolated testing environments

- Implementing integration tests with controlled test data to verify interactions with real resources, such as utilizing Docker containers to create realistic testing environments

- Applying the Repository pattern to isolate database interaction logic and simplify testing, ensuring that code is robust and behaves as expected under various conditions

Could you elaborate on how you organize and manage test data during the execution of integration tests?

During integration testing, I employ the following methods to organize and manage test data:

- Utilizing object factories to generate consistent test data, ensuring that the tests are reliable and repeatable

- Setting up test databases that can be easily reset and restored for each test suite, facilitating a stable testing environment

- Using migration mechanisms to maintain the correct structure of the test database, ensuring that the database schema is always aligned with the application requirements

- Creating scripts for automatically populating test databases with necessary data before initiating tests, which helps in simulating real-world scenarios during testing

Could you discuss the benefits of using Docker containers during integration testing in C# projects?

Utilizing Docker containers during integration testing allows for the creation of conditions closely resembling a real environment. This facilitates easier configuration and dependency management, ensuring a consistent testing environment. Moreover, Docker can be easily integrated with CI/CD tools, simplifying the automation of the testing process and ensuring a streamlined development pipeline.

How do you implement and scale property-based testing in your C# projects?

Property-based testing involves creating tests that validate system properties using randomly generated data. In my projects, I use libraries such as FsCheck (for .NET projects) to automatically generate test cases. This approach helps in uncovering edge cases and subtle bugs that might be overlooked during traditional testing, thereby enhancing the robustness of the application.

Which tools and methods do you use for analyzing and optimizing the performance of unit and integration tests?

To analyze and optimize the performance of tests, I utilize the following tools and techniques:

- Profiling tests to identify slow portions of the test suite, helping in pinpointing areas where optimization can make a significant difference
- Parallel execution of tests to reduce the overall testing time, ensuring that the development process remains agile
- Employing caching and other techniques to minimize the initialization time of the testing environment, which helps speed up the testing process
- Optimizing test data and scenarios to decrease test execution time, which fosters quicker feedback loops and iterative development

Could you discuss how you use code coverage analysis tools to assess the quality of test coverage in your projects?

Certainly – I utilize code coverage analysis tools such as Coverlet or dotCover to assess the quality of test coverage. These tools help in identifying uncovered code areas and analyzing the effectiveness of the test suites. This contributes to continuous improvement in code quality and a reduction in the number of bugs, ensuring that the application maintains high standards of reliability and performance.

Could you explain your approach to creating and managing automated tests in projects with a microservices architecture?

In projects with a microservices architecture, I focus on creating comprehensive sets of unit and integration tests for each microservice separately. I also integrate contract testing to verify interactions between different services. Test automation is a key factor in maintaining reliability and a fast development cycle in microservice ecosystems.

How do you determine which level of testing (unit, integration, system) should be used to verify specific aspects of the system?

The choice of testing level depends on the specific aspect of the system that needs to be verified. Unit tests are ideal for testing individual components or functions. Integration tests help in verifying the interaction between different components of the system. Meanwhile, system tests allow for evaluating the overall behavior of the system, ensuring it meets the specified requirements.

Could you share your experience in creating flexible and scalable test architectures that can adapt to changes in the system?

When developing flexible and scalable test architectures, I focus on utilizing well-defined abstractions and design patterns. These allow for easy adaptation of tests to system changes. A key strategy is to develop tests that are independent, reusable, and easily scalable, which simplifies adaptation to future changes in the system.

Can we discuss your experience using containers to simulate external services during integration testing?

Certainly – utilizing containers such as Docker for simulating external services during integration testing can be highly beneficial. This approach enables the creation of isolated and controlled testing environments, where specific conditions for testing can be accurately reproduced. Containers also facilitate the automation of test scenarios and integration with CI/CD pipelines, making the testing process more streamlined and efficient.

Could you talk about approaches to testing asynchronous code in C# and the main challenges one might encounter?

Testing asynchronous code in C# demands a special approach. I typically use asynchronous test methods and frameworks that support asynchronous testing. One of the main challenges is managing side effects and states that can influence test results. This also includes correctly anticipating asynchronous operations and handling exceptions that might occur during asynchronous execution, ensuring the tests are robust and can handle real-world scenarios effectively.

As we draw this chapter to a close, it is our hope that you are now fortified with the knowledge and insight to implement unit testing seamlessly in your C# projects. This practice, a beacon of quality assurance, serves to not only detect bugs early but also facilitates smoother code integrations and enhancements. Armed with the strategies and techniques delineated in this section, you are poised to elevate your coding craftsmanship to new heights, fostering applications that stand the test of time. As you move forward, may the principles of unit testing serve as your steadfast ally in the pursuit of software excellence.

Summary

In this chapter, we embarked on a comprehensive exploration of fundamental principles that govern maintainable and efficient programming in C#. From techniques of crafting clean, coherent code to a detailed walkthrough of the essential development tools, we have equipped you with a robust toolkit that will facilitate streamlined navigation through the complex landscape of C# programming.

This segment serves as a springboard, aiding you in significantly enhancing your programming skills by leveraging the best practices and premier tools that are accessible for C#. Armed with a solid foundational understanding, we warmly invite you to advance to the subsequent section of this insightful journey.

In the upcoming chapter, we will immerse ourselves in a deep study of C# libraries and frameworks, powerful allies in achieving greater efficiency and effectiveness in your project executions. Furthermore, we will delve into insightful strategies and invaluable tips for gearing up for technical interviews, empowering you to successfully exhibit your newly honed skills. Let us forge ahead to the next exhilarating phase of your pathway to achieving expertise in C# programming.

Additional reading

- *Clean Code with C# - Second Edition*, by Jason Alls

  https://www.packtpub.com/product/clean-code-with-c-second-edition/9781837635191

- *Real-World Implementation of C# Design Patterns*, by Bruce M. Van Horn II

  https://www.packtpub.com/product/real-world-implementation-of-c-design-patterns/9781803242736

- *.NET MAUI for C# Developers*, by Jesse Liberty and Rodrigo Juarez

  https://www.packtpub.com/product/net-maui-for-c-developers/9781837631698

6

Deep Dive into C# Libraries and Frameworks

Embarking on a journey through the dynamic and expansive domain of **C#** development becomes considerably smoother when you are well-acquainted with its core libraries and frameworks.

In this chapter, we aim to serve as your reliable guide, steering you through the vital and powerful resources that C# proudly presents. We venture deep into the functionalities of the **Entity Framework**, a powerhouse for data management, and explore the vast potential of **ASP.NET Core** in the sphere of web development. Moreover, we cast a spotlight on the remarkable capabilities of **MAUI/Xamarin**, opening doors to the exciting world of cross-platform mobile development.

In this chapter, we'll cover the following main topics:

- Essential C# libraries and frameworks
- Entity Framework and data access
- ASP.NET Core for web development

Exploring essential C# libraries and frameworks

In the vibrant world of programming, the ability to utilize libraries and frameworks proficiently stands as a hallmark of an adept developer. As we venture into the realm of C#, a language renowned for its versatility and robustness, it becomes imperative to familiarize ourselves with the essential libraries and frameworks that augment its capabilities. This chapter unfolds as a guided journey, introducing you to the pivotal tools and resources that have cemented C# as a powerhouse in the software development landscape. Brace yourselves as we delve deep into the intricacies of C# libraries and frameworks, unlocking the potential that can propel your coding skills to unprecedented heights.

What libraries and tools would you recommend for developing automated testing systems in C#?

When it comes to building automated testing systems in C#, several libraries and tools can significantly facilitate this process. Here are some that I would highly recommend:

- **NUnit**: A well-regarded library for unit testing. It offers attributes to specify test cases and assert the expected results, helping to create a robust testing framework.

- **xUnit**: This is another widely used framework for unit testing; it is known for being more modern and extensible compared to NUnit. It allows for more precise control over test running and more options for creating reusable test code.

- **Moq**: This library is instrumental in creating mock objects for unit testing, helping to isolate units of code for more accurate and efficient testing.

- **Selenium**: A powerful tool for controlling a web browser through the program. It's functional for browser automation and can be used effectively for testing web applications by automating user actions.

- **Playwright**: This is a recent addition to the automation landscape, allowing for the scripting of actions in multiple web browsers, which can be used for both testing and web scraping.

- **SpecFlow**: A tool that supports **behavior-driven development** (BDD), enabling the description of test cases in natural, business-readable language, fostering better communication and collaboration among stakeholders.

Additional tools and libraries can be explored based on the specific requirements of your project, including integration with continuous integration and continuous delivery/deployment (CI/CD) pipelines and compatibility with other tools in your technology stack.

Could you delve deeper into the process of optimizing application performance using C# libraries and tools?

Optimizing the performance of applications in C# is a multi-faceted process involving various strategies and approaches. Here are some essential steps and methodologies to consider:

- **Code profiling**: Utilizing tools such as the **Visual Studio** profiler helps in identifying bottlenecks in the code. It's crucial to regularly profile the code to spot potential areas where optimizations can be made.

- **Asynchronous programming**: Implementing asynchronous methods can significantly improve the responsiveness of your application. It helps to reduce the waiting time and makes the application more scalable by efficiently using system resources.

- **Database query optimization**: Leveraging ORM tools, such as **Entity Framework** or **Dapper**, for optimal database operations can significantly enhance performance. This includes using lazy loading wisely, optimizing LINQ queries, and avoiding N+1 query problems.

- **Caching**: Employing caching systems, such as **MemoryCache** or **Redis**, can reduce the database load and enhance the application's performance. It helps to store frequently accessed data in the memory to avoid redundant database calls, thereby speeding up data retrieval processes.

- **Parallelization**: Utilizing the **Task Parallel Library** helps to parallelize tasks, thus improving the application's throughput. Implementing parallel algorithms where applicable can significantly reduce the time taken for CPU-bound operations.

Furthermore, it is beneficial to stay updated with the latest advancements in the **.NET** ecosystem and continuously explore new libraries and tools that can potentially enhance your application's performance. Regular code reviews, adhering to best practices, and adopting a performance-oriented mindset are key to building high-performing applications in C#.

What libraries would you recommend for implementing a microservices architecture in C# projects?

To implement a microservices architecture in C# projects, I would recommend utilizing the following libraries and tools:

- **ASP.NET Core**: A lightweight and flexible platform that is highly favored for creating microservices. It allows for the development of high-performance and modern microservices architectures, offering various features to build scalable and maintainable services.

- **Docker**: A vital tool for containerizing and facilitating the easy deployment of microservices. It ensures that the application runs the same regardless of where it's deployed, thus enhancing the scalability and maintainability of the services.

- **RabbitMQ** or **Kafka**: These are robust tools for implementing reliable messaging systems between microservices. They allow for asynchronous communication and can help in decoupling services, making the system more resilient and scalable.

- **Ocelot** or **YARP**: An API gateway that assists in managing routing and load balancing between microservices. It acts as a reverse proxy to forward requests to appropriate microservices, handling various cross-cutting concerns such as authentication and logging.

- **IdentityServer**: A tool that facilitates the implementation of authentication and authorization in a microservices architecture. It helps to secure microservices and allows for centralized identity management, which is crucial in a microservices environment.

What memory management strategies would you recommend when processing large datasets in C#, and what approaches might be useful in this case?

When processing large datasets in C#, I would recommend adopting the following strategies and utilizing these approaches:

- **Data streaming**: Utilize streams to handle large volumes of data in chunks instead of loading the entire dataset into memory simultaneously, thus preventing memory overflow and ensuring efficient memory usage.

- **Garbage collector (GC) optimization**: Enhance memory management by avoiding frequent memory allocations and garbage collections, which can potentially slow down the application. Understanding and optimizing the garbage collection process can lead to improved performance.

- **Memory-mapped files**: Employ memory-mapped files for the efficient management of large data volumes. This technique allows you to work with large files while keeping memory usage under control, enhancing the application's performance.

- **Parallel computing libraries**: Utilize libraries, such as the **Task Parallel Library** (TPL), for parallel data processing and optimal system resource utilization. This approach allows for the efficient handling of large datasets by distributing the workload across multiple processors, thus speeding up the computation process.

- **System.IO.Pipelines**: This library is a crucial tool for efficient data stream processing in C#. It enables the easy implementation of high-performance data-processing pipelines by breaking down data into smaller pieces and handling them asynchronously. This can significantly enhance the performance of an application when dealing with large datasets, reducing memory pressure and improving processing speed.

What is the .NET Foundation, and can you name some projects that are part of it?

The **.NET Foundation** is an independent organization established to foster innovation in the .NET developer community. It provides resources and support for open source projects related to the .NET ecosystem. Numerous projects are part of the .NET Foundation, including but not limited to the following:

- **Orleans**: A framework that provides a straightforward approach to building distributed high-scale computing applications, without the need to learn and apply complex concurrency or other scaling patterns.

- **ASP.NET Core**: A framework for building modern web applications and services, offering features that enable the development of high-performance web APIs and apps.

- **Entity Framework** : An object-relational mapper (ORM) facilitating the work with databases in .NET, allowing developers to work with database objects and data using .NET objects.

- **ML.NET**: A library offering machine learning (ML) capabilities within the .NET ecosystem, providing tools and services for building custom ML models using C# or F# without requiring expertise in ML.

- **NuGet**: A package manager for .NET, facilitating the discovery, installation, and management of thousands of useful .NET libraries and tools.

- **Roslyn**: A compiler and APIs for analyzing and generating C# and visual basic code, enabling developers to build code analyzers, refactoring providers, and other code-aware tools.

These projects, and many others within the .NET Foundation's umbrella, demonstrate a commitment to fostering a robust, innovative, and collaborative .NET community.

What do the "Community Toolkit" projects entail, and what is their primary goal?

The **Community Toolkit** projects comprise a collection of tools, libraries, and components developed by the community to simplify and enhance the development process within the .NET ecosystem. The primary goal of these projects is to provide developers with resources for quick and efficient application development, offering ready-to-use components that can be easily integrated into their projects.

What key features make Entity Framework a popular choice for working with databases in C#?

The key features that make **Entity Framework** a popular choice for working with databases in C# include the following:

- **Object-relational mapper (ORM)**: This allows you to work with databases using object-oriented paradigms, facilitating the mapping between object code and relational databases

- **Language Integrated Query (LINQ)**: It enables the formulation of database queries using LINQ, simplifying the writing and reading of queries

- **Code-first approach**: This permits developers to define models and their relationships in code, followed by automatically generating a database schema from this code

- **Database migrations**: A tool for database version control that allows the tracking and management of changes in the database schema

- **Lazy loading**: A feature for the automatic loading of related data upon request, helping to optimize performance and resource utilization

Can you name and characterize a few popular libraries for web development on the ASP.NET Core platform?

A few popular libraries for web development on the ASP.NET Core platform include the following:

- **Model View Controller (MVC)**: A framework for creating web applications with a clear separation of responsibilities between the model, view, and controller

- **SignalR**: A library for implementing real-time web functionalities through web sockets and other technologies

- **Blazor**: A framework for building interactive web interfaces using C# instead of JavaScript

- **Entity Framework Core**: An ORM for working with databases, facilitating easy integration and interaction with databases in ASP.NET Core applications

What capabilities do Xamarin and MAUI offer for developing cross-platform mobile applications?

Xamarin and **MAUI** provide a range of capabilities for developing cross-platform mobile applications, including the following:

- **Unified code base**: Both Xamarin and MAUI allow for the creation of applications for different platforms (iOS, Android, etc.) using a single code base, thus promoting code reuse and reducing development time

- **Native performance and experience**: MAUI enables developers to build applications that offer native performance and user experience by allowing access to native APIs

- **Flexible UI design**: MAUI, an evolution of Xamarin, offers new functionalities for creating flexible user interfaces with .NET MAUI graphics and reusable controls, making the UI design process more streamlined and efficient

- **Community and corporate support**: As part of the Microsoft ecosystem, MAUI benefits from strong community and corporate support, providing developers with a rich set of resources, including documentation, tutorials, and community forums

- **Integration with modern development tools**: Xamarin and MAUI integrate well with modern development tools, such as Visual Studio, offering features such as XAML Hot Reload for a more productive development experience

By leveraging these capabilities, developers can build cross-platform mobile applications more efficiently while ensuring high performance and a native-like user experience.

Could you recommend a few libraries for creating RESTful APIs in C#?

I would recommend the following for creating RESTful APIs in C#:

- **ASP.NET Web API**: A framework that facilitates the easy creation of HTTP services accessible from any client, including browsers and mobile devices

- **ServiceStack**: A high-performance framework for creating web services, supporting various formats, including JSON, XML, and others

- **Swashbuckle**: A library integrated into Swagger UI for automatic API documentation generation, enhancing the ease of developing and maintaining APIs

In your opinion, what are the best libraries for developing graphical interfaces in C#?

For developing graphical interfaces in C#, I would recommend the following libraries:

- **Windows Presentation Foundation (WPF)**: A robust framework for developing desktop applications with rich graphical interfaces

- **WinForms**: A traditional framework for creating desktop applications utilizing window forms, offering a wide array of tools and controls

- **Universal Windows Platform (UWP)**: A framework for developing applications that can run on all devices equipped with Windows 10, enhancing the uniformity of applications across different devices

- **Avalonia**: A cross-platform framework for creating graphical interfaces, allowing development across various operating systems, promoting flexibility and broader reach

- **MAUI**: Enables the creation of mobile applications with a shared graphical interface component for both Android and iOS, fostering code reuse and streamlined development

What are the main frameworks available for unit testing in C#, and what are their distinctive features?

For unit testing in C#, the following main frameworks are available, each having its distinctive features:

- **NUnit**: A popular unit testing framework boasting a rich set of functionalities and attributes to facilitate test organization and execution

- **xUnit**: A modern testing framework supporting parallel test execution and integrated assertions, fostering efficient and effective testing processes

- **MSTest**: An integrated framework for unit testing in Visual Studio, characterized by its simplicity and ease of use and integration, serving as a reliable tool for developers

- **Moq**: A library that specializes in creating mock objects, which is often used in conjunction with other unit testing frameworks to test interactions between components, enhancing the depth and reliability of testing efforts

Could you name and explain a few popular libraries for multimedia processing in C# and the criteria for selecting them?

Here are a few popular libraries for multimedia processing in C#:

- **NAudio**: A library that specializes in audio processing, offering functionalities to play, record, and manipulate audio files with ease

- **Accord.NET**: A comprehensive library providing a wide array of functionalities for image, video, and audio processing, facilitating multimedia application development

- **Emgu CV**: A .NET wrapper for OpenCV, enabling operations such as image processing and facial recognition, fostering the development of computer vision applications

The criteria for selecting a library include support for the required formats and functions, community backing and documentation, and ease of integration and utilization in your project, ensuring a smooth development process.

Which C# libraries would you recommend for real-time data processing?

For real-time data processing in C#, I would recommend the following libraries:

- **SignalR**: A library that facilitates the easy addition of real-time functionality regarding your applications, enabling real-time interaction between client and server and enhancing the responsiveness and interactivity of your applications

- **RabbitMQ**: A popular message broker service that is suitable for implementing high-performance solutions for real-time message exchange, fostering seamless communication in distributed systems

- **Redis**: A high-performance in-memory database management system capable of being utilized for real-time data-processing solutions, enhancing the speed and efficiency of data handling in your applications

- **Apache Kafka**: A scalable and high-performance data stream processing platform, allowing for the implementation of complex solutions for real-time data processing, which facilitates the development of robust data pipelines and analytics systems

Could you name and describe a few renowned libraries for task automation and scripting in C# projects?

Certainly. Here are a few renowned libraries for task automation and scripting in C# projects:

- **PowerShell SDK**: Allows for the integration and execution of PowerShell scripts directly from C# code, facilitating the automation of various administrative and management tasks

- **Roslyn**: A .NET compiler and API for code analysis and generation, which can be utilized for automating tasks related to code analysis and modification, enhancing code quality and maintainability

- **Fluent automation**: A library for web application testing automation, allowing for the creation of scripts for automatic browser control, enhancing the testing efficiency and coverage

Could you name and describe a few popular libraries and protocols for implementing client-server communication in C#?

Here are a few popular libraries and protocols for implementing client-server communication in C#:

- **Windows Communication Foundation (WCF)**: Covers a wide range of protocols and patterns for building client-server applications, providing a unified and comprehensive framework for communication

- **gRPC**: A modern, high-performance protocol for client-server communication based on **HTTP/2** and **Protocol Buffers**, ensuring efficient and scalable communication

- **SignalR**: Facilitates the easy implementation of real-time bi-directional communication between client and server, enhancing application interactivity and responsiveness

- **REST/HTTP**: Utilizes the HTTP protocol to implement RESTful APIs, allowing for organized interaction between clients and servers through standard HTTP methods and facilitating interoperable and scalable solutions

What modern alternatives to Entity Framework could you recommend for working with databases in C#, and what are their advantages?

Modern alternatives to Entity Framework for working with databases in C# include the following:

- **Dapper**: A lightweight ORM that offers high performance and flexibility when working with databases, providing a streamlined approach to data access.

- **NHibernate**: A full-featured ORM with rich mapping and configuration capabilities, offering a comprehensive solution for complex data management tasks.

- **Micro ORM**: This category includes small ORMs that provide basic functionality for database operations without additional overhead, allowing for faster and more direct database interactions.

- **Linq2db**: An open source ORM that allows developers to work with databases using LINQ syntax in C#. It provides a type-safe data access layer, allowing for the compile-time validation of queries, which can help to catch errors before runtime. It supports a wide range of database providers and offers good performance and flexibility, making it a valuable tool for developers looking to maintain the benefits of LINQ while working with databases.

The advantages of these modern alternatives, when compared to Entity Framework, include greater performance and flexibility and the ability to have more detailed control over database operations, enhancing application efficiency and maintainability.

Could you discuss the features and recommendations for using gRPC in C# projects?

gRPC is an open standard for high-performance and modern remote procedure call (RPC) communication. Here are some features and recommendations for its use in C# projects:

- **High performance**: gRPC utilizes the HTTP/2 protocol, offering high-performance and low bandwidth usage, ensuring efficient communication

- **Support for multiple programming languages**: gRPC supports many popular programming languages, including C#, facilitating cross-language development and integration

- **Contract-first API development**: Through Protocol Buffers, gRPC promotes contract-based API development, which simplifies maintenance and scalability, ensuring well-defined and consistent interfaces

- **Streaming**: gRPC supports data streaming, enabling the implementation of complex interaction scenarios, enhancing application capabilities in real-time communication

- **Suitability in modern architectures**: gRPC is well-suited for modern microservices architectures and distributed systems, providing a robust and scalable solution for contemporary software development needs

How can the Orleans framework facilitate the simplification of developing distributed systems and microservices in C#?

The **Orleans** framework can greatly aid in simplifying the development of distributed systems and microservices in C# through the following means:

- **Abstraction of distributed system complexity**: Orleans abstracts away much of the complexity of building distributed systems by automating the management of distributed instances, also known as virtual actors. This means developers can focus more on business logic rather than the intricacies of distributed computing, thereby simplifying the programming model.

- **Virtual actor model**: Orleans employs a virtual actor model where actors are single-threaded components with an isolated state, making concurrency management simpler. This programming model promotes the building of systems that are easier to reason about, as developers can work with the high-level abstraction that automatically manages the distribution of actors across a cluster of servers.

- **Scalability**: The framework facilitates the easy scalability of applications by automatically distributing the workload among servers, which facilitates the efficient use of resources and improves application performance as demand increases.

- **Fault recovery**: Orleans ensures fault handling and the recovery of actors after failures. It reduces the complexity of developing resilient systems and minimizes downtime, ensuring that actor activations can be restored on other servers in the event of a failure.

- **State preservation**: Orleans allows for the storage of actor states in external repositories, which simplifies the development of fault-tolerant applications by ensuring data persistence and consistency across system components.

- **Digital Twins concept**: Orleans can be utilized to implement the digital twins concept, where virtual representations (twins) of physical or other complex digital assets are created. These digital twins can communicate and interact with each other in a distributed environment, facilitating complex simulations, real-time monitoring, and control systems, offering a powerful tool for building sophisticated, distributed IoT, and AI applications.

Through these features and concepts, Orleans facilitates the development of robust, scalable, and efficient distributed systems and microservices, making it easier for developers to create complex applications in C#.

Could you name a few libraries for computational science and data processing in C#?

Hare a few libraries for computational science and data processing in C#:

- **Math.NET Numerics**: This library provides a wide range of mathematical and numerical methods, supporting complex computations and analyses in various scientific and engineering domains

- **Accord.NET**: This is a comprehensive framework for scientific computing that includes methods for ML, statistical analyses, and image processing, offering a robust toolset for data science and analytics applications in C#

What libraries and tools would you recommend for developing security and encryption systems in C#?

For developing security and encryption systems in C#, I would recommend the following libraries and tools:

- **System.Security.Cryptography**: A suite of classes in .NET that offer a broad spectrum of cryptographic services, including encryption, decryption, hashing, and digital signatures
- **Bouncy Castle**: A popular library for cryptography that supports a wide range of cryptographic algorithms and protocols
- **PCLCrypto**: A portable library that facilitates cryptographic operations across various platforms, offering flexibility and code reuse
- **Libsodium**: A modern, easy-to-use, and secure library for cryptography, offering various tools for secure communication and data encryption

Can you provide an overview of popular libraries for graphics processing and data visualization in C#?

Here are a few popular libraries for graphics processing and data visualization in C#:

- **OxyPlot**: An open source framework for creating graphs and charts in .NET applications, offering a variety of visualization tools and options
- **LiveCharts**: A lightweight library for data visualization that enables the creation of animated, interactive graphs and charts, enhancing data presentation and analysis
- **ScottPlot**: A library designed for the quick and easy creation of scientific graphs in .NET, catering to data scientists and researchers
- **Microsoft chart controls**: A set of controls from Microsoft for creating various types of charts and diagrams in .NET applications, offering a rich set of features and customization options
- **GGPlot**: A .NET port of the popular R ggplot2 library, offering data visualization using high-level syntax and facilitating the creation of complex, multi-faceted visualizations

What other frameworks and libraries in C#, besides Xamarin/MAUI, would you recommend for mobile application development?

For mobile application development in C#, besides Xamarin/MAUI, you might consider the following frameworks and libraries:

- **Uno platform**: A framework that allows for the development of mobile applications for various platforms (Windows, Android, and iOS) with a single codebase in C#, promoting code reuse and reducing development time

- **Flutter with Dart and C#**: Although Flutter primarily uses Dart as its main language, you can employ C# for writing business logic through the Flutter platform, utilizing plugins and packages for integration, thus leveraging C#'s capabilities in a Flutter project

- **React Native with C#**: Similar to Flutter, you can integrate C# into React Native projects through various plugins and packages, allowing for the creation of mobile applications that take advantage of both technologies

- **Avalonia**: While primarily being a framework for creating cross-platform desktop applications, Avalonia can also be utilized for mobile developments, offering a unified approach to multi-platform development

As we conclude our expedition, we hope that you have garnered an enriched understanding of the indispensable C# libraries and frameworks. These utilities serve not just as tools but as trusted allies in the journey of crafting remarkable software solutions. Remember, the mastery of these frameworks isn't an endpoint but a continual process of exploration and learning. We encourage you to experiment, innovate, and, above all, cultivate a deep-seated curiosity that drives you to unearth the boundless possibilities that lie within the dynamic ecosystem of C#. On this note, we bid you adieu with the confidence that you are well on your way to becoming a proficient C# developer, equipped with the knowledge and skills to navigate the complex yet rewarding world of software development.

With the foundations of C# now firmly within your grasp, let us turn the page and delve into the realm of data management with Entity Framework.

Introduction to Entity Framework and data access

In the contemporary era of software development, efficient data handling is a cornerstone of robust and scalable applications. As we embark on this chapter, we prepare to unravel the nuances of Entity Framework, a pivotal tool in the C# developer's arsenal for seamless data access and manipulation. Recognized for its ability to bridge the gap between complex databases and object-oriented programming paradigms, Entity Framework stands as a beacon of innovation and efficiency. Let us commence this journey of understanding, where we explore the dynamic synergy between Entity Framework and adept data access strategies, paving the path for proficient and streamlined development.

What is Entity Framework, and what role does it play in the .NET ecosystem?

Entity Framework (EF) is an **object-relational mapping (ORM)** framework that allows developers to interact with databases using .NET objects. It simplifies database interactions by automating many aspects of data management. Within the .NET ecosystem, EF provides a unified and cohesive approach to data manipulation and retrieval. It integrates seamlessly with LINQ, enabling developers to write database queries directly in C# code, enhancing the efficiency and maintainability of data-related operations.

What are the main mapping strategies in EF, and what are their distinctive characteristics?

In EF, there are three primary mapping strategies, each with its unique characteristics:

- **Database first**: This approach involves generating models and context based on an existing database. It is convenient when you already have a database with a defined structure, facilitating a straightforward mapping between the database schema and the object model.

- **Model first**: In this case, the model is created first, from which the database schema is then generated. This allows developers to focus on defining a domain model initially, promoting a design-driven approach to database schema creation.

- **Code first**: Developers initially create classes representing the domain model objects, and then EF uses these classes to generate the database schema. This offers more control over the code and the database structure, fostering a code-centric development process where the database schema evolves with the codebase.

Each of these strategies has its advantages and disadvantages, and the choice depends on the specific needs of the project and the requirements of the development process, allowing for flexibility and alignment with different project methodologies.

How is transaction management implemented in EF, and can you provide an example?

Transaction management in EF can be handled using the methods provided by the `DbContext` class. Here is an example of a transactional operation in EF:

```
using (var context = new MyDbContext())
{
    using (var transaction = context.Database.BeginTransaction())
    {
        try
        {
            context.Entities.Add(new Entity { Name = "Entity1" });
            context.SaveChanges();
            context.Entities.Add(new Entity { Name = «Entity2» });
            context.SaveChanges();
            transaction.Commit();
        }
        catch (Exception)
        {
```

```
            transaction.Rollback();
        }
    }
}
```

In the preceding example, two addition operations are carried out within a single transaction. If any of them fails, the transaction is rolled back, reversing all changes.

What features (such as "lazy loading") are available in EF for performance optimization?

EF offers several features for performance optimization, including the following:

- **Lazy loading**: This mechanism automatically loads related data as they are requested. It can help reduce the database load by preventing the loading of large amounts of data simultaneously.

- **Eager loading**: This approach involves loading the main data along with related data all at once. This can be implemented using the `Include` and `ThenInclude` methods.

- **AsNo tracking**: This method is used to disable change tracking for queries, which can enhance performance for read-only operations.

- **Stored procedures**: You can utilize stored procedures to optimize certain database operations, facilitating complex operations and enhancing security.

Can you discuss the advantages and disadvantages of using the code-first approach compared to the database-first approach in EF?

Here are some pros and cons of the code-first and database-first approaches:

- **Code-first approach**:

  - Advantages:

    - Greater flexibility and control over the code

    - Easier to make changes to the model and migrate these to the database

    - Promotes a code-first development practice where the focus is initially on business logic

  - Disadvantages:

    - It can be challenging to use with large, existing databases

    - There might be a need to manually manage complex migrations

- **Database-first approach**:

  - Advantages:

    - Ideally suited for projects with existing databases

    - It can be a quicker way to start working with large databases

  - Disadvantages:

    - Less control over the automatically generated code

    - Changes in the database may require additional synchronization code or new code generation

Both approaches have their place in development, and the choice between them often depends on the specific circumstances of the project; this allows for tailored strategies that align with project goals and existing infrastructure.

How does EF handle concurrent data access situations?

In EF, concurrent data access situations can be managed using optimistic locking. This is typically achieved through the usage of the [ConcurrencyCheck] or [Timestamp] attributes in the models. When a concurrency conflict arises (i.e., two users trying to update the same record simultaneously), EF throws a DbUpdateConcurrencyException, which can be caught and handled appropriately, perhaps by prompting the user to review the changes and try again.

Can you explain how LINQ is utilized in EF to formulate and execute SQL queries?

In EF, LINQ is utilized to formulate and execute SQL queries directly from C# code. This allows developers to construct database queries in the form of C# expressions, which are then automatically translated by EF into corresponding SQL queries. By using LINQ, various types of data operations, including selection, insertion, updating, and deletion, can be performed using the convenient syntax of object-oriented programming.

What tools and methodologies are recommended for conducting database migrations in EF?

For conducting database migrations in EF, the following tools and methodologies are recommended:

- **EF migrations**: These are a set of tools that allow for the automatic generation of migration scripts based on changes in the models. Commands such as 'Add-Migration', 'Update-Database', and others can be utilized to manage migrations.

- **SQL scripts**: You can manually create and apply SQL scripts for complex migrations or when greater control over the migration process is required.

- **Seed data**: This is used to populate the database with certain data during migration, facilitating the initialization of essential data in the database.

Can you describe some commonly used repository patterns when working with EF?

The repository pattern is a design pattern that isolates data access logic in a separate class, facilitating the easier testing and maintenance of the code. Here are a few commonly used repository patterns when working with EF:

- **Generic repository**: This pattern creates a generic repository class that can be used for any entity type, reducing code duplication

- **Repository and unit of work**: This pattern combines the repository pattern with the "unit of work" pattern, allowing for the grouping of several operations in a single transaction, simplifying transaction management

What best practices would you recommend for the effective management of connections and sessions in EF to achieve high performance and scalability?

For the effective management of connections and sessions in EF and to achieve high performance and scalability, the following best practices are recommended:

- Utilize short lifecycles for connections and contexts to minimize the risk of blockages and conflicts

- Employ connection pooling to reduce the overhead of opening new connections

- Optimize queries using techniques, such as lazy and eager loading, cautiously to avoid the N+1 query problem or loading too much data at once

- Use asynchronous methods for database queries to enhance performance and scalability

- Implement caching strategies to reduce the number of database queries and increase performance

- Conduct the profiling and optimization of SQL queries to enhance performance and avoid bottlenecks

Utilizing these practices can help create more efficient and scalable applications based on EF.

What is the "N+1 query problem" in EF, and what methods do you use to prevent performance issues arising from it?

The **N+1 query problem** in EF occurs when the code executes one query to retrieve the main entities and then an additional query for each entity to fetch related data, leading to *N* additional queries for *N* entities, which can severely degrade performance. Essentially, it means making one too many database calls, which can be highly inefficient and slow down the application.

To prevent the **N+1 query problem** in EF, I employ the following strategies:

- **Eager loading**: Use the `.Include` and `.ThenInclude` methods to load related data in one query

- **Explicit loading**: Load related data separately using the `.Load` method

- **Selective loading**: Only load necessary fields through projection (using the `.Select` method)

- **Utilizing caching**: To reduce the number of queries to the database

- **Query optimization**: The careful analysis and optimization of queries to avoid unnecessary operations

Can you discuss strategies for optimizing LINQ queries in EF for the efficient handling of large volumes of data?

Here are several strategies for optimizing LINQ queries in EF when dealing with large volumes of data:

- **Projection**: Using the `.Select` method to select only necessary fields instead of loading the entire object

- **Pagination**: Using the `.Skip` and `.Take` methods to limit the number of returned rows

- **Query compilation**: Using compiled queries to enhance the performance of repetitive queries

- **Asynchronous operations**: Using asynchronous methods to enhance I/O performance

- **Batching**: Grouping several operations into a single transaction to reduce the costs associated with individual transactions

How do you configure and adapt the Identity framework in projects using EF for managing user access and authentication?

When configuring and adapting the Identity framework in projects using EF, I typically undertake the following steps:

- **Identity configuration**: Configuring Identity settings through the `AddIdentity` and `ConfigureServices` methods in the `Startup.cs` file

- **Extending user and role classes**: Creating custom user and role classes by inheriting them from the base Identity classes

- **Configuring security policies**: Defining and setting up security policies for role-based or permission-based access control

- **Customizing the authentication process**: Adjusting authentication parameters, such as utilizing external identity providers

- **Database migration**: Executing migrations to create Identity tables in the database

Can you share any complex scenarios you have encountered during database migration in EF and how you resolved them?

Yes, here are a few complex situations I encountered during database migration in EF, along with the ways I addressed them:

- **Schema conflicts**: These can occur when changing the structure of models. I resolved this by carefully planning the changes and utilizing methods, such as `HasColumnOrder`, to specify the column order.

- **Dependency issues**: These can arise when removing or modifying elements that are referenced by other parts of the schema. I tackled this by updating dependencies before executing the migration.

- **Performance issues**: During the migration of large volumes of data, a decrease in performance can occur. I resolved this by optimizing queries and using batching to reduce the number of transactions.

Can you provide examples of integrating EF with other technologies or frameworks to enhance its functionality?

Yes, here are a few examples of integrating EF with other technologies and frameworks:

- **ASP.NET Core Identity**: To implement user and role management functionality

- **Dapper**: To optimize certain queries using a more low-level ORM

- **Hangfire**: To integrate with a library for scheduling tasks and background operations

- **GraphQL**: To create an API that allows clients to request only the necessary data, integrated with EF for executing database queries

- **Redis**: To integrate a caching system for improving performance and scalability

Using these integrations can help expand the capabilities of EF and create more powerful and flexible applications.

What is your approach to unit testing and integration testing in an environment where EF is extensively used?

In an environment where EF is extensively utilized, my approach to testing includes the following strategies:

- **Unit testing**:

  - Mocking: I use mocking to simulate database behavior, utilizing libraries, such as Moq or NSubstitute

  - In-memory database: I employ an in-memory database to create an isolated testing environment

- **Integration testing**:

  - Test database: I establish a separate test database to conduct integration tests

  - Data seeding: I use data seeding techniques to initialize the testing environment before each test

- **Automated testing**: I automate the testing process using frameworks, such as xUnit or NUnit, to create and execute test suites

What design patterns and architectural solutions would you recommend for building high-performance and scalable systems based on EF?

For building high-performance and scalable systems based on EF, I recommend the following patterns and solutions:

- **Repository pattern**: To abstract data access logic and facilitate data source replacement

- **Unit of Work pattern**: To group several operations into a single transaction

- **Command query responsibility segregation** (CQRS): To separate read and write logic, enhancing performance and scalability

- **Domain-driven design** (DDD): To concentrate on business logic and ensure design flexibility

- **Microservices architecture**: To construct scalable and independent modules that can be deployed separately

Can you discuss your experience in optimizing database performance in the context of using EF?

Yes, here are a few strategies I have employed to optimize database performance in the context of using EF:

- **Lazy loading**: I attempted to avoid the N+1 query problem through the mindful use of lazy loading and eager loading techniques

- **Indexing**: I optimized queries by properly indexing the database tables
- **Batch operations**: I utilized batch operations to reduce the number of individual queries to the database
- **Caching**: I implemented caching to decrease the load on the database by storing frequently queried data in the memory
- **Asynchronous programming**: I adopted asynchronous programming to enhance performance in scenarios with high I/O operations

How do you integrate DDD approaches into EF, and what key decisions have you had to make?

When integrating DDD approaches into EF, I have utilized the following strategies and made the subsequent decisions:

- **Rich domain model**: I developed a rich domain model that encapsulates business logic and rules
- **Aggregates**: I used aggregates to group related objects and ensure data consistency
- **Repositories**: I implemented repositories to provide an abstraction layer for data access
- **Domain events**: I utilized domain events to document significant changes in the domain, facilitating the development of decoupled systems
- **Bounded contexts**: I defined bounded contexts to isolate different parts of the business domain and ensure the clear separation of responsibilities

Can you elaborate on the use of AOP for implementing interceptors and filters in projects utilizing EF?

Aspect-oriented programming (**AOP**) serves as a powerful tool for implementing interceptors and filters in projects utilizing EF. Here are several ways I utilize AOP:

- **Logging**: Implementing the automatic logging of operations by using aspects to intercept methods and record information in logs
- **Transaction management**: Managing transactions through aspects, which allow for the centralization of transaction management logic
- **Caching**: Implementing aspects for the automatic caching of frequently invoked method results
- **Error handling**: Centralizing error handling through aspects, which helps to avoid duplicating error handling code
- **Authorization**: Implementing aspects to verify access to methods based on authorization rules

Utilizing AOP enables the creation of clean and flexible code, simplifying the implementation of interceptors and filters.

Could you mention some of the lesser-known but powerful features of EF and how they can be utilized more effectively?

Certainly, several lesser-known but powerful features of EF include the following:

- **Shadow properties**: These can be used to store additional information that is not part of the main model

- **Global query filters**: These allow you to automatically apply filters to all queries, which can be useful for functionalities such as soft deletion

- **Alternate keys**: These can be used to specify additional unique keys besides the primary keys

- **Custom conventions**: This feature allows you to customize the ways EF Core interprets models

- **Interceptors**: These can be utilized to intercept and modify SQL queries before execution

Do you have experience in adapting EF for interaction with unconventional databases? Can you provide a few examples?

I have experience adapting EF to work with unconventional databases. Here are a few examples:

- Using EF with in-memory databases for testing

- Adapting EF to work with document-oriented databases, such as **MongoDB**, by using specialized providers

- Implementing custom providers to integrate with unconventional database management systems (DBMs)

Have you encountered unforeseen issues while working with EF, and how did you resolve them?

Yes, here are a few unforeseen issues I encountered and the ways I resolved them:

- **Performance issues due to the incorrect use of lazy loading**: I resolved this by assessing and optimizing LINQ queries

- **Concurrent access conflicts**: I addressed this by implementing optimistic concurrency control

- **Database migration issues**: I handled this by manually managing migrations and adjusting migration scripts

Have you integrated EF with alternative data management approaches, for instance, with NoSQL databases? How was this implemented?

Yes, I have experience in integrating EF with alternative data management approaches. Here is how it was implemented:

- Utilizing a hybrid architecture where some parts of the application used relational databases (through EF) and others used NoSQL databases

- Employing the repository pattern to abstract data sources and provide a uniform interface for interacting with different types of databases

- Creating custom data providers to integrate EF with NoSQL databases

Have you had experience optimizing EF for use in high-load or real-time systems? What strategies and tools were applied?

Yes, I have experience optimizing EF for high-load systems. Here are several strategies and tools that I have utilized:

- **Asynchronous programming**: To enhance efficiency and scalability (the asynchronous methods of EF were employed)

- **Caching**: To reduce the load on the database by caching a portion of the queries

- **LINQ query optimization**: To increase performance through the analysis and optimization of LINQ queries

- **Utilization of indexes**: To improve query performance through the appropriate creation and utilization of indexes in the database

Can you compare your experience working with EF in new ("greenfield") projects to working with existing ("brownfield") projects? What challenges did you encounter, and what strategies were applied?

In **greenfield** projects, there's the advantage of starting with a clean slate, allowing developers to design and implement a database structure and data models that adhere to current best practices and design patterns, aiming for scalability, efficiency, and performance from the beginning. Conversely, **brownfield** projects involve working with pre-existing databases, where developers are tasked with modifying or enhancing legacy systems, which may introduce constraints due to outdated structures or previously implemented, less optimal design choices.

In **greenfield** projects, the challenge is to create an efficient and scalable system, which is met by applying best practices to database design and architecture from the start. Meanwhile, in **brownfield** projects, the challenge involves working within the constraints of existing systems. The strategies here include careful refactoring and incremental improvements to integrate modern solutions without disrupting legacy operations.

Can you provide examples of the successful integration of EF into technologies or frameworks that are not typically associated with the .NET ecosystem?

Certainly, one example would be integrating EF into frontend frameworks, such as **Angular** or **React**, to create comprehensive web applications. Another example might be utilizing EF in conjunction with **NoSQL** databases, such as MongoDB, to implement hybrid data management solutions. This involves creating custom data providers and using the repository pattern to abstract and unify interaction with various types of databases.

As we draw the curtain on this enlightening section, we hope that you now hold a foundational grasp of EF and its pivotal role in data access. The journey of learning is perennial, and we encourage you to delve deeper, exploring the multi-faceted avenues that EF opens up in the realm of data management and application development. Remember, a skilled craftsman constantly hones his tools, and in the world of software development, knowledge is your most potent tool. We part with the anticipation that you will forge ahead, leveraging the potent capabilities of EF to craft applications that are not only robust but also finely attuned to the ever-evolving demands of the digital landscape.

In transitioning from the structured world of databases, we now shift our focus to the dynamic realm of web development.

ASP.NET Core for web development

In the vibrant sphere of web development, ASP.NET Core emerges as a front-runner, encapsulating a wealth of features that facilitate the creation of dynamic, scalable, and modern web applications. As we step into this section, we aim to equip you with the foundational knowledge and skills to harness the full potential of this powerful framework. With its roots deeply embedded in the Microsoft ecosystem, ASP.NET Core offers a seamless amalgamation of performance, security, and flexibility. Join us as we embark on a journey through the intricate corridors of ASP.NET Core, fostering a deeper comprehension and appreciation for the boundless opportunities it presents in the realm of web development.

Why should one consider using ASP.NET Core for web application development compared to other popular frameworks?

ASP.NET Core is a compelling choice for web application development for various reasons:

- **High performance**: ASP.NET Core is well-known for its performance. The framework is lightweight and has been benchmarked to be faster than other popular frameworks in many scenarios. Performance optimizations are provided out of the box and can be further enhanced by the developer.

- **Cross-platform capability**: It is a cross-platform framework, meaning it can run on various operating systems such as Windows, Linux, and macOS. This flexibility ensures that applications can reach a wider audience and can be hosted on different platforms, providing more hosting options.

- **Modularity**: The modular architecture of ASP.NET Core allows developers to include only the necessary components in their applications. This not only makes the application lighter but also reduces its surface area for attacks, potentially increasing security.

- **Security**: ASP.NET Core comes with built-in features to protect against many common web vulnerabilities, such as CSRF, XSS, and SQL injection. Microsoft regularly updates the framework to address new security threats.

- **Community and support**: There is a robust and active community around ASP.NET Core. Microsoft provides long-term support for the framework, ensuring that applications can be maintained with up-to-date tools and security features. Additionally, the vast community contributes to the availability of resources, third-party libraries, and troubleshooting support.

Compared to other frameworks, ASP.NET Core stands out for its enterprise readiness, scalability, and the backing of Microsoft, which can be crucial for businesses requiring reliable and long-term support for their applications.

Can you explain the concept of Middleware in ASP.NET Core and its implementation?

Middleware in ASP.NET Core is a piece of software that's assembled into an application pipeline to handle requests and responses. For each component, it provides the following actions:

- Chooses whether to pass the request on to the next component in the pipeline
- Can perform work before and after the next component in the pipeline

The concept is central to ASP.NET Core applications, which are built from multiple middleware components. This allows for building a pipeline for requests and responses, where each middleware instance can perform a specific task, such as authentication, error handling, logging, or serving static files.

When a request is made to an ASP.NET Core application, it travels through the configured middleware pipeline. Each middleware aspect has the opportunity to process the request and decide if it should pass it to the next aspect in the pipeline or not. This allows for a highly configurable request handling process, where you can add, remove, or change the order of middleware components to suit your application's needs.

Implementation-wise, Middleware components are C# classes that implement the `IMiddleware` interface, although, in practice, they're often set up as simple classes with a specific convention-based method signature:

```
public async Task InvokeAsync(HttpContext context, RequestDelegate
next)
{
```

```
    // Do work that can't be done by the next middleware
    await next(context); // Call the next middleware in the pipeline
    // Do other work that can happen after the next middleware
}
```

To use middleware, you add it to your application's request pipeline configuration in the `Configure` method of the `Startup` class, like so:

```
public void Configure(IApplicationBuilder app)
{
    app.UseMiddleware<YourMiddlewareClass>();
    // Other middleware
}
```

In .NET 6 and onwards, including .NET 7, the typical `Startup.cs` class was replaced with a new minimal hosting model that simplifies the bootstrapping and configuration process of an ASP.NET Core application. This model makes use of the `Program.cs` file, which is used to set up the app's services and middleware in a more streamlined and top-level statement syntax.

```
app.Use(async (context, next) =>
{
    // Custom middleware logic before calling the next middleware
    await next();
    // Custom middleware logic after calling the next middleware
});
```

Or, we can use the following middleware class:

```
app.UseMiddleware<YourMiddlewareClass>();
```

This flexible system allows ASP.NET Core applications to be tailored to specific needs by plugging in various middleware components.

What is the difference between Middleware and Filters in ASP.NET Core?

Middleware and **Filters** in ASP.NET Core serve similar purposes—they handle incoming and outgoing HTTP requests and responses. However, there are key differences:

- **Scope of Application**: Middleware has components that operate at the application level and are used to handle HTTP requests and responses across the entire pipeline.

  Filters are applied at the level of controllers and actions, making them more specific to **MVC** and **Razor Pages**.

- **Processing stages**: Middleware works in the earlier stages of request processing—it encounters the request soon after it enters the system and before it reaches MVC.

  Filters perform tasks after routing has determined which controller and action will be executed. They can intervene at various stages of action execution, such as before or after the controller action method.

- **Functionality**: Middleware is often used for tasks such as authentication, logging, and serving static files.

  Filters can be used to customize authentication, authorization, error handling, caching, and other tasks that are specific to particular actions or controllers.

- **Control over processing**: Middleware does not have direct access to the MVC execution context, such as the action context or results operating at a lower level.

  Filters can interact with the MVC execution context and modify it.

Therefore, the choice between using middleware or Filters depends on the scope of the application, the desired flexibility, and the specific needs for request or response handling in an ASP.NET Core application.

How can user authentication and authorization be implemented in ASP.NET Core?

In ASP.NET Core, you can implement user authentication and authorization using built-in services and middleware. Here are the primary steps to achieve this:

1. **Setting up Identity**: Utilize ASP.NET Core Identity to manage users and their roles

2. **Authentication**: Configure authentication using appropriate schemes (for example, JWT, OAuth, cookies, etc.)

3. **Authorization**: Employ authorization policies to define the access rules to the resources in your application

4. **Applying attributes**: Utilize the ' [Authorize] ' attribute to enforce access restrictions at the controller or action levels

5. **Validation and handling**: Add appropriate error handling and credential verification to ensure the secure operation of your web application

How can sessions and states be managed in ASP.NET Core?

Managing sessions and states in ASP.NET Core can be carried out via the following mechanisms:

- **Sessions**: Use the session service to store and retrieve data at the session level. Before using sessions, you need to configure the session middleware in the ConfigureServices and Configure methods in the Startup class.

- **Cookies**: Utilize cookies to store information on the client side.

- **Caching**: Employ caching mechanisms to temporarily store frequently used data, reducing the load on the database or other external systems.

- **Application state**: Although server-level application state management is limited in ASP.NET Core, you can still use means, such as databases or distributed caching systems, to store the global state of the application.

What are the main differences between JWT tokens, sessions, and cookies in the context of authorization and user state preservation?

- **JSON web token (JWT)**: It is an open standard that defines a way to securely transmit information between parties in the form of a JSON object. JWTs are often used for authentication and authorization in web applications.

- **Sessions**: Sessions are used to store user state information between requests. Session data are stored on the server, and the client is given a unique session identifier, which can be stored in cookies.

- **Cookies**: These are small text files stored on the client side and are used to preserve information between browser sessions. Cookies can be used to store session identifiers, user preferences, and more.

What are the primary design patterns recommended for use when developing web applications on ASP.NET Core?

When developing web applications on ASP.NET Core, the following design patterns are often utilized:

- **Model View Controller (MVC)**: This pattern is integral to ASP.NET Core, offering a clear division between data models, user interfaces (views), and control logic (controllers). It aligns well with ASP.NET Core's emphasis on the separation of concerns, making it easier to manage complex applications.

- **Repository pattern**: In ASP.NET Core, this pattern is useful for abstracting data access logic from business logic. It helps to manage data operations, making the code more maintainable and testable, especially in applications with complex data models.

- **Unit of Work**: This pattern complements the repository pattern in ASP.NET Core by managing transactions across multiple repositories. It ensures consistency and atomic operations, which are crucial in applications that handle complex transactions.

- **Dependency injection**: ASP.NET Core has built-in support for dependency injection, making it simpler to implement. This pattern is key for creating loosely coupled, easily testable components, representing a core principle in ASP.NET Core application development.

- **Command query responsibility segregation (CQRS)**: This pattern separates read and write operations into distinct models, which can optimize performance and scalability, especially in complex applications with diverse data operation requirements.

How would you organize exception handling in an ASP.NET Core web application to ensure reliability and security?

To organize exception handling in ASP.NET Core, the following approaches can be utilized:

- **Custom middleware**: Develop custom middleware aspects to intercept and handle exceptions effectively

- **Global exception handler**: Utilize a global exception handler using methods such as `UseExceptionHandler` or `UseDeveloperExceptionPage`, depending on the environment (development or production)

- **Logging**: Integrate with logging systems to record exception details and monitor the application's state

- **Status codes**: Configure appropriate HTTP status codes to inform the client about the nature of the error, facilitating improved user experience and system reliability

What tools and strategies would you recommend for testing web applications on ASP.NET Core?

For testing web applications on ASP.NET Core, the following tools and strategies are recommended:

- **xUnit**: A popular framework for unit testing in the .NET ecosystem

- **Moq**: A library for creating mock objects, which simplifies unit testing by isolating components

- **Selenium**: A tool for browser automation that allows for functional testing of web applications

- **Postman**: A tool for API testing, enabling the easy creation and execution of requests to web applications

- **Integration testing**: Use classes, such as `TestServer` and `WebApplicationFactory`, for the integration testing of web applications

- **Continuous integration and continuous delivery/deployment (CI/CD)**: Implement CI/CD pipelines to automate the testing and deployment processes, ensuring rapid feedback and consistent deployments

What strategies and approaches have you used to optimize the performance of ASP.NET Core web applications in high-traffic systems?

To optimize the performance in high-traffic systems, the following strategies can be employed:

- **Caching**: Utilize caching mechanisms to reduce the load on the database and improve response times

- **Asynchronous programming**: Implement asynchronous operations to enhance the performance of web applications by allowing the non-blocking execution of code

- **Load balancing**: Employ load balancers to evenly distribute the load among servers, ensuring the better utilization of resources and preventing server overloads

- **Database query optimization**: Analyze and optimize SQL queries to enhance database operation efficiency, avoiding potential bottlenecks

- **Conducting stress testing**: Regularly conduct stress tests to identify and eliminate system bottlenecks, preparing the application to handle real-world load scenarios more effectively

- **Redis**: A multi-faceted tool used for ensuring efficient distributed locking, enabling rapid session management in web applications, and facilitating high-performance data caching

How have you utilized the innovations and features of ASP.NET Core to create innovative web solutions? Can you provide specific examples or cases?

By using ASP.NET Core, various innovations can be leveraged to create innovative web solutions, such as the following:

- **Blazor**: This feature can be utilized to build interactive web interfaces using C# instead of JavaScript, facilitating the development of more dynamic and responsive web applications

- **SignalR**: It enables the implementation of real-time functionalities in web applications, allowing the creation of chat applications, games, and other interactive services that require real-time updates and communications

- **gRPC**: A framework that can be used to create high-performance, strongly typed APIs, enhancing communication between distributed systems

- **Containerization and microservices**: Leveraging **Docker** and **Kubernetes** to create scalable and easily deployable web applications, facilitating efficient development and deployment workflows

How can you ensure the secure storage of database connection strings and other confidential data during development?

To ensure the secure storage of confidential data during the development phase, the following approaches can be adopted:

- **Secret manager**: A tool that allows for the local storage of confidential data during development without including them in the project code, thus preventing the accidental exposure of sensitive information

- **Environment variables**: Utilizing environment variables to store and transfer confidential data securely, segregating sensitive information from the application's codebase

- **Azure Key Vault or similar services**: Employing specialized services for the centralized and secure storage of confidential data, facilitating the secure access and management of sensitive information across different environments and deployments

What are the main differences between ASP.NET and ASP.NET Core, and why should Core be chosen for new projects?

The primary differences and advantages of using ASP.NET Core compared to ASP.NET include the following:

- **Cross-platform capability**: ASP.NET Core can be utilized across various operating systems, including Windows, Linux, and MacOS, whereas ASP.NET is restricted to Windows. This flexibility facilitates the development process and allows for a broader reach.

- **Open source**: ASP.NET Core is open source, promoting greater transparency and opportunities for the developer community to contribute and innovate.

- **Modularity and flexibility**: ASP.NET Core offers a more modular and flexible architecture, making it easier to add or remove components, thereby enhancing the adaptability of web applications to changing requirements.

- **Container support**: It offers superior support for containers and microservices, simplifying deployment and scaling processes, which is beneficial for creating modern, scalable applications.

- **Improved performance**: ASP.NET Core is optimized for higher performance compared to traditional ASP.NET, enabling the development of more efficient and responsive web applications.

How is container and microservice support implemented within ASP.NET Core?

In ASP.NET Core, support for containers and microservices is realized through the following features:

- **Docker integration**: The easy creation of Docker images for ASP.NET Core applications facilitates deployment and management in containerized environments, offering streamlined deployment processes

- **Microservice architecture**: The ability to break the application into several independent microservices, each of which can be deployed and scaled separately, allowing for more scalable and maintainable systems

- **Orchestration**: Smooth integration with orchestration systems, such as Kubernetes, aids in automating the deployment, scaling, and management of containerized applications, promoting efficient and automated operational workflows

- **Configuration and secret management**: Tools are available for the centralized and secure management of configurations and secrets in microservice environments, ensuring the safe handling of sensitive information

- **API gateway**: Support for utilizing API gateways to route and aggregate requests to various microservices enhances the organization and security of microservice architectures

What strategies and practices do you recommend for maintaining security in web applications developed based on ASP.NET Core?

To ensure security in web applications developed on ASP.NET Core, I recommend employing the following strategies and practices:

- Utilizing HTTPS to encrypt data in transit, safeguarding sensitive information during communication

- The authentication and authorization of users using built-in features of ASP.NET Core Identity, ensuring secure access control mechanisms

- Protecting against common web attacks, such as SQL Injection, XSS, and CSRF, by using built-in security mechanisms, mitigating vulnerabilities and potential exploits

- Employing security header policies, such as **content security policy (CSP)**, to reduce the risk of potential attacks, adding an extra layer of security to your web application

- Regularly updating dependencies and components to the latest secure versions, keeping the application safe from known vulnerabilities

- Implementing logging and monitoring activities for quick detection and response to security incidents, facilitating proactive security management

How can SQL and NoSQL databases be integrated and utilized in ASP.NET Core projects?

The integration and utilization of SQL and NoSQL databases in ASP.NET Core projects can involve the following steps:

1. Choosing an appropriate ORM or library to work with the specific type of database (for instance, EF for SQL databases), facilitating efficient data management

2. Configuring connection strings and other configuration parameters in the `appsettings. json` file, setting up the necessary configurations for database connections

3. Creating data models and configuring mappings to represent the database structure in the code, organizing the data structure for application usage

4. Using LINQ to formulate and execute queries to SQL databases and the relevant APIs for NoSQL databases, facilitating efficient data retrieval and manipulation

5. Implementing repositories or services to manage data operations, such as adding, updating, deleting, and retrieving, creating a structured approach to data management in the application

What are the recommended approaches to developing and deploying highly available and scalable web applications based on ASP.NET Core?

For the development of highly available and scalable web applications using ASP.NET Core, the following approaches are recommended:

-   Utilize stateless applications to facilitate horizontal scaling

-   Consider utilizing cloud services for automatic scaling and resource management, enhancing the scalability and reliability of the applications

-   Use a **content delivery network** (**CDN**) for distributing static content, which can help to reduce server load and improve content delivery speed

-   Optimize database operations by implementing caching and connection pooling to enhance performance and reduce latency

-   Implement monitoring and logging to identify and address issues in real-time, ensuring continuous service availability and performance optimization

How can ASP.NET Core be integrated within cloud services and platforms?

ASP.NET Core can be integrated within various cloud services by using the SDKs or APIs provided by cloud service providers. For instance, the **Azure** SDK can be used for integration with Azure, and the **AWS** SDK for AWS integration. Additionally, consider using libraries for authentication, data storage, and working with message queues, among other functionalities, to streamline the integration process and take advantage of cloud platform features.

What are the key components of ASP.NET Core, and what are their roles in web development?

The primary components of ASP.NET Core include the following:

- **Kestrel**: A lightweight, high-performance web server that serves as the foundational server for ASP.NET Core applications
- **Middleware components**: These can be used for processing HTTP requests in a pipeline, allowing for modular and customizable request handling
- **MVC**: A design pattern for developing web applications that incorporate models, views, and controllers, facilitating an organized and maintainable code structure
- **Razor Pages**: An alternative approach to creating web interfaces that simplifies the programming model for ASP.NET Core applications
- **Dependency injection**: A built-in system for dependency injection, promoting code modularity and testability
- **Configuration**: A system for managing settings in a structured and centralized manner, facilitating configuration management across different environments

How does routing work in ASP.NET Core, and how can it be configured?

In ASP.NET Core, routing is utilized to determine how HTTP requests are handled within the application. The routes are defined by using templates that specify which controller and action will handle a particular request. To configure routing, the `UseRouting()` and `UseEndpoints()` methods can be used in the request processing pipeline, allowing for a structured and customizable routing setup.

What popular libraries and packages are recommended for developing web applications on ASP.NET Core?

During the development process on ASP.NET Core, the following libraries and packages are often utilized:

- **EF Core**: An ORM for working with databases, facilitating data access and management

- **AutoMapper** or **Mapster**: For automating the mapping between objects, reducing the amount of boilerplate code required for object transformations

- **Serilog** or **NLog**: These are used for logging and helping to track and diagnose issues in the application

- **Swagger** and **Swashbuckle**: These are used for API documentation to aid in creating professional and interactive API documentation

- **Polly**: This is used for implementing resilience patterns to enhance the stability and reliability of the application in the face of transient faults and failures

How do you create and integrate custom Middleware aspects in ASP.NET Core projects?

To create and utilize custom middleware aspects in ASP.NET Core projects, adhere to the following steps:

1. Create a class that incorporates an `Invoke` or `InvokeAsync` method, which accepts `HttpContext` as a parameter

2. Utilize the aforementioned methods to handle HTTP requests within middleware

3. Register middleware in the request processing pipeline by using the `UseMiddleware` method in the `Startup` class

This structure allows for the streamlined integration of custom middleware aspects into your ASP. NET Core projects, facilitating enhanced request handling and project functionality.

What methods of dependency injection are present in ASP.NET Core, and how do they contribute to the development of flexible and testable applications?

In ASP.NET Core, there are three primary types of dependency injection: **singleton**, **scoped**, and **transient**. These methods promote the creation of flexible and testable applications by separating specific implementations from interfaces, which simplifies the testing and maintenance of the code. Here is a detailed explanation of each:

- **Singleton**:

  - Definition: In this method, a single instance of the service is created and shared across the entire application, and it exists for the lifetime of the application

  - Contribution to flexibility and testability: Singleton services improve application flexibility with global state access but can complicate testability due to persistent states between tests

  - Resource optimization: As only a single instance is created, this helps in optimizing resources, especially for services that are expensive to create or maintain

- State persistence: Singleton services can retain their data state persistently throughout the application lifecycle

- Ease of configuration: Simplifies configuration by centralizing service instance management

- Testing challenges: It might pose challenges in testing scenarios where isolated service instances are required, as the shared instance can retain its state between test cases

- **Scoped**:

  - Definition: A new instance of the service is created once per request or per "scope". The created instance is shared across components during a single HTTP request.

  - Contribution to flexibility and testability: Scoped services provide a balance between the broad availability of singletons and the isolated, per-use basis of transients, enhancing flexibility by sharing a state within a request while still allowing for clean, separate instances in different requests, thereby improving testability.

  - Data isolation: Helps to isolate data for individual requests, which can prevent potential issues related to concurrent access and data consistency.

  - Resource management: Facilitates better resource management by allowing the creation of service instances on a per-request basis.

  - Simplified testing: This makes it easier to test applications by allowing the creation of isolated service instances for each test case or request scenario.

- **Transient**:

  - Definition: Transient services are created each time they are requested. This means a new instance is provided to each controller and every service or component that requests it.

  - Contribution to flexibility and testability: Transient services increase flexibility by providing fresh, independent instances to every component that requires them, ensuring no shared state across operations, which greatly aids in creating isolated, predictable unit tests for components.

  - Isolated instances: Ensures that each component gets a fresh, isolated instance, preventing the potential side effects from shared states.

  - Fine-grained control: Offers fine-grained control over service instances, allowing developers to manage the lifecycle and dependencies more precisely.

  - Facilitates testing: Simplifies testing by enabling the creation of separate instances for each test, which can be configured or mocked independently.

By utilizing these dependency injection methods, developers can create applications that are more modular, maintainable, and testable. It encourages the separation of concerns and adherence to the SOLID principles, fostering the development of robust and scalable applications in ASP.NET Core.

How do you plan to organize automated testing for a web application developed on ASP.NET Core?

To organize automated testing in ASP.NET Core, the following approaches can be utilized:

- **Unit testing**: Employing frameworks, such as xUnit or NUnit, to test individual parts of the code, ensuring the reliability of the code components

- **Integration testing**: Creating tests that verify the interaction between system components, providing a holistic view of system functionality and the integration points

- **UI testing**: Using tools such as **Selenium** for automating user interface testing, ensuring the user interface functions correctly and meets user requirements

- **CI/CD**: Setting up continuous integration and delivery pipelines to automate the testing and deployment process, enhancing the development lifecycle and facilitating quicker releases

What challenges have you encountered during the deployment of large-scale web applications on ASP.NET Core, and how did you overcome them?

During the deployment of large-scale web applications on ASP.NET Core, several challenges might be encountered, including performance optimization, resource management, security assurance, database migration, and maintaining a state when both the old and new services are running concurrently. Here's how these challenges can be mitigated:

- **Performance optimization**: To ensure optimal performance, it's vital to conduct regular performance testing and optimize the code and resources based on the insights gathered. Implementing caching strategies and optimizing database queries are some of the steps that can be taken to enhance performance.

- **Resource management**: Effective resource management involves optimizing server resources to prevent bottlenecks and ensure smooth operation even during peak times. This might include strategies such as load balancing and utilizing cloud resources effectively.

- **Security assurance**: Security is a paramount concern in large-scale deployments. Implementing modern security practices, such as SSL encryption, utilizing secure coding practices to prevent vulnerabilities, and regularly updating the system to patch any security holes are essential steps.

- **Database migration**: Large-scale deployments often involve database migrations, which can be challenging. Utilizing migration scripts and tools that facilitate smooth migration without data loss is crucial. It is also essential to have backup strategies in place to prevent data loss and to test the migration process thoroughly before implementation to identify and fix any potential issues.

- **Supporting a state across old and new services**: During the transition phase, where both old and new services are running concurrently, maintaining state consistency can be a significant challenge. Implementing strategies, such as feature flags, to gradually transition users to new services and utilizing stateful distributed databases that can synchronize states across both systems are ways to ensure a seamless transition.

- **Scaling**: Scaling strategies, including both horizontal (adding more machines) and vertical scaling (adding more power to the existing machines), can be employed to handle increased load and ensure stability.

By adopting these strategies, it is possible to overcome challenges and ensure the robust, scalable, and secure deployment of large-scale web applications on ASP.NET Core. Continuous monitoring and adapting strategies based on real-time insights can further enhance the reliability and performance of the deployment.

How can you integrate ASP.NET Core with modern frontend frameworks such as Angular or React? Do you have practical experience with this?

Integrating ASP.NET Core with modern frontend frameworks, such as Angular or React, can be achieved by using several approaches:

- **Creating single-page applications (SPAs)**: ASP.NET Core can serve as the back end for SPAs developed with Angular or React, facilitating a seamless user experience

- **Using templates**: ASP.NET Core offers project templates for Angular and React, which simplify the integration process by providing a structured setup

- **API integration**: You can create RESTful APIs in ASP.NET Core to facilitate data exchange by using the frontend part of the application

What strategies do you propose for ensuring data security and user confidentiality in web applications developed on ASP.NET Core?

To ensure data security and user confidentiality in web applications developed on ASP.NET Core, the following strategies can be employed:

- **Data encryption**: Utilize robust encryption algorithms to safeguard data confidentiality

- **Authentication and authorization**: Implement reliable authentication and authorization systems to restrict access to sensitive information, thereby protecting user privacy and data integrity

- **Protection against common attacks**: Shield your web application from prevalent attacks, such as SQL injection, cross-site scripting (XSS), and cross-site request forgery (CSRF), by leveraging the built-in security mechanisms of ASP.NET Core

Can you provide some examples of the successful use of ASP.NET Core in complex business projects or innovative developments?

ASP.NET Core has been successfully applied in various high-traffic and innovative projects. Here are a few examples:

- **Financial platforms**: Developing reliable and scalable financial platforms capable of handling a large volume of transactions efficiently, showcasing the robustness of ASP.NET Core in handling complex computational tasks

- **E-commerce**: Crafting intricate e-commerce solutions that offer high levels of security and can withstand substantial traffic, demonstrating the framework's scalability and reliability

- **Educational platforms**: Creating interactive and innovative educational platforms that utilize virtual reality and other cutting-edge technologies, underscoring the flexibility of ASP.NET Core in incorporating new technologies

- **Healthcare and telemedicine**: Developing platforms for providing online medical services and remote patient health monitoring, highlighting the versatility of ASP.NET Core in facilitating healthcare advancements

These projects exemplify the flexibility and potency of ASP.NET Core as a tool for developing modern web applications that meet the demands of various business domains.

As we reach the terminus of this enlightening section, we trust that your perspective on web development has been enriched through the lens of ASP.NET Core. This framework, with its modernized approach and robust capabilities, stands ready to be the cornerstone of your future web development projects. It is our aspiration that you carry forth this knowledge as a beacon, guiding you in the crafting of web solutions that are not only efficient but also innovative. As we part ways, remember that the journey with ASP.NET Core is far from over; it is a dynamic field that is ever-evolving and ripe with opportunities for further exploration and mastery. Forge ahead with curiosity and determination as you sculpt the next generation of web experiences by using ASP.NET Core.

Summary

As we draw this enriching chapter to a close, we are optimistic that you now find yourself significantly better prepared, with a deeper understanding and appreciation for the essential C# libraries and frameworks. The insights and guidance encapsulated within these pages not only aspire to bolster your development skills but also stand to robustly prepare you to face the rigors of technical interviews with a newfound confidence.

Remember, the secret to mastering coding challenges is not confined to mere knowledge acquisition; it extends to the strategic and efficient application of this knowledge. We fervently hope that the expertise and insights accrued from this chapter will serve as a robust pillar in your evolving journey as a C# developer, gearing you up to embrace and conquer the diverse and thrilling challenges that the tech arena continually presents.

With a solid grasp of C# libraries and ASP.NET now under your belt, in the next chapter, we'll transition smoothly into covering the practical strategies for acing coding challenges during interviews, ensuring you're well-prepared on all fronts for the multi-faceted role of a modern C# developer.

Additional reading

- *Web Development with Blazor - Second Edition*, by Jimmy Engström

  https://www.packtpub.com/product/web-development-with-blazor-second-edition/9781803241494

- *Microsoft Azure For .NET Developers [Video]*, by Trevoir Williams

  https://www.packtpub.com/product/microsoft-azure-for-net-developers-video/9781835465059

7

Overcoming Challenges in C# Technical Interviews and Tips for Tackling Coding Challenges during Interviews

Embarking on the journey to secure a role in C# development can be both exhilarating and daunting, largely because it hinges on the process of technical interviews. This chapter serves as a beacon, guiding you through the intricate paths of preparation and execution for C# programming interviews. It strives to be a comprehensive resource, encompassing a review of pivotal C# concepts and programming paradigms and offering a glimpse into the real-world applications of C#.

This chapter addresses the technical aspects of interview preparation, from optimizing computer performance and setting up the ideal development environment, thereby ensuring that candidates can showcase their skills in the most conducive environment.

In this chapter, we'll cover the following main topics:

- Reviewing C# programming concepts and topics
- Reflecting on real-world examples of C# applications
- Common C# technical interview questions and problems

Reviewing C# programming concepts and topics

To set the foundation for a successful interview, it's imperative to revisit and reinforce our understanding of C# programming concepts and topics. In this section, we will delve deep into the intricacies of C# programming, refreshing your memory on essential principles and paradigms that form the backbone of C# development.

The concepts and principles upon which the C# programming language is based are foundational for software development. A detailed study and profound understanding of these concepts are key to creating efficient, optimized, and reliable programs. Let's take a detailed look at the fundamental concepts and principles of the C# programming language.

Data types

Data types in C# define the nature of data that can be stored and manipulated within a program. They serve as the foundation for creating variables and objects and determine the operations that can be performed on the data. Here are some examples:

- `int` and `long`: Used for storing integer values
- `float` and `double`: Used for floating-point numbers
- `char`: Used for single characters
- `string`: Used for strings of text
- `bool`: Used for Boolean values, which are typically true or false

Understanding data types is crucial as they determine the kind of information that can be stored and the operations that can be performed, enabling developers to create robust and effective solutions.

Operators

Operators in C# perform actions on operands and produce results. They are essential for conducting operations such as arithmetic, comparison, assignment, and logical operations. They include the following:

- **Arithmetic operators**: +, -, *, /, and % for performing arithmetic operations
- **Comparison operators**: ==, !=, <, >, <=, and >= for comparing values
- **Logical operators**: &&, ||, and ! for creating logical expressions
- **Bitwise operators**: &, |, ^, ~, << and >> for manipulating with bits

A thorough understanding of operators is important for implementing logic and conducting operations within the program, allowing for the development of dynamic and interactive software applications.

Loops

Loops in C# allow you to repeat a block of code multiple times. They are essential for automating repetitive tasks, reducing code duplication, and enhancing development productivity. The main types of loops include the following:

- `for`: Used when the number of iterations is known

- `foreach`: Used for iterating over collections where the number of iterations is determined by the number of items in the collection
- `while`: Used when the number of iterations is unknown
- `do-while`: Guarantees the execution of the code block at least once

Understanding loops is crucial as they enable developers to efficiently manage repetitive tasks and conditions, leading to cleaner and more efficient code.

Conditional statements

Conditional statements in C# enable you to perform different actions depending on whether a specific condition has been met. They are vital for implementing logical checks and branching the flow of program execution. The main conditional statements are as follows:

- `if-else`: Used to perform actions based on the truthfulness of a condition
- `switch-case`: Used to choose one block of code to execute from multiple possibilities

Grasping conditional statements is fundamental for controlling the flow of programs and implementing decision-making logic in software development.

Classes and objects

Classes and objects are fundamental concepts of object-oriented programming in C#. Let's take a closer look:

- **Classes** serve as templates that define the structure and behavior of objects. They can contain fields, methods, properties, and other class members.
- **Objects** are specific instances of classes and represent the implementation of the defined class.

A clear understanding of classes and objects is indispensable in C# programming as it lays the foundation for designing and implementing sophisticated and robust software solutions. These concepts empower developers to model real-world entities and their interactions, encapsulate functionality, and create reusable and maintainable code.

Inheritance and polymorphism

Inheritance and polymorphism are key principles of object-oriented programming that ensure code reusability and flexibility:

- **Inheritance** allows a new class to be created that inherits properties and methods from an existing class, promoting code reusability and establishing a hierarchical relationship between classes

- **Polymorphism** allows objects to interact through a common interface, making the system more modular and scalable, and enabling objects of different types to be treated as objects of a common supertype

Understanding these principles is pivotal for designing efficient and versatile object-oriented software solutions.

Encapsulation and abstraction

These concepts assist in managing access to an object's data and implementing a high level of abstraction in programming:

- **Encapsulation** protects the internal state of an object and prevents unauthorized external access, allowing strict control over the data and ensuring data integrity
- **Abstraction** allows implementation to be separated from the interface and supports the creation of systems with higher levels of flexibility and scalability, enabling developers to reduce programming complexity and increase efficiency

Mastery of these concepts is crucial for developing robust and maintainable software systems, thus ensuring data integrity and reducing complexity.

Arrays and collections

Arrays and collections in C# are used for storing data and allow data to be organized in a manner that facilitates easy access and manipulation:

- **Arrays** are static collections capable of storing a fixed number of elements of a single type
- **Collections** are dynamic and can store a variable number of elements; they come in different types, such as lists, dictionaries, stacks, queues, and so on

A proper understanding of arrays and collections is essential for efficient data storage and manipulation, enabling developers to handle data more effectively in diverse scenarios.

Delegates and events

Delegates are types that safely encapsulate a method and allow variables to be defined that can hold references to these methods, enabling callback mechanisms and event handling.

Events use delegates to notify about state changes, allowing one object to inform other objects about certain occurrences.

Comprehending delegates and events is vital for developing interactive and responsive software applications, allowing for the implementation of event-driven programming paradigms and enhancing the software's adaptability and responsiveness to user actions or system events.

Language Integrated Query (LINQ)

LINQ enables the use of query expressions to interact with data, irrespective of its source. It facilitates easy filtering, sorting, grouping, and transformation of data, providing a seamless and integrated way to query objects, databases, and XML documents.

Understanding LINQ is essential as it provides a uniform and model-independent querying capability, streamlining data manipulation and retrieval processes and offering enhanced readability and maintainability.

Asynchronous programming

Asynchronous operations allow a program to perform other tasks while waiting for a long-running operation to complete, such as reading from a file or downloading data from the internet. Asynchronous programming in C# utilizes the `async` and `await` keywords to create asynchronous code.

Mastery of asynchronous programming is crucial as it enhances application responsiveness and scalability, especially when dealing with I/O-bound or network-bound operations, improving the **user experience** (**UX**) and overall application performance.

Multithreading

Multithreading in C# is used to execute multiple tasks simultaneously, boosting the program's productivity, especially when performing high-load or blocking operations. The main components of multithreading are as follows:

- **Threads**: The fundamental units of execution. These allow programs to operate in parallel, maximizing the utilization of CPU resources.

- **Tasks**: These have a higher level of abstraction over threads, which facilitates the creation of asynchronous code, making it easier to manage and coordinate parallel operations.

- **Concurrent collections**: These are specialized data structures that have been optimized for multithreaded access, such as `ConcurrentDictionary` and `ConcurrentQueue`.

A deep understanding of multithreading concepts is paramount for developing high-performance applications, optimizing resource utilization, and ensuring smooth and responsive UXs, even under heavy loads or during extensive computations.

Thread synchronization primitives

Thread synchronization primitives are crucial elements when developing multithreaded programs in C#. They allow safe management of access to shared resources, ensuring the stability and reliability of programs.

In the context of C# multithreading, various synchronization primitives are used to manage concurrent access to shared resources. These include the following:

- **Lock statement**: `lock` is a basic mechanism for blocking access to an object or a section of code so that only one thread can execute the given code at a time. It is a simple and convenient synchronization mechanism for protecting critical sections of code.

- **Monitor**: The `Monitor` class allows objects to be locked and unlocked, offering more control and flexibility compared to `lock`, such as the ability to try to acquire a lock with a timeout.

- **Mutex**: `Mutex` controls access to a shared resource between different processes, unlike `lock` and `Monitor`, which only operate within one process.

- **Semaphore**: `Semaphore` manages access to a limited number of resources, allowing several threads to use these resources simultaneously.

- `AutoResetEvent` and `ManualResetEvent`: These classes allow one thread to wait for a signal from another thread to continue execution. `AutoResetEvent` automatically returns to the non-signaled state after release, while `ManualResetEvent` remains in the signaled state until it's explicitly reset.

Attributes and reflection

Attributes and **reflection** are important concepts in C# as they add flexibility and dynamism to the code. Attributes are used for adding metadata to program elements such as classes, methods, and properties, which can alter their behavior during runtime. Reflection allows for dynamically introspecting, analyzing, and interacting with types in the program – for example, obtaining information about classes and their members, creating object instances, invoking methods, and reading and writing fields and properties.

Exception handling

Exception handling is a critical part of any programming language, and C# is no exception. It allows for detecting and handling errors that occur during program execution, preventing crashes and unforeseen outcomes. Standard constructs such as `try`, `catch`, `finally`, and `throw` allow exceptions to be managed and error-handling strategies to be implemented to ensure program robustness and data accuracy.

Lambda expressions and anonymous functions

Lambda expressions and **anonymous functions** are fundamental concepts in C# that allow functions to be declared and defined in place, often used as arguments for other functions. They are notable for their ability to provide concise, expressive syntax for representing functionality, especially when used with higher-order functions and LINQ.

Generics

Generics in C# enable the creation of classes, interfaces, and methods that can operate with different data types without losing type safety and performance. They play a key role in creating versatile and flexible collections, services, and other components that can work with any data type.

Interfaces and abstract classes

Interfaces and **abstract classes** in C# serve to define contracts and base functionality that must be implemented or inherited by specific classes. They enable developers to create modular, flexible, and extensible systems, maintaining code clarity and comprehensibility.

Development environment

The **development environment** in C# provides the tools and resources necessary for effective software development. Some of them are as follows:

- **.NET SDK**: This software development kit includes compilers, libraries, and other resources for developing applications in C#.

- **NuGet Packages**: A package management system that allows for the easy integration of third-party libraries and components into C# projects.

- **Visual Studio**: This powerful **integrated development environment** (**IDE**) is a standard for C# development. It grants developers access to a plethora of tools for writing, testing, and debugging code, as well as managing projects and resources.

- **Visual Studio Code**: An open source, cross-platform, lightweight editor with extension support that can be configured for C# development and beyond.

- **Rider**: JetBrains' Rider is an alternative IDE for C# that offers high productivity and convenience to developers by integrating ReSharper and other JetBrains tools to enhance development.

Testing

Testing is a critically important phase of software development, ensuring the high quality and reliability of programs. Here are some common testing types:

- **Unit testing**: Testing individual components of the program (modules) to verify their correctness and reliability

- **Integration testing**: Examining interactions between different parts of the system to detect integration errors

- **Mocking frameworks**: Tools that allow mock objects to be created to simulate the behavior of external dependencies during testing

Having concluded our review of C# programming concepts and topics, you should now feel more grounded in the fundamental principles of C#. This solid foundation will be your steadfast ally as you face technical questions and coding challenges in your upcoming interviews, enabling you to approach them with confidence and clarity.

Next, we will bridge this theory with practice by reflecting on real-world examples of C# applications.

Reflecting on real-world examples of C# applications

Moving forward, it is crucial to bridge the gap between theoretical knowledge and practical application. This section is dedicated to exploring real-world examples of C# applications, providing you with valuable insights into how C# is implemented in various domains and industries.

C# in the gaming industry

In the realm of game development, Unity stands out as a paramount game development engine, predominantly recognized for its extensive use of C# for scripting and managing intricate gameplay dynamics. This seamless integration renders the engine exceptionally versatile, permitting developers to create immersive gaming experiences across an array of platforms, including PCs, mobile devices, consoles, and VR devices.

C# offers multiple benefits when used in game development, particularly within the Unity engine. Here are several advantages that make C# a preferred choice for developers in the gaming sector:

- **Object-oriented programming**: C#'s object-oriented programming paradigm is instrumental in the construction of complex game systems, allowing for the encapsulation, inheritance, and polymorphism of game objects, thereby facilitating clean and manageable code structures

- **Strict typing**: The strict typing system of C# enables developers to catch errors during the compilation phase, promoting robustness and reducing the likelihood of runtime errors, which are often hard to trace and fix

- **Seamless integration with Unity**: The harmonious integration of C# with Unity provides developers with the tools needed to leverage advanced game engines and create high-quality, immersive games with rich environments and intricate gameplay mechanics

- **Rich community and documentation**: A substantial developer community and exhaustive documentation act as indispensable reservoirs of knowledge, aiding developers in troubleshooting, learning new techniques, and keeping abreast of the latest advancements in game development

Additional insights and capabilities

Beyond the aforementioned advantages, the combination of Unity and C# opens up a plethora of possibilities and capabilities for game developers:

- **Physics engine integration**: The integration of Unity and C# enables the simulation of realistic and accurate physics, allowing for the creation of more lifelike and immersive gaming experiences

- **Multimedia processing**: C# plays a crucial role in processing audio and visual elements within Unity, facilitating the development of diverse multimedia effects and contributing to a deeper, more enveloping gaming experience

- **Automation through scripting**: C# scripting in Unity permits the automation of various developmental tasks and the dynamic modification of object behaviors, streamlining the development process and enhancing gameplay variability

- **Networking capabilities**: C# excels in developing network code, paving the way for the creation of engaging multiplayer games, where players can connect, compete, and cooperate

Real-world game examples

Several noteworthy games have been developed using C# and Unity, exemplifying the power and versatility of this combination:

- **Hollow Knight**: This indie game, characterized by its unique artistic style and captivating gameplay, has garnered widespread acclaim and a substantial fan base. It showcases the potential of Unity and C# in creating memorable gaming experiences.

- **Monument Valley**: This award-winning game, celebrated for its inventive design and thoughtful gameplay mechanics, underscores the creative possibilities afforded by the Unity platform and C# scripting.

C#'s symbiotic relationship with Unity has significantly impacted the gaming industry, fostering innovation and enabling the development of a diverse range of games. Its object-oriented nature, strict typing system, seamless integration with advanced game engines, and comprehensive community support make it an invaluable asset for game developers aiming to push the boundaries of what is possible in game design and execution.

C# in web development – ASP.NET and C#

In the domain of web development, ASP.NET, enriched by C#, emerges as a refined framework that empowers developers to construct diverse web applications, shape the server-side logic of websites, devise web services, and design APIs with unparalleled efficacy and precision. This synergy allows for the crafting of robust, secure, and scalable solutions that can serve a multitude of use cases and industries.

Advantages of C# in web development

The integration of C# with ASP.NET brings forth a multitude of advantages, propelling it as a preferred choice for web developers. Here are some of the notable benefits:

- **Exceptional performance**: ASP.NET Core, with its advanced features and optimizations, is revered as one of the most high-performing frameworks in the web development ecosystem, enabling the swift execution of complex tasks

- **Enhanced security**: The synergy of C# and ASP.NET provides a robust set of security features and best practices, enabling developers to build secure, reliable applications that are resistant to various threats and vulnerabilities

- **Efficient development process**: The abundant libraries, tools, and resources available for C# and ASP.NET streamline the development workflow, reducing development time and effort and ensuring a smooth development experience

- **Superior scalability**: The combination of C# and ASP.NET allows for the development of highly scalable applications that can efficiently handle increasing loads and user demands, ensuring uninterrupted service availability

Real-world web applications

Several prominent web applications and services have been developed using C# and ASP.NET, illustrating the practical applications and reliability of this combination:

- **Stack Overflow**: This eminent platform, revered as a knowledge hub for developers, has been meticulously crafted using C# and ASP.NET. It stands as a testament to the power and versatility of this amalgamation in creating resource-rich, high-performance web platforms.

- **Microsoft's products and services**: A host of Microsoft's products, services, and websites are born out of the union of C# and ASP.NET, delivering secure, scalable, and high-performance solutions to users worldwide.

The collaboration of C# with ASP.NET in web development has paved the way for the creation of state-of-the-art web applications, services, and APIs, demonstrating remarkable versatility, security, and performance. Whether it is building community-driven platforms such as Stack Overflow or developing scalable, reliable solutions for global enterprises such as Microsoft, the combination of C# and ASP.NET has proven to be a formidable asset in the web development arena.

C# in mobile development – Xamarin and C#

In the domain of mobile development, Xamarin, in synergy with C#, enables developers to create versatile applications with a unified code base that can run seamlessly across different platforms while maintaining the native look, feel, and responsiveness. Xamarin utilizes the .NET framework to interface with the native APIs of different mobile operating systems, allowing developers to leverage the full range of native functionalities.

Advantages of C# in mobile development

The combination of Xamarin and C# offers a range of benefits that streamline the mobile development process and enhance the final product's quality:

- **Cross-platform capability**: Xamarin and C# allow developers to write a universal code base that can be deployed on various mobile platforms, reducing redundancy and ensuring consistency across devices

- **Enhanced productivity**: Xamarin's integration with C# enables the incorporation of object-oriented classes and interfacing with .NET APIs, which accelerates the development process and improves overall efficiency

- **Native efficiency and aesthetics**: Xamarin provides access to the native features and specifications of different platforms, allowing the development of applications that not only look and feel native but also deliver high performance

- **Extensive library access**: Developers can leverage a wealth of .NET and NuGet libraries that facilitate and expedite the development trajectory, offering pre-built functionalities and solutions

Real-world mobile application instances

Several applications exemplify the efficacy and adaptability of Xamarin and C# in mobile development:

- **OCSM Mobile**: This application is a testament to the capability of Xamarin and C# in creating robust managerial tools. It aids users in overseeing projects, monitoring progress, and coordinating tasks, demonstrating the versatility and efficiency of this combination.

- **Insight Timer**: A renowned application in the realm of meditation and wellness, Insight Timer leverages Xamarin and C# to provide a multi-platform experience, offering users a plethora of resources for self-improvement and mental well-being.

Additional technical insights

Xamarin, coupled with C#, brings forth additional technical nuances that are pivotal for mobile development:

- **Access to native APIs and services**: Xamarin allows developers to tap into the native APIs and services inherent to Android and iOS, ensuring optimal performance, resource allocation, and UX

- **MAUI** or **Xamarin.Forms**: This framework simplifies the process of creating cross-platform user interfaces with XAML, making the development and maintenance of interfaces more manageable and efficient

- **Technological integration**: Xamarin facilitates the integration of C# and .NET with various technologies and programming paradigms, allowing developers to utilize best practices and tools specific to each platform

The amalgamation of Xamarin and C# has enriched the landscape of mobile development, enabling the creation of high-quality, versatile applications that run uniformly across diverse platforms while retaining native aesthetics and performance. Whether it's developing robust project management tools such as OCSM Mobile or creating wellness applications such as Insight Timer, Xamarin and C# have proven to be invaluable assets in addressing a spectrum of user needs and preferences.

C# in scientific research and development

C# plays a pivotal role in the realm of scientific research and development, serving as a cornerstone for extensive data processing, analytics, computer modeling, and scientific data visualization. Its integration with the .NET framework provides a robust foundation for developing complex scientific models and efficiently representing research outcomes through powerful libraries and tools such as Math.NET and ML.NET. These tools are crucial for conducting advanced data analysis, statistical modeling, artificial intelligence, and machine learning, thus enabling the scientific community to push the boundaries of research and discovery.

Advantages of C# in scientific research

The use of C# in scientific research offers several significant advantages, especially in terms of productivity, security, and integration with diverse technologies:

- **Enhanced productivity**: C# is distinguished by its speed and efficiency, which are crucial for handling vast volumes of data and conducting complex calculations, thus accelerating the pace of scientific discoveries and innovations

- **Extensive libraries and tools**: The rich ecosystem of libraries and tools available in C# and .NET facilitates the development of scientific applications by providing a myriad of resources and functionalities, thereby reducing development time and effort

- **Robust security and reliability**: The strict typing and object-oriented features of C# enhance the security and reliability of scientific applications, ensuring the integrity and confidentiality of data and processes

- **Seamless integration with .NET**: The harmonious synergy between C# and .NET allows access to a plethora of technologies and services, enabling comprehensive and advanced scientific research and development

Applications in research and development

C# has been instrumental in the creation of numerous applications and solutions aimed at solving complex scientific problems and advancing research in various fields. These applications leverage C#'s robust features and extensive libraries to perform intricate computations, simulate scientific phenomena, and visualize data in a meaningful way.

Technical insights

C#'s technical prowess in scientific research is evident through its ability to do the following:

- **Model complex systems**: The robustness of C# allows for the modeling of intricate systems and phenomena, enabling researchers to gain deeper insights into the workings of the natural world

- **Visualize data proficiently**: C# aids in the proficient depiction of research outcomes and scientific data, allowing for the clearer communication of findings and the facilitation of knowledge dissemination

- **Integrate advanced technologies**: The integration capabilities of C# with the .NET framework allow for the incorporation of cutting-edge technologies and methodologies, fostering innovation and the development of groundbreaking solutions in the scientific domain

C#'s significance in scientific research and development is undeniable, acting as a catalyst for innovation and discovery through its advanced features, extensive libraries, and seamless integration with the .NET framework. Whether it's modeling intricate scientific phenomena, visualizing complex datasets, or integrating advanced technologies, C# continues to empower scientists and researchers to explore uncharted territories, uncover new knowledge, and contribute to the advancement of science and technology.

Now that we have explored several real-world applications of C#, the practical understanding you've acquired will be instrumental in visualizing and solving real-world problems during your interviews. This reflection should equip you with a more nuanced perspective on applying C#, enhancing your ability to relate theoretical concepts to practical scenarios.

To further optimize your preparation, we will discuss strategies to minimize distractions in the next section.

Common C# technical interview questions and problems

Embarking on the journey to secure a role as a C# developer can often be met with a mixture of excitement and nervous anticipation. As we delve into this section, we aim to alleviate some of that nervousness by arming you with a compendium of common technical interview questions and problems that you might encounter. With a focus on C#, a language revered for its versatility and depth, this section serves as your trusted companion, guiding you through potential interview landscapes and offering insights into the intricacies of tackling technical queries with confidence and expertise. Set forth with us as we navigate this preparatory guide, which is designed to hone your skills and set you on a path to success in your upcoming interviews.

How can the Singleton pattern be implemented in C#? Are there any potential issues to be aware of, and how can they be avoided?

The **Singleton** pattern in C# can be implemented using a static instance of the class coupled with a private constructor. One of the primary concerns to be aware of is the multithreading environment, which might lead to the creation of multiple instances. This can be circumvented by employing locking mechanisms or lazy initialization. Here is a basic example of its implementation:

```
public sealed class Singleton
{
    private static readonly Singleton instance = new Singleton();
```

```
private Singleton() {}

public static Singleton Instance
{
    get { return instance; }
}
}
```

Potential issues such as multithreading can be mitigated by incorporating thread-safety measures in the implementation, thus ensuring that only a single instance of the class is created, even in a multithreaded environment.

How does C# facilitate multithreaded programming? Can you discuss the various methods of implementing multithreading and their advantages and disadvantages?

In C#, multithreaded programming can be achieved through the use of thread classes, task-based asynchronous programming, or asynchronous programming. Each of these methods has its pros and cons:

- **Thread**: This method offers full control over threads but is relatively complex to manage and can lead to performance issues if misused.

- **Task**: This method operates at a higher level of abstraction, making multithreading management easier but can obscure some nuances of low-level thread management.

- **Asynchronous programming**: This method allows readable and efficient code to be written. However, it can be complex to understand and debug, especially in intricate systems.

Each method serves different use cases and selecting one depends on the specific requirements and complexities of the program.

How would you approach exception handling in a complex C# project? Discuss various strategies for handling exceptions and their impact on the program's stability

In a complex C# project, exception handling can be orchestrated using a multi-tiered exception handling approach, where specific exceptions are handled at lower levels and general exceptions at higher levels. It is essential to employ the **fail-fast** principle for critical errors and attempt to recover the system in the case of less serious exceptions. This helps in maintaining the program's stability and facilitates debugging.

Implementing robust logging systems alongside proper exception handling can provide insights into various issues and assist in resolving them more efficiently.

Can you discuss how delegates are implemented and utilized in C#? How do they differ from interfaces and abstract classes?

Delegates in C# are types that represent methods directly, allowing for the declaration, assignment, and passing of methods as parameters, facilitating the creation of flexible and adaptable systems. They differ from interfaces and abstract classes in that they focus solely on representing methods, not grouping related methods or properties, which is typically done in interfaces and abstract classes.

Delegates provide a way to define and encapsulate method signatures, making it possible to create event-driven programming patterns and callbacks, adding to the versatility and functionality of the C# programming landscape.

Can you provide a detailed overview of the type system in C# and discuss how the language ensures type safety?

The **type system** in C# encompasses various data types, including simple types (such as `int`, `float`, and `bool`), complex types (such as classes and structures), and collection types (such as arrays and lists). C# ensures type safety through type checking at compile time, which helps prevent type errors during runtime and promotes the development of reliable and stable applications. This proactive approach minimizes runtime errors and fosters the creation of secure and efficient code.

What strategies would you employ to handle large data processing in C# through parallel programming and asynchronous operations?

To handle large volumes of data in C#, I would utilize parallel programming and asynchronous operations to enhance the system's performance and resource efficiency. This can be achieved using methods such as the **Task Parallel Library** (**TPL**), which facilitates the easy implementation of parallel loops and tasks, and asynchronous programming with the `async` and `await` keywords for non-blocking I/O operations. These strategies aid in distributing the computational workload across multiple cores and optimizing resource utilization, thereby accelerating data processing speeds.

How would you approach the implementation of data caching in C# to enhance system performance, and which caching strategies do you consider most effective?

Data caching in C# can be implemented using various strategies, such as object-level caching or database query caching. This can be accomplished using built-in caching mechanisms or by utilizing third-party libraries. Additionally, considering different caching policies such as **Least Recently Used** (**LRU**) can be beneficial in optimizing resource use and enhancing performance. Effective caching not only improves the responsiveness of the system but also helps reduce the load on the database or the network, thereby facilitating the development of scalable and high-performing applications.

What strategies and methods do you use for unit testing in C#? How do you plan to achieve a high level of code coverage with tests?

For unit testing in C#, I would utilize frameworks such as *MSTest, NUnit* or *xUnit* to create and manage test cases. To achieve a high level of code coverage with tests, I would practice **test-driven development** (TDD), which encourages writing tests before developing functionality, and use tools for code coverage analysis to identify areas that require additional testing. This method ensures robustness in the developed features and facilitates the early identification and rectification of issues, promoting a more reliable and maintainable code base.

Can you provide examples of complex algorithmic problems you have solved in C# and explain how you approached their solutions?

Some complex algorithmic problems I might solve in C# include optimization tasks, such as finding the shortest path in a graph using Dijkstra's algorithm, or searching and sorting tasks using various algorithms such as quicksort or binary search. The approach to solving these problems typically involves analyzing the problem, developing an efficient algorithm, and implementing and testing it using C#. This process entails a careful evaluation of the problem's characteristics and requirements, followed by the application of appropriate data structures and algorithms to create optimized, scalable solutions.

Can you discuss several modern methods and practices for enhancing the productivity and scalability of C# applications? Are there any specific tools or libraries you would recommend for this purpose?

To optimize productivity and scalability in C#, various approaches can be employed, including asynchronous programming, parallel computing, and memory optimization through intelligent resource management. Several tools and libraries that could be utilized include TPL for parallel programming, MemoryCache for data caching, and performance profilers such as JetBrains dotTrace for identifying and eliminating bottlenecks in your code. These tools and practices enable developers to build highly efficient and scalable applications, taking full advantage of modern hardware and software capabilities while maintaining code readability and maintainability.

Can you explain the memory management mechanism in C# and strategies to prevent memory leaks?

In C#, memory management is based on the automatic garbage collection system, which automatically releases memory that is no longer in use. To prevent memory leaks, developers should avoid holding long-term references to objects and utilize the `using` directive to manage resources that require manual release appropriately. Being cautious with event handlers and removing any unused event subscriptions can also aid in preventing potential memory leaks. Following these strategies will help you in developing robust and memory-efficient applications.

How can you utilize the Facade design pattern in C# to organize complex system interfaces?

The **Facade** design pattern can be implemented in C# by creating a class that offers a simplified interface to a complex system of classes or libraries. This facade consolidates the functionalities of intricate systems into a single interface, facilitating easier access and utilization of the system. It serves as a unified frontend interface that interacts with multiple subsystems, enhancing modularity and making the system more user-friendly and comprehensible.

How would you analyze and optimize the performance of a C# application using profilers and other tools?

To analyze and optimize the performance of a C# application, I would employ profilers such as JetBrains dotTrace or Visual Studio Diagnostic Tools to identify bottlenecks and performance issues. These tools assist in analyzing code execution and resource utilization, allowing developers to find and remedy issues impacting performance. Besides this, implementing code reviews and utilizing benchmarking tools can provide insights into the code's efficiency, helping in further optimization and ensuring a smooth and responsive application experience.

What is understood by algorithm complexity, and how is it calculated?

Algorithm complexity refers to a theoretical assessment of the efficiency of algorithms in terms of execution time and memory usage. This complexity is usually measured in **Big O** notation, which describes the behavior of the algorithm in the worst-case scenario. For instance, for the bubble sort algorithm, the complexity in the worst case would be $O(n2)$, where n is the number of elements in the array. Understanding algorithm complexity aids in choosing the most efficient algorithm for a particular task, ensuring optimal performance.

Can you explain the concept of recursion in programming and provide examples of its application in C#?

Recursion is a programming technique where a function calls itself either directly or indirectly. Recursion can be useful for solving problems that can be broken down into smaller, similar tasks. In C#, recursion can be implemented by creating a method that calls itself with a condition to exit to avoid an infinite loop. Examples include recursive implementation of the factorial calculation algorithm or a tree traversal algorithm. Utilizing recursion can often lead to more elegant and simpler solutions for problems that are naturally recursive, although you must be cautious to avoid stack overflow; you can do this by defining a clear base case.

How do you plan to implement a custom data structure, such as a queue or stack, in C#? What key aspects should you consider to ensure optimal performance and data safety?

When implementing a custom data structure in C#, I would primarily focus on defining appropriate interfaces and classes. To ensure high performance, it is crucial to optimize operations for adding, removing, and accessing elements. Regarding data safety, I would meticulously work on memory management, avoiding memory leaks, and ensuring proper exception handling. Implementing proper encapsulation to safeguard data and considering thread safety to avoid concurrent modification issues are also vital aspects to be considered.

Can you share your experience in integrating C# applications with other programming languages and platforms? What were the primary challenges you encountered, and how did you overcome them?

When integrating C# applications with other programming languages and platforms, I encountered three primary challenges:

- **Compatibility**: Different systems often have varying interfaces, which can lead to compatibility issues. To address this, I applied the **Adapter** pattern effectively. This pattern acts as a bridge, allowing two incompatible interfaces to work together. It involves creating an adapter class that wraps the non-compatible interface and exposes a new interface that matches what the C# application expects. This encapsulation of the communication process abstracts the complexities of interfacing with different systems, particularly when dealing with legacy systems or APIs that require specific data formats or protocols.

- **Data exchange**: Exchanging data between systems in a format that each understands is critical. For this, REST APIs were essential. These APIs provide a standard method for communication using HTTP requests and responses that are language and platform-independent. This uniformity ensures that data exchange is seamless and consistent, irrespective of the underlying technology stack of the systems involved.

- **Dependency management**: Managing dependencies between disparate systems can be complex. To mitigate this, I utilized middleware to manage these dependencies and orchestrate interactions between the C# application and other services. Middleware can handle request routing, authentication, logging, and other cross-cutting concerns, which simplifies the integration process and reduces the coupling between the C# application and external components.

By adopting these strategies, I ensured that the C# application could integrate smoothly with other systems while maintaining a clear and structured code base that is easy to maintain and scale.

How would you construct a high-performance logging mechanism for a large-scale distributed application in C#?

To construct a high-performance logging mechanism in C#, I would employ asynchronous operations for log writing to minimize latency. Additionally, I would utilize structured logging to retain detailed information about each operation. Centralized log storage could be implemented using systems such as the ELK Stack or Graylog, facilitating easy search and analysis of logs. Implementing batch processing and utilizing efficient data storage formats would further enhance the performance and effectiveness of the logging system.

How do you ensure data protection and security against potential attacks in your C# projects?

To ensure data protection and security in my C# projects, I employ several strategies, including utilizing the latest versions of frameworks and libraries, conducting regular security updates, implementing data encryption at both the application and database levels, and incorporating authentication and authorization mechanisms. Additionally, I conduct regular security audits and penetration tests to identify and mitigate potential vulnerabilities. This proactive approach helps fortify the application against various potential threats, ensuring a robust and secure system.

Can you share your experience in implementing a microservice architecture in C#? What were the main challenges and learning moments during this process?

When implementing a microservice architecture in C#, one of the primary challenges was decomposing the system into separate microservices to ensure flexibility and scalability. A significant learning moment was facilitating effective communication between microservices through well-planned APIs and applying patterns such as the **Circuit Breaker** pattern to prevent network failures. These strategies helped in maintaining system resilience and ensuring smooth inter-service communication, enhancing the overall efficiency of the system.

Can you describe how the concept of LINQ is implemented in C# and give examples of its application for manipulating data collections?

In C#, LINQ is a set of extensions that enable queries to be performed on various data sources directly from the programming language. LINQ can be used to work with collections, XML, databases, and more. For instance, to filter and sort a collection of objects, you can use the following syntax:

```
var result = from s in students
             where s.Age > 20
             orderby s.Name
             select s;
```

The preceding code snippet demonstrates how LINQ can facilitate data manipulation in C#, providing a streamlined and readable way to perform complex queries on collections.

How do you utilize delegates and events to create modular and flexible systems in C#?

In C#, delegates and events are used to implement loose coupling between the components of a system. Delegates can serve as function pointers, allowing for the dynamic alteration of program behavior. Events enable objects to notify other objects about certain state changes. For instance, you can create a logging system that responds to specific events in the system while utilizing events and delegates to facilitate message transmission between components. This approach aids in building systems that are both modular and adaptable, enhancing their maintainability and scalability.

How would you implement multithreading in C# using TPL?

To implement multithreading in C# using TPL, I would utilize the *Task* and *Parallel* classes for asynchronous and parallel code execution. For instance, the `Task.Run` method can be used for launching tasks asynchronously, while the `Parallel.For` or `Parallel.ForEach` methods facilitate parallel iterations in a loop. This not only simplifies the implementation of multithreading but also optimizes performance by leveraging all available processor cores, thus enhancing the system's responsiveness and throughput.

How would you organize an error and exception handling system in a large C# project to ensure its reliability and stability?

To ensure reliability and stability in a large C# project, I would implement a centralized exception handling system that encompasses logging, notifications, and possibly automatic failure recovery mechanisms. This can be achieved through the usage of try-catch blocks in critical execution paths, coupled with the application of global exception handlers to capture unforeseen exceptions and gather detailed error information for further analysis and system improvement. Such a structured approach helps in maintaining system integrity and facilitating swift recovery in the event of failures.

Can you explain how to use attributes in C# for annotating code with metadata?

In C#, attributes can be used to add metadata to assemblies, classes, methods, and more. They allow you to specify additional information that can be utilized at runtime for various purposes, such as object serialization or access control. Here's a basic example of using an attribute to annotate a method:

```
[Obsolete("This method is deprecated, use NewMethod instead.")]
public void OldMethod()
{
```

```
    // ...
}
```

The preceding snippet demonstrates how attributes can be used to annotate code with metadata, thereby providing guidelines or restrictions that assist in code management and documentation.

How can you implement the Observer pattern in C# to create an event notification system?

The **Observer** pattern can be implemented in C# using delegates and events. In this pattern, observers subscribe to notifications from a specific object (subject) and receive notifications when certain events occur. Here is a basic example:

```
public class Subject
{
    public event EventHandler<string> Notify;

    public void TriggerEvent(string message)
    {
        Notify?.Invoke(this, message);
    }
}

public class Observer
{
    public void OnNotify(object sender, string message)
    {
        Console.WriteLine("Observer received: " + message);
    }
}

// Usage:
 var subject = new Subject();
 var observer = new Observer();
 subject.Notify += observer.OnNotify;
 subject.TriggerEvent("Event occurred");
```

The preceding code snippet demonstrates how the Observer pattern can be utilized in C# to establish a notification system where observers can dynamically subscribe to or unsubscribe from particular events, promoting a flexible and modular system design.

Can you share your experience working with NoSQL databases in C# projects?

In practice, I frequently utilized NoSQL databases in C# projects, especially when handling large volumes of unstructured or semi-structured data. These databases, such as MongoDB or CouchDB, provide the flexibility to work with data and easily scale the system. I use specialized libraries and software development kits to integrate NoSQL databases with C# projects, simplifying data handling and ensuring high performance. These databases facilitate efficient data storage and retrieval, enhancing the scalability and adaptability of the project.

How can you apply the Factory and Singleton design patterns to create scalable and flexible systems in C#?

The **Factory** and **Singleton** design patterns can be immensely beneficial when it comes to building scalable and flexible systems in C#:

- **Factory**: The Factory pattern helps isolate object creation logic from the main client code, fostering system flexibility and scalability. This also facilitates the addition of new object types without modifying the existing code, thereby enhancing the maintainability and extensibility of the system.

- **Singleton**: The Singleton pattern ensures that a class has only one instance throughout the system and provides a global access point to this instance. This can be useful for managing resources that should be limited to a single instance, ensuring consistency and preventing potential conflicts in resource usage.

Both of these patterns can be used together or separately, depending on the specific requirements of the project, and can contribute to a well-organized, robust, and efficient system design.

How do you organize and plan the testing phase during the development process of a software product in C#?

During the organization of the testing phase in the development process of a software product in C#, I adopt a structured approach that encompasses several key elements:

- **Developing a detailed testing plan**: This involves defining clear test objectives, identifying test scenarios, outlining success criteria, and selecting appropriate tools and frameworks for test automation. This plan serves as a roadmap for the testing process and helps in tracking progress.

- **Comprehensive test coverage**: I focus on covering all the crucial parts of the system with various types of tests, including the following:

  - **Unit tests**: To test individual components in isolation and ensure that they function as intended

  - **Integration tests**: To validate the interactions between different components of the system

  - **System tests**: To verify the behavior of the entire system as a whole

- **Continuous testing**: Incorporating testing into the **continuous integration and continuous delivery/deployment (CI/CD)** pipeline to facilitate early detection of issues and streamline the testing process.

- **Performance and load testing**: This involves conducting performance tests to ensure that the system can handle the expected load and identify areas where optimizations may be needed.

- **User acceptance testing (UAT)**: This involves collaborating with stakeholders to conduct UAT to validate that the system meets the business requirements and user expectations.

- **Documentation and knowledge transfer**: This ensures that all test cases, scripts, and results are well-documented to facilitate knowledge transfer and future reference.

Through this organized approach, I aim to ensure the high quality and reliability of the product, fostering a development environment that is both efficient and effective.

Can you discuss the approaches and strategies you use to ensure data security in your C# projects?

To ensure data security in my C# projects, I employ a multifaceted approach that encompasses several strategies:

- **Data encryption**: This involves implementing encryption algorithms to protect sensitive data both at rest and during transmission. This includes utilizing protocols such as SSL/TLS for secure communications.

- **Secure storage of credentials**: This involves utilizing secure methods for storing sensitive credentials, such as using secret management systems or secure vaults, to prevent unauthorized access.

- **Adherence to security standards**: Following the latest security standards and best practices when working with networks helps prevent vulnerabilities and potential breaches.

- **Principle of least privilege**: This involves applying the principle of least privilege to data access, ensuring that individuals and systems have only the necessary access rights to perform their roles, thereby minimizing the potential impact of a security breach.

- **Security audits and code reviews**: Regularly conducting security audits and code reviews helps with identifying and mitigating potential vulnerabilities. This involves utilizing automated tools as well as manual reviews to identify security issues.

- **Data backup and recovery**: This involves implementing robust data backup and recovery strategies to safeguard data integrity and availability, ensuring that data can be restored in the event of a loss or corruption.

- **Security training and awareness**: This involves promoting security awareness among the development team through training and workshops to foster a security-conscious culture.

By embracing these strategies, I strive to safeguard data integrity and confidentiality in my projects, building robust defenses against potential security threats and vulnerabilities.

How do you implement and optimize interaction with network protocols and APIs in your C# projects?

Implementing and optimizing interaction with network protocols and APIs is a critical aspect of developing robust and efficient C# projects. Here's a comprehensive approach that I typically employ:

- **Asynchronous programming**: I make extensive use of asynchronous programming models available in C# to enhance system performance and responsiveness. This approach helps in non-blocking I/O operations, thus allowing the system to perform other tasks while awaiting responses, which significantly improves the overall efficiency of the application.

- **Utilizing appropriate libraries and frameworks**: Depending on the specific requirements of the project, I select and utilize appropriate libraries and frameworks that simplify the process of making network requests and handling responses. Libraries such as HttpClient are commonly used for this purpose.

- **Caching**: To optimize API interactions and reduce network load, I employ caching strategies. This involves storing the results of frequent API calls locally to prevent unnecessary network requests, which can significantly improve system response time and reduce server load.

- **Batch requests**: Where possible, I use batch requests to group multiple API calls into a single request. This strategy reduces the number of network calls and can lead to performance improvements, especially in scenarios where a series of dependent API calls are required.

- **Error handling and retry logic**: I implement comprehensive error handling and retry logic to manage network-related errors gracefully. This helps in providing a robust UX by reducing the likelihood of failed requests affecting the UX.

- **API rate limiting awareness**: Being aware of and respecting API rate limits to prevent exceeding the allowable number of requests, thus helping me potential bans or restrictions imposed by the API provider.

- **Security considerations**: I ensure secure interactions with APIs by implementing necessary security measures such as SSL/TLS encryption, and validating and sanitizing inputs to prevent injection attacks.

- **Monitoring and analytics**: I incorporate monitoring and analytics tools to track the performance of network interactions, identify bottlenecks, and make informed decisions on optimizations based on real-time data.

- **Documentation and collaboration**: I maintain up-to-date documentation of the API integrations to facilitate collaboration and knowledge sharing among the development team.

- **Testing**: I conduct comprehensive testing, including unit tests, integration tests, and performance tests, to validate the reliability and efficiency of the network interactions implemented in the project.

By adopting these strategies and practices, I aim to deliver a more efficient, agile, and robust system, optimizing the interaction with network protocols and APIs to provide a seamless and high-performing UX.

Can you share your experience in developing real-time systems in C#?

I have a rich experience in developing real-time systems in C#. Developing real-time applications involves several critical considerations to ensure that the system can respond to inputs or events within a specified time frame. Here are some of the strategies and practices I adhere to:

- **Asynchronous programming**: I frequently employ asynchronous programming techniques to enhance the system's efficiency. This helps in managing I/O-bound operations more effectively, allowing the system to remain responsive even when handling tasks that might take some time to complete.

- **Code optimization**: A significant focus is placed on optimizing the code to facilitate quick responses to real-time events. This includes adopting best coding practices, such as avoiding complex nested loops and utilizing efficient algorithms to enhance the speed of operations.

- **Memory and resource management**: Proper utilization of memory and resource management mechanisms is crucial to maintain a high level of performance and stability. This involves avoiding memory leaks, effectively managing resources, and ensuring the timely release of unused resources to prevent potential bottlenecks.

- **Real-time communication**: Implementing real-time communication protocols such as WebSockets or SignalR can facilitate seamless data exchange between the server and clients, enhancing the interactivity and responsiveness of the application.

- **Concurrency control**: Developing strategies for effective concurrency control can ensure data integrity and consistency, especially in scenarios where multiple processes or threads are accessing shared resources simultaneously.

- **Scalability considerations**: The system should be designed to be scalable to handle increasing loads efficiently. This might involve implementing load balancing strategies and optimizing the database for high concurrency.

- **Monitoring and logging**: Incorporating monitoring and logging mechanisms can help track the system's performance in real-time and identify any issues promptly, allowing for quicker troubleshooting and resolution.

- **Testing and simulation**: Conducting rigorous testing, including load testing and simulation of real-time scenarios, allows the system's performance to be validated under various conditions and ensures it meets the required real-time criteria.

- **UX focus**: I ensure that the UX remains smooth and responsive, with a particular focus on minimizing delays and providing immediate feedback on user actions.

- **Continuous improvement**: I embrace a culture of continuous improvement, where the system is regularly updated and optimized based on real-world feedback and performance metrics.

Through my experience, I have found that a successful real-time system in C# is built on a foundation of well-designed architecture, optimized code, and effective resource management, complemented by a user-centric approach to delivering a seamless and responsive UX.

How do you integrate and implement artificial intelligence and machine learning models in your C# projects?

Integrating and implementing artificial intelligence and machine learning models into C# projects is a nuanced process that involves leveraging a variety of tools and methodologies. Primarily, I utilize libraries and frameworks such as ML.NET, a powerful, open source, and cross-platform framework developed by Microsoft. This framework facilitates the easy implementation and utilization of machine learning models directly within C# applications, offering functionalities ranging from data processing to model training and evaluation.

In addition to ML.NET, I often employ the SciSharp Stack, a collection of open source projects that provide a .NET binding to popular Python libraries. This enables seamless integration and utilization of well-established Python libraries, such as TensorFlow and NumPy, directly within the C# environment. The SciSharp project broadens the horizon for C# developers, allowing them to leverage a rich ecosystem of AI and ML tools that were previously confined to the Python sphere.

By utilizing a combination of ML.NET, the SciSharp project, and RESTful APIs, I can build robust and sophisticated artificial intelligence and machine learning functionalities within C# projects, paving the way for innovative solutions and applications in the evolving landscape of technology.

As we wrap up this insightful chapter, we hope that you feel fortified and ready to tackle the challenges that lie ahead in the technical interview arena. The questions and problems that have been explored within these pages are not merely hurdles to overcome but opportunities to showcase your proficiency and passion for the C# language. We encourage you to continue exploring, practicing, and sharpening your skills; the world of technology is ever-evolving and brimming with new challenges to conquer. Remember, every interview is a learning experience and a step forward in your journey to becoming a seasoned C# developer. Armed with knowledge and bolstered by practice, you are well on your way to having a remarkable impact on the dynamic world of software development.

Summary

As we conclude this chapter, it is pivotal to recognize that the journey to mastering C# technical interviews is multifaceted, requiring a harmonious blend of technical acumen, practical application, and interpersonal skills. The strategies, insights, and recommendations elucidated in this chapter aim to serve as a robust framework, empowering you to navigate the challenges and nuances of C# technical interviews with confidence and poise. It is not just about acquiring knowledge; it is about strategically applying that knowledge, coupled with effective communication and problem-solving skills, as this sets apart successful candidates.

Concurrently, we've prepared you for the technical interview battleground by dissecting common C# interview questions and problems, providing you with a toolkit of strategies to navigate these challenges with confidence and expertise. This dual approach ensures that as you close this chapter, you emerge as a more capable and resourceful C# developer, ready to tackle the industry's demands and turn coding challenges into opportunities for showcasing your technical prowess.

In the next chapter, you'll learn how to navigate the subtleties of interview processes, enhance the soft skills that set you apart, and cultivate a network that supports your career growth as a C# developer.

8

Building Soft Skills and Expanding Your Network

Having delved into the technical nuances of C# interviews in *Chapter 7, Overcoming Challenges in C# Technical Interviews and Tips for Tackling Coding Challenges during Interviews*, we will now underscore the value of soft skills, which are often deemed as the linchpin in the professional world. In the technology-driven age we live in, the realm of technical interviews has expanded beyond mere verbal interactions and written tests.

This chapter is meticulously crafted to address the manifold aspects of interview preparation, from minimizing distractions during preparation to the essential soft skills to ace the interviews.

In this chapter, we'll cover the following main topics:

- Minimizing distractions during preparation
- Optimizing computer performance and setting up the development environment for live coding exercises during the interview
- Common interview challenges and handling strategies
- The essence and development of soft skills for C# developers

Minimizing distractions during preparation

A focused mind is key to effective learning and preparation. In this section, we will delve into strategies to minimize distractions, helping you create an environment conducive to concentrated study and in-depth learning.

Effective learning and preparation necessitate complete focus. When studying a complex programming language such as C#, any distractions can hinder your progress and diminish your understanding. In this chapter, we will explore strategies to help you minimize distractions and create an environment conducive to deep learning and comprehensive material absorption.

Designate a specific study space

Choosing the right study space is crucial. It should be quiet, comfortable, and, most importantly, free from distractions. Find an area where you can fully concentrate on learning C#.

Comfort

Comfort also plays a significant role in learning. Ensure that your chair and desk are comfortable and that you have adequate space to work. Proper lighting is also critical to avoid eye strain.

Noise minimization

Avoid places with high noise levels since noise can significantly disrupt concentration. If absolute silence is unattainable, consider using noise-canceling headphones or playing white noise or relaxing music.

Workspace organization

Your workspace should be organized and clutter-free. Ensure that all necessary learning materials are within reach to avoid constant interruptions.

Remove distractions

Avoid having smartphones, your TV, and other entertainment sources at hand. If possible, keep them in another room to minimize the temptation to check notifications or news.

A routine

Consistency matters. Strive to study every day at the same time and place to form a habit and maintain a rhythm.

To summarize, allocating a specific study space is the first and most crucial step for successful learning in C#. When in the right environment, your concentration, motivation, and learning ability significantly improve.

Turn off notifications

In an era where information is at our fingertips, managing distractions is essential for effective learning. Notifications, although useful, can often interrupt the flow of study and negatively impact concentration.

The importance of a distraction-free environment

Notifications from various apps and services can significantly distract and hinder the learning process. They disrupt concentration and reduce the efficiency of learning C#. Consider putting your devices in *Do Not Disturb* mode or using specialized apps that block distracting notifications while studying.

Notifications in Windows

In Windows, you can manage notifications through the **Action Center** area. Open **Settings**, then navigate to **System | Notifications & actions** to disable unwanted notifications. Additionally, you can enable **Focus Assist** to temporarily block all notifications.

Notifications in macOS

In macOS, you can manage notifications via **System Preferences | Notifications**. Here, you can configure notifications for each app individually or enable **Do Not Disturb** mode to prevent notifications from appearing.

Mobile devices

Don't forget to also turn off notifications on mobile devices, such as smartphones and tablets. Most operating systems offer a *Do Not Disturb* feature that allows all notifications to be blocked temporarily.

Use specialized apps

There are apps such as *Freedom* or *Cold Turkey* that help block distracting apps and websites for a specified period, which can be beneficial while studying.

To summarize, turning off notifications is a crucial step in creating an environment conducive to concentration and in-depth study of C#. Managing notifications helps you avoid unnecessary distractions and improves focus on the material.

Organize your workspace

Ensure that your desk is clean and tidy. The presence of superfluous items can distract you from studying. Keep only the materials and tools that are genuinely necessary close at hand.

Cleanliness and order

A clean and orderly desk fosters concentration and helps with avoiding distractions. Remove all unnecessary items, leaving only what is essential for studying C# on your desk.

Only the essentials at hand

Keep only the materials that are genuinely necessary close by. Superfluous books, papers, and other items can be distracting.

Ergonomics

Proper workspace organization also involves considering ergonomics. A comfortable chair, a suitably chosen desk, and good lighting can help reduce fatigue and strain during prolonged computer work.

Digital organization

Workspace organization also involves managing your digital space effectively. Ensure that your computer desktop is not cluttered with files, and organize your files and folders efficiently.

Proper time allocation

Managing your time is also a part of organizing your workspace. Develop a schedule and stick to it, allocating sufficient time to study every aspect of C#.

To summarize, meticulously organizing your workspace can significantly impact your productivity and learning ability. A simple yet effective workspace is key to successful learning in C#.

Plan breaks

Studying programming is mentally demanding. Constant strain can lead to fatigue and decreased productivity. Schedule short breaks every 45 to 60 minutes to rest and recuperate.

The importance of breaks

Breaks are a crucial part of the learning process. They help prevent fatigue and burnout and contribute to improved concentration and retention of information while studying C#.

Pomodoro Technique

One way to plan breaks is to use the *Pomodoro Technique*. This method involves alternating short work periods (usually 25 minutes) with short breaks (5 minutes). After four cycles, a longer break (15 to 30 minutes) should be taken.

Stay active

During breaks, it is beneficial to stand up and move around. Minor physical exercises or just a walk can enhance blood circulation and relieve tension.

Mindful resting

It is also crucial to give your mind a rest. During breaks, try not to think about studying. You might wish to read a book, listen to music, or simply enjoy the silence.

To summarize, properly planned breaks play a key role in effective learning and preventing fatigue. They allow you to maintain a high level of concentration and enhance material absorption when studying C#.

Set your goals

Before starting to learn, determine exactly what you want to achieve. This will help you stay focused on the task and avoid distractions.

The importance of goal-setting

Setting clear and specific goals is a foundational step in the process of learning C#. It helps maintain motivation and focus and directs your efforts in the right direction.

Short-term and long-term goals

Identify both short-term and long-term goals. Short-term goals should be specific and measurable – for example, learning the basics of C# syntax in a week. Long-term goals can be more general and ambitious, such as becoming a professional C# developer.

Break goals into tasks

Break each goal into small, manageable tasks. This makes the learning process less overwhelming and helps you track progress.

Set deadlines

Assign specific deadlines for achieving each goal and task. Deadlines create a sense of responsibility and help maintain focus and discipline.

Monitor progress

Regularly check your progress on each task and goal. This will help you stay motivated and make necessary adjustments to your learning plan if needed.

To summarize, setting goals is critically important on the path to mastering C#. Goals provide direction and meaning to your efforts, allow you to assess your progress, and keep you motivated throughout the entire learning journey.

With this knowledge of strategies to minimize distractions, you are now better equipped to maintain focus and optimize your preparation time. Remember, a distraction-free environment is paramount for quality learning and will greatly contribute to your overall preparedness and success in the interviews.

Next, we will address the significance of optimizing computer performance and setting up the development environment for live coding exercises during the interview.

Optimizing computer performance and setting up the development environment for live coding exercises during the interview

As we progress, the importance of a stable and optimized computer environment cannot be overstated. In this section, we will explore ways to optimize computer performance and set up the development environment, ensuring the smooth execution of live coding exercises during interviews.

System cleanup

The primary objective of a system cleanup is to improve the computer's performance by eliminating unnecessary files and applications. This process frees up valuable disk space, enhances system speed, and ensures a smoother user experience, which is particularly crucial when performing tasks such as live coding exercises during interviews. Over time, computers accumulate a significant amount of unnecessary files, including temporary files, cached data, and remnants of uninstalled programs. These clutter the system, reducing available storage space and potentially degrading overall performance. Regular system cleanups are essential to maintaining optimal computer functionality.

Let's look at the steps you should follow to clean up your system:

1. **Remove unnecessary files and applications:**

    I.   Navigate to your system's settings and look for options related to storage management or cleanup

    II. Utilize built-in tools to identify and remove temporary files, system cache, and unused applications

    III. Consider using third-party cleanup tools for a more thorough cleanup, but ensure they are from reputable sources to avoid security risks

2. **Empty the recycle bin:**

    After deleting files, always remember to empty the recycle bin or trash to free up storage space permanently

3. **Organize files and folders:**

    I.   Regularly review and organize the files and folders on your computer

    II. Delete obsolete and redundant files

    III. Archive older files that are not frequently accessed by external storage solutions or cloud storage

4. **Uninstall unused programs:**

    I.   Go through the list of installed programs and uninstall those that are no longer needed

    II. Pay attention to programs that may have been pre-installed on your computer but are not useful to you

5. **Optimize disk space:**

    I.   Use Disk Cleanup tools to remove old system restore points and other unnecessary system files

    II. Consider using a disk defragmenter tool on HDDs (not required for SSDs) to optimize file storage and improve disk performance

By routinely performing these tasks, you'll not only recover valuable disk space but also improve the overall performance and longevity of your system. It's a practice that complements regular maintenance and helps ensure that your computer remains fast, responsive, and capable of meeting your daily needs.

Updating the operating system and software

The core objective of updating the operating system and software is to ensure that all system components and installed applications are running the latest versions, which usually offer enhanced performance, improved security, and new features. This is crucial for maintaining a stable and optimized environment, especially when it comes to intricate tasks such as live coding exercises during interviews.

Operating systems and software applications frequently release updates to patch vulnerabilities, fix bugs, and introduce new features. Running outdated software can expose the system to security risks and may lead to performance issues. Regular updates are crucial to maintaining system stability and security and ensuring access to the latest features and improvements.

Here are the steps you should follow to update your operating system and software:

1. **Update the operating system**:

    I.   Regularly check for system updates and install them promptly

    II.   Enable automatic updates if available, ensuring that the system is always up to date with the latest security patches and enhancements

2. **Update software applications**:

    I.   Keep all installed software and applications updated to their latest versions

    II.   Use built-in update features in applications or refer to the official websites to download updates

    III. Consider using software that offers automatic update features to reduce manual intervention

3. **Update drivers**:

    I.   Regularly update the drivers for hardware components to ensure optimal performance and avoid compatibility issues

    II.   Use official sources to download driver updates to avoid security risks

4. **Review software regularity**:

    Regularly review installed software and remove applications that are no longer needed, ensuring that only the necessary software is kept updated

5. **Use reliable sources**:

    Always use official and reliable sources to download updates to avoid security risks associated with downloading from untrusted sites

Regular maintenance, including updating your operating system, software, and drivers, is crucial for the health of your computer. By following these steps, you'll ensure that your system is secure, runs smoothly, and continues to provide a dependable computing experience. It's a proactive approach to safeguard your digital life and enhance your technology's usability and longevity.

Optimizing startup programs

The primary goal of optimizing startup programs is to enhance the system's boot time by managing applications that run automatically when the computer starts. This ensures a swift and responsive system right from startup, which is particularly essential when you're preparing for tasks such as live coding exercises during interviews. Startup programs are those applications that are configured to launch automatically when the system boots up. While some of these are crucial for the system's functionality and user convenience, others may not be necessary and can significantly slow down the startup time. Managing these programs effectively can result in a faster, more efficient computer startup and overall improved system performance.

Follow these steps to optimize the startup programs in your system:

1. **Identify startup programs**:

    I.   Open your system's task manager and navigate to the startup tab to view all programs set to run at startup

    II.   Assess the list and identify which programs are essential and which ones are not needed at startup

2. **Disable unnecessary programs**:

    I.   Once unnecessary startup programs have been identified, disable them to prevent them from running at startup

    II.   Be cautious not to disable any system-critical programs that are required for the proper functioning of your computer

3. **Prioritize essential programs**:

    I.   Some startup programs may be necessary for system functionality or user convenience

    II.   Prioritize these essential programs, ensuring they are allowed to run at startup

4. **Regularly review startup programs**:

    I.   Periodically review the list of startup programs, especially after installing new software, and adjust them as needed

    II.   Remove any obsolete or redundant programs that may have been added over time

5. **Optimize your system settings**:

  I.   Explore the system settings for any available options to optimize or accelerate the boot process

  II. Adjust settings carefully, understanding the implications of each change to avoid undesired system behavior

In the context of C# development, ensuring that your development tools and essential applications are prioritized in the startup process can lead to a more efficient development experience. Regular maintenance and careful management of startup programs are essential practices that contribute to the overall performance and responsiveness of your development environment.

Setting up the development environment

Setting up a development environment is essential for efficient coding, especially during live coding interviews. Properly configuring your IDE and development tools ensures a smooth, interruption-free experience, allowing you to concentrate on coding rather than troubleshooting your environment. Let's learn how to create a productive setup for software development tasks.

Configuring the IDE and development tools

The main objective of configuring the IDE and development tools is to establish a productive and error-free development environment. Proper configuration is crucial for conducting live coding exercises during interviews, as it ensures the smooth operation of coding tools and avoids unnecessary disruptions. The IDE and other development tools form the backbone of software development, providing the necessary functionalities to write, test, and debug code. Configuring these tools appropriately is essential for maximizing productivity and minimizing the likelihood of encountering issues during the development process.

Here are the steps to configure the IDE and development tools:

1. **Choose the right IDE**:

  I.   Select an IDE that best suits your development needs and preferences. Popular IDEs for C# development include Visual Studio and Rider.

  II. Consider the system requirements, features, and support provided by the IDE before making a choice.

2. **Install the required plugins and extensions**:

  I.   Identify and install any plugins or extensions that can enhance the functionality of your IDE and streamline your workflow

  II. Ensure that the added plugins are compatible with your IDE version to avoid conflicts and issues

3. **Set up version control:**

    I.   Configure version control systems such as Git within your IDE to manage code changes effectively and collaborate with other developers

    II.   Regularly commit your changes and keep your repositories organized

4. **Configure build tools:**

    I.   Set up and configure build tools and automation scripts that will compile and run your code efficiently

    II.   Regularly update the build tools to the latest versions to leverage new features and improvements

5. **Optimize your IDE's settings:**

    I.   Customize your IDE settings to suit your coding preferences, including themes, code formatting, and keyboard shortcuts

    II.   Adjust the settings for optimal performance, allocating sufficient resources to the IDE to avoid slowdowns and crashes

6. **Keep development tools updated:**

    Regularly check for updates to your IDE and development tools and install them so that you can benefit from bug fixes, security patches, and new features

By following these steps, you'll be able to establish a robust development environment that can significantly improve your productivity and coding quality. Regular updates and personalization of the environment will keep your setup efficient and aligned with your development practices.

Establishing a reliable internet connection

The primary goal of establishing a reliable internet connection is to ensure uninterrupted access to online resources, collaboration tools, and communication platforms, particularly during live coding exercises in interviews where a stable connection is crucial. A stable and fast internet connection is a prerequisite for most modern software development tasks. It is imperative for accessing online documentation, collaborating with other developers, using cloud-based tools, and conducting research. Any interruptions or instability in the connection can lead to delays, disruptions, and decreased productivity.

Follow these steps to ensure that you have a reliable internet connection:

1. **Choose a reliable internet service provider (ISP):**

    I.   Select an ISP known for its reliability, speed, and customer service

    II.   Consider the bandwidth needs based on the number of users and the types of online activities involved in your work

2. **Optimize your Wi-Fi settings**:

   I.   If a wired connection is not feasible, optimize your Wi-Fi settings by choosing a less congested channel and placing your router in a central location

   II.   Use Wi-Fi extenders or mesh networks to improve coverage in larger areas

3. **Monitor bandwidth usage**:

   I.   Regularly check the network's bandwidth usage to identify any unnecessary high-bandwidth activities that could be affecting the connection's stability and speed

   II.   Manage the bandwidth allocation efficiently, prioritizing development-related activities

4. **Have a backup connection**:

   I.   Consider having a backup internet connection, such as a mobile hotspot, to avoid disruptions in case the primary connection fails

   II.   Regularly test the backup connection to ensure its reliability when needed

By following these steps, you can create a more dependable and efficient internet setup, minimizing disruptions and ensuring that your online work proceeds smoothly. Regularly managing your connection and being prepared with a backup plan is key to avoiding costly downtime and maintaining productivity.

Testing the setup

The main objective of testing your setup is to ensure that all components of the development environment, including hardware, software, and development tools, are functioning seamlessly together. This is crucial for identifying and resolving any potential issues before they can impact activities such as live coding interviews.

Regularly testing your complete setup helps in maintaining a smooth and efficient development environment. It involves verifying the functionality and compatibility of installed development tools, libraries, and IDEs, as well as ensuring that hardware and system configurations are optimized for performance. Regular testing can preemptively identify issues, allowing for timely resolutions and reducing the risk of disruptions during critical tasks.

You must perform the following steps to test the setup:

1. **Perform system checks**:

   I.   Regularly check the health and performance of the system, ensuring that there are no hardware issues or resource bottlenecks that could impact the development environment

   II.   Use system diagnostics tools to monitor system parameters such as CPU usage, memory consumption, and disk activity

2. **Verify your development tools and IDEs:**

   I.   Test all installed development tools and IDEs to ensure that they are functioning correctly and are free of bugs and errors

   II.   Verify that all plugins, extensions, and additional components are compatible and do not conflict with each other

3. **Check your libraries and dependencies:**

   I.   Validate that all the required libraries, frameworks, and dependencies are correctly installed and configured

   II.   Ensure that there are no missing or outdated components that could lead to errors or compatibility issues

4. **Conduct test runs:**

   I.   Regularly perform test runs of code to verify that the development environment has been configured correctly for building, running, and debugging applications

   II.   Address any issues that are encountered during test runs, such as compilation errors, runtime exceptions, or performance bottlenecks

5. **Optimize your configuration settings:**

   I.   Review and optimize the configuration settings of your operating system, development tools, and IDEs for maximum performance and stability

   II.   Adjust settings such as memory allocation, cache sizes, and build options to suit your development needs and system specifications

6. **Validate your internet connection and online services:**

   I.   Test the reliability and speed of your internet connection, especially if the development environment relies on online services, cloud platforms, or remote repositories

   II.   Verify the availability and functionality of any online platforms, APIs, or services that are integral to the development process

By methodically testing and optimizing each component of your development environment, you can create a stable and responsive setup that enhances your productivity and minimizes potential disruptions during your development work. It's a strategy that pays dividends by ensuring that you can focus on coding rather than resolving setup issues.

Preparing for potential technical issues and immediate solutions

You must preemptively identify, mitigate, and resolve any technical glitches, hardware failures, or software errors that might occur, especially during live coding interviews where instant resolution is essential to maintain the interview's flow and integrity.

Technical glitches are inherent in software development realms, ranging from minor hassles to substantial failures, potentially impeding productivity. Effective preparation and having contingency plans ready are crucial to reducing the downtime and stress caused by unforeseen technical issues.

Here are the steps you should follow to be prepared for potential technical issues and be ready with immediate solutions:

1. **Have immediate solutions for failures**:

    I.   Have an alternate computer or device ready, ensuring it's configured with all the necessary tools and environments so that you can switch promptly if the primary one fails

    II.   Establish an alternate, reliable internet connection, such as a mobile hotspot, to swiftly switch if the primary connection drops

2. **Convey issues during interviews**:

    I.   If any technical issue arises during the interview, communicate it promptly and clearly to the interviewer, explaining the problem and the steps you are taking to resolve it.

    II.   Maintain professionalism and composure. Avoid showing frustration or panic. Focus on resolving the issue or suggesting alternative solutions.

3. **Installation and update precautions**:

    I.   Refrain from installing new, untested, or non-essential software or updates immediately before the interview to avoid unforeseen complications or incompatibilities

    II.   Ensure that the system and all the software have been updated, tested, and stable well before the interview day

4. **System and equipment checks**:

    I.   Conduct thorough checks of all equipment, software, and services to be used well before the interview, addressing any identified issues preemptively

    II.   Arrange contingency plans for all critical components, ensuring minimal disruption if any component fails

5. **Optimal system health and backup solutions**:

   I.   Regularly monitor system health and have backup solutions ready for immediate deployment in case of failure

   II.   Regularly back up essential data and configurations by using reliable solutions, ensuring they are updated and securely stored

6. **Knowledge and documentation**:

   I.   Maintain a well-documented knowledge base of solutions to past technical issues to be able to efficiently resolve future problems

   II.   Stay informed about the latest developments, updates, known issues, and solutions related to your development environment and tools

Now, let's take a look at some best practices:

- **Regular maintenance and inspection**: Ensure that hardware is regularly cleaned, inspected, and maintained to prevent unexpected failures

- **Clear and concise communication**: Maintain clear and concise communication with interviewers or team members when technical issues arise, focusing on solutions rather than problems

- **Alternate solutions ready**: Always have alternate solutions and workarounds ready for critical components of your development environment to ensure continuity in case of failures

Having established a seamless and efficient development environment, you can now approach live coding sessions during interviews with increased confidence and peace of mind. A well-optimized computer environment will allow you to focus solely on solving problems and writing efficient code, without being impeded by technical glitches or disruptions.

Next, we'll delve into common interview challenges and strategies to handle them effectively.

Common interview challenges and handling strategies

Technical interviews can be fraught with challenges and unexpected scenarios. This section will shed light on common interview challenges and arm you with effective strategies and solutions to navigate them successfully.

Understanding and analyzing the problem

Understanding the problem can enable candidates to swiftly comprehend and deconstruct complex C# challenges during interviews. These skills demonstrate a candidate's proficiency in dissecting problems and forming coherent, efficient solutions within C# frameworks.

Here's some guidance for candidates for defining and analyzing issues effectively:

- **Define and analyze the issue:**

  - **Objective:**

    - To quickly and accurately understand the core of the problem that needs to be solved during the interview

  - **Strategies:**

    - Actively listen to the interviewer and ask clarifying questions to comprehend all aspects of the problem. This will help in confirming your understanding of the requirements and constraints of the problem in a C# context, such as object types, data structures, and algorithmic constraints.

    - Paraphrase the problem in your own words to ensure your understanding aligns with what is expected. It is crucial to avoid misunderstandings, especially regarding the expected output and the constraints of the problem.

    - Develop a concise action plan before commencing the solution development, outlining the approach, methods, and tools needed, particularly focusing on C# syntax and libraries.

- **Time management:**

  - **Objective:**

    - To manage your time efficiently during the interview so that you have the opportunity to solve the problem promptly

  - **Strategies:**

    - Prioritize tasks and allocate time for analysis, planning, and implementation of the solution. This will ensure well-structured and optimized C# code, considering performance and readability.

    - Monitor the time closely and adjust the working pace according to the circumstances, keeping in mind the compilation and execution time for C# code.

    - Allocate sufficient time for testing and optimizing the solution while considering possible edge cases and optimizing for performance and readability in C#.

- **Adapt to unexpected situations:**

  - **Objective:**

    - To respond appropriately to any unexpected questions or tasks that may arise during the interview

- **Strategies:**

  - Maintain composure and demonstrate flexibility in thinking, especially when dealing with unfamiliar C# concepts or libraries

  - Be prepared to quickly alter approaches and strategies depending on new requirements, adapt the code to new constraints, or modify the algorithm accordingly

  - Clarify unknown details of the task and react swiftly to new information, ensuring that the C# code that's been developed adheres to the newly presented constraints and requirements

To summarize, preparing for a technical interview requires the ability to quickly analyze and solve problems, manage time effectively, and adapt to unexpected situations, especially in a C# development environment where specific syntax and libraries are involved.

Skills in defining and analyzing problems, along with flexibility and adaptability, are key to success in technical interviews. It's crucial to demonstrate a deep understanding of C# concepts, syntax, and best practices while maintaining clear and effective communication throughout the interview process.

Effective communication and creative thinking

Communication is crucial in interviews, allowing candidates to convey their innovative ideas and C# solutions. These skills enhance mutual understanding and showcase the candidate's ability to creatively and analytically optimize solutions in C# environments. Let's take a closer look:

- **Communicate with the interviewer:**

  - **Objective:**

    - To effectively communicate with the interviewer, demonstrate your thought process, and provide clear and comprehensible answers

  - **Strategies:**

    - Express your thoughts and ideas clearly and coherently, avoiding ambiguous terms and jargon, particularly those not commonly used in C# development environments.

    - Respond to questions thoroughly and accurately, addressing all parts of the inquiries and avoiding evasive answers. Relate your responses to C# programming concepts and practices whenever it's relevant.

    - Ask clarifying questions to understand the interviewer's expectations and clarify any ambiguities, ensuring alignment on C# coding standards, algorithms, and problem-solving approaches.

- **Creative thinking and problem-solving**: These skills are vital, allowing candidates to devise innovative and effective solutions to complex C# problems during interviews. These skills highlight a candidate's ability to think outside the box and apply novel approaches to optimize C# code and algorithms:

  - **Objective**:

    - To demonstrate the ability to approach problem-solving innovatively and creatively

  - **Strategies**:

    - Strive to find alternative solutions that may be more effective or creative, applying C# features and libraries that are most suited to the problem at hand.

    - Explore various methods and techniques for problem-solving to have a broader arsenal of ideas during the interview. This may include understanding and applying advanced C# concepts and design patterns.

    - Experiment with different approaches and strategies, evaluating their advantages and disadvantages, and optimizing the C# code for performance, readability, and maintainability.

In conclusion, effective communication and creative thinking are crucial components of a successful technical interview, especially when discussing and solving problems related to C# programming.

The ability to articulate your thoughts and ideas clearly, as well as demonstrating creativity and an innovative approach to problem-solving in C#, can significantly enhance your chances of success. It is vital to relate your responses and strategies to C# principles and best practices, ensuring clarity and relevance in the context of the interview.

Managing stress and psychological preparation

These skills are crucial as they empower candidates to maintain composure and focus when facing challenging C# questions during interviews. These skills reflect a candidate's resilience and ability to perform optimally under pressure in C# development scenarios. Let's take a closer look:

- **Stress management strategies**:

  - **Objective**:

    - To learn and apply techniques and strategies to maintain self-control and focus during the interview

  - **Strategies**:

    - Developing healthy habits such as regular physical exercise and proper nutrition can help in reducing stress levels, improving overall mood, and enhancing cognitive function, all of which are crucial for solving complex C# problems during the interview.

- Utilizing relaxation techniques such as meditation or breathing exercises before and during the interview to maintain composure and clarity of thought. This is particularly important when you're facing unexpected challenges in C# code or algorithms.

- Employing positive thinking and success visualization to maintain an optimistic attitude and confidence is essential for articulating thoughts clearly and solving C# related problems efficiently.

- **Psychological preparation**:

  - **Objective**:

    - To maintain a calm and focused state of mind during the interview

  - **Strategies**:

    - Preparing for possible interview scenarios and understanding your emotional reactions to them is crucial. Rehearse explaining C# concepts, coding on a whiteboard, or solving problems under time constraints.

    - Learning self-regulation techniques to manage anxiety and negative emotions can help in maintaining focus on C# coding challenges and responding to interviewers' questions more effectively.

    - Practicing in conditions that are as realistic as possible develops psychological resilience, whether it's simulating interview pressure or solving C# problems in a constrained environment.

Overall, managing stress and psychological preparation are crucial for overcoming the difficulties and challenges of a technical interview. These strategies are particularly important for staying focused and thinking clearly when discussing and solving C# related problems.

The ability to maintain calm, concentrate, and manage emotions and reactions can make the interview process less stressful and more productive. It is essential to maintain a balanced and focused mind to articulate C# solutions and concepts effectively and to approach problem-solving innovatively and logically.

Post-interview strategies and learning from experience

Strategies that are employed after the interview and the ability to learn from previous experiences are essential, helping candidates improve their methodologies and develop their C# skills for subsequent interviews. These approaches indicate a candidate's dedication to ongoing growth and mastery in C# development contexts:

- **Learning from experience**:

  - **Objective**:

    - To analyze and learn from your mistakes and experiences after each interview for further professional development

- **Strategies**:

  - Meticulously analyze your responses and behavior during the interview and identify weaknesses and areas for improvement. Reflect on your application of C# concepts, coding structures, and problem-solving approaches.

  - Document your observations and conclusions after each interview and create an action plan for continuous improvement, focusing on enhancing your C# knowledge and programming skills.

  - Seek and analyze feedback from interviewers for a better understanding of your strengths and weaknesses, particularly concerning C# development principles and practices.

- **Post-interview strategies**:

  - **Objective**:

    - To utilize time and resources effectively after the interview to maximize your chances of future success

  - **Strategies**:

    - Send thank-you notes to interviewers and maintain contacts for future collaboration. Express your gratitude for the opportunity to discuss and solve C#-related problems and express your eagerness for future engagements.

    - Reflect on your performance, evaluate what could have been done better, and plan the next steps. Identify areas where your C# coding and problem-solving skills can be improved.

    - Leverage the experience and knowledge you've acquired to prepare for future interviews, explore new technologies and methods in C# development, and stay updated on best practices and industry trends.

To summarize, post-interview strategies and learning from experience are pivotal for continuous improvement and development in software engineering, especially in mastering C# development.

A systematic analysis of your experience, learning from mistakes and feedback, and planning and executing subsequent steps can aid you in achieving professional success. It's crucial to focus on enhancing technical proficiency in C#, maintaining a learning mindset, and applying lessons learned in practical C# development scenarios.

Equipped with an understanding of potential challenges and strategies to overcome them, you are now better prepared to tackle any unforeseen situations during your interviews. Facing challenges with a composed and strategic mindset will not only enhance your problem-solving capabilities but also leave a lasting impression on your interviewers.

Following this, we will explore the crucial role of soft skills for C# developers.

The essence and development of soft skills for C# developers

Within the dynamic realm of C# development, soft skills are fundamental, serving as a cornerstone for building a flourishing and well-rounded career. This section intricately explores the synergistic relationship between soft skills and technical proficiency, demonstrating how their seamless integration fosters enhanced communication and collaboration and establishes a positive professional atmosphere. The emphasis on the importance of soft skills is a central theme of this discourse, portraying the continual refinement and cultivation of these skills as an enduring journey. The harmonious blending of technical knowledge and interpersonal abilities is crucial, enabling the creation of a balanced and effective working environment and facilitating substantial contributions to teamwork and the realization of broad organizational goals.

Cultivating soft skills in C# development

Developers possessing not only technical acumen but also soft skills are often more valued within teams. Their ability to listen, communicate, and collaborate can enhance team efficiency and ensure smoother project executions.

The importance of soft skills

Soft skills are often regarded as equally important as technical skills in software development. They aid in communication, conflict resolution, and time management, which are crucial for effective teamwork.

Communication

Effective communication is a pivotal soft skill for C# developers. It involves active listening, clear and accurate expression of thoughts and ideas, and the ability to understand others.

Team interaction

C# developers should be proficient in collaborating effectively with other team members since software development is often a collective effort. They need to be able to be receptive to criticism, consider the opinions of others, and work together to achieve common goals.

Customer service

Interacting with clients and providing high-quality service are also important skills. Developers should be capable of identifying client needs, resolving their issues, and delivering timely and efficient solutions.

Self-management

The ability to manage time, set priorities, and self-motivate are important soft skills for C# developers. Developers who can self-motivate and organize their time effectively typically demonstrate higher productivity and work quality.

Empathy and emotional intelligence

Developers with high emotional intelligence can better understand and manage their own emotions and those of their colleagues and clients, fostering a more harmonious working environment.

Problem-solving and critical thinking

These skills are indispensable for developers as they navigate the complexities of coding and debugging, enabling them to identify and implement effective solutions efficiently.

Adaptability and learning agility

In the ever-evolving field of technology, the ability to quickly learn and adapt to new tools, technologies, and methodologies is crucial for staying relevant and maintaining career growth.

Conflict resolution

Being able to effectively resolve disputes and maintain a positive, collaborative environment is crucial, especially when working in teams with diverse viewpoints and approaches.

Time management

Balancing multiple tasks, setting priorities, and meeting deadlines are essential skills that can significantly impact project outcomes and overall productivity.

By integrating these soft skills with their technical knowledge, C# developers can optimize their performance, contribute more effectively to their teams, and enhance their career prospects. They should continuously strive to improve these skills through learning, practice, feedback, and reflection to stay competitive in the evolving tech landscape.

Effective time management and being able to integrate technical skills with soft skills are key for C# developers to advance their careers and positively impact team projects, as the next section will discuss.

Technical and soft skills – balance and harmony

While technical skills are pivotal for developers, soft skills can act as the *lubricant* that facilitates teamwork. Developers who can communicate effectively with other team members, project managers, or even clients often find common ground and resolve issues more swiftly.

Skill equilibrium

Developers capable of balancing their technical and soft skills tend to be the most effective in their roles. This balance aids them in not only writing high-quality code but also in communicating effectively with colleagues and clients.

Team harmony

Mutual respect and understanding within a team result from the harmony between technical and soft skills. This creates a productive and positive work environment where every team member can contribute.

Developing both skill sets

Developers should continuously work on enhancing both technical and soft skills. They can attend courses, read books, participate in workshops and seminars, and seek feedback from peers and mentors.

Examples and strategies

Provide examples of successful developers who adeptly combine technical and soft skills and discuss their strategies for achieving balance and harmony. Explore how they employ both skill sets in problem-solving and goal attainment.

The importance of balance

Balanced technical and soft skills enable C# developers to adapt to various work situations, interact effectively with diverse individuals, and influence decisions at all project levels.

Continuous learning

Developers should remain abreast of the latest industry trends, technologies, and best practices, and be open to learning new tools and methodologies to stay competitive in the field.

Active listening

Active listening is a crucial component of effective communication. It helps in understanding others' viewpoints and responding appropriately, fostering better relationships with team members and clients.

Feedback and reflection

Regularly seeking and reflecting on feedback can help developers identify areas for improvement and growth, both in technical and soft skills.

Time management and prioritization

Effective management of time and priorities is crucial for meeting deadlines and maintaining work-life balance, thereby reducing stress and increasing productivity.

Conflict resolution strategies

Developing strategies for resolving disagreements and conflicts constructively can lead to healthier work relationships and more cohesive teams.

Networking and relationship-building

Building a strong professional network and maintaining positive relationships with colleagues, mentors, and other industry professionals can open up opportunities for learning and career advancement.

By incorporating these additional details, advice, and examples, C# developers can gain a deeper understanding of the significance of a balanced skill set and can better navigate their professional journeys.

Networking and cultivating strong relationships are as critical as technical expertise for C# developers, paving the way for professional growth and learning opportunities. Next, we'll delve into practical strategies for honing soft skills to complement technical abilities.

Strategies for developing soft skills

It is recommended that C# developers attend soft skills training sessions, read relevant literature, and participate in communication groups. They may also seek a mentor or a coach for personal skill development. Let's take a look at some effective strategies for developing soft skills.

Identifying strengths and weaknesses

Developers should first identify their soft skills' strengths and weaknesses. They can use self-assessments, peer feedback, or professional evaluations to pinpoint areas for improvement.

Setting goals

After identifying areas of improvement, developers should set **Specific, Measurable, Achievable, Relevant, and Time-bound (SMART)** goals to enhance their soft skills.

Choosing learning methods

There are various ways to develop soft skills, such as reading books, attending workshops and seminars, taking online courses, and participating in discussion groups and networks.

Practicing and applying skills

Soft skills can only be honed through regular practice and application in real-world situations. Developers should seek opportunities to use and improve their soft skills daily.

Receiving feedback

Regular and constructive feedback from peers, mentors, or clients is crucial for the continuous development of soft skills. It helps identify areas for improvement and assess the effectiveness of the adopted strategies.

Monitoring and refinement

After setting and executing a soft skills development strategy, it is important to regularly review progress, adjust learning methods, and modify goals based on the outcomes.

Maintaining a positive attitude

A positive and proactive attitude can help developers overcome challenges and create a conducive work environment, fostering collaboration and mutual respect among team members.

Effective communication

Developers should practice articulating their thoughts clearly and concisely and be open to understanding and acknowledging the perspectives of others to build strong professional relationships.

Time management

By prioritizing tasks efficiently and allocating time judiciously, developers can maintain a healthy work-life balance, improve their productivity, and reduce stress levels.

Emotional intelligence

Developing emotional intelligence enables developers to better understand and manage their own emotions and those of others, promoting a harmonious and cooperative work environment.

Networking

Building a robust professional network provides access to a wealth of knowledge and opportunities for learning and career advancement, and helps with staying informed about industry trends and best practices.

Continuous learning and adaptation

Developers should be committed to lifelong learning, staying updated with the latest technologies and methodologies, and adapting to the evolving needs of the industry.

By incorporating these additional details, advice, and examples, C# developers can gain comprehensive insights into the importance of continual soft skill development and can effectively navigate their professional growth paths.

The commitment to continuous learning and adaptability is essential for developers, ensuring they remain at the forefront of their field. Now, let's explore how the development of soft skills can significantly influence a C# developer's career trajectory and open up new avenues for advancement.

The impact of soft skills on career growth

Soft skills can open the doors to leadership positions, project management roles, or even higher executive positions for developers. They can also help developers stand out among competitors during job interviews.

The role of soft skills in professional development

Soft skills can play a pivotal role in developers' career advancement, aiding them to adapt, interact, and distinguish themselves in a professional environment.

Leadership and management

Possessing soft skills can enhance developers' leadership and management capabilities, potentially leading to advanced positions and leadership roles.

Interaction and communication

Effective communication skills and the ability to interact constructively can improve relationships with colleagues, clients, and superiors, fostering professional growth.

Competitive advantage

Soft skills can serve as a competitive advantage in the job market, helping developers stand out during interviews and providing more opportunities for career advancement.

Development strategies

Developers should employ strategic approaches to develop their soft skills, such as learning, mentoring, practicing, and continuous self-improvement, to climb the career ladder.

Conflict resolution

Developers with strong conflict resolution skills can efficiently handle disagreements and disputes, maintaining a harmonious working environment and facilitating cooperation among team members.

Problem-solving and critical thinking

Developers benefit significantly from enhancing their problem-solving and critical thinking skills, enabling them to identify, analyze, and resolve issues more effectively, thereby contributing to project success.

Active listening

Active listening is crucial for understanding the needs, concerns, and feedback of colleagues and clients, leading to better collaboration and more effective solutions.

Adaptability

In the ever-evolving tech landscape, adaptability is key. Developers who readily embrace new technologies, methodologies, and challenges are more likely to excel in their careers.

Networking skills

Building relationships within and outside the organization can open up new opportunities, provide insights, and contribute to personal and professional growth.

Customer-centric approach

A customer-centric approach that focuses on understanding and addressing customer needs and expectations can lead to improved satisfaction and loyalty, impacting the organization's success positively.

By incorporating these additional details, advice, and examples, developers can gain a more comprehensive understanding of the significance of soft skills in shaping their career trajectories and achieving success in C# development.

Adopting a customer-centric approach is key to enhancing satisfaction and fostering loyalty, which is instrumental in an organization's success. This segues into our next topic, where we will examine how creativity and critical thinking serve as vital soft skills for problem-solving and innovation in C# development.

Exploring additional soft skills

Creativity and critical thinking can aid developers in problem-solving and innovating. These skills can also assist them in adapting to rapidly changing technological trends.

Creativity

Creativity is a crucial soft skill that helps C# developers generate innovative ideas and solve problems in unconventional ways.

Critical thinking

Critical thinking enables developers to analyze information, evaluate arguments, and solve problems based on logic and reason, which is crucial during coding and testing processes.

Learning and development

Developers should be open to learning and continually improving their soft skills through education, self-study, reading, and attending seminars and workshops.

Resilience

Developers need resilience to cope with challenges, setbacks, and failures, learning from them and bouncing back stronger.

Attention to detail

Attention to detail is essential for identifying and correcting errors in code, ensuring the delivery of high-quality software products.

Initiative

Taking the initiative and proactively tackling tasks and challenges can demonstrate a developer's commitment and can lead to career advancement opportunities.

In this unified exploration, we delved into the specific and essential soft skills that are required for excelling and distinguishing yourself in the competitive and diverse realm of C# development. This comprehensive synthesis offers detailed insights into the spectrum of soft skills that are imperative for navigating and flourishing in the multifaceted environment of C# development. By highlighting these pivotal soft skills, this section serves as a guide to aspiring C# developers who wish to be more adaptable and comprehensive in their roles. The relentless pursuit of refining these skills is essential, serving as a driving force for personal advancement and shared success in professional domains. Maintaining a persistent curiosity and openness to learning is crucial, with every enhancement being a progressive step toward achieving aspirational goals in the dynamic and varied sphere of C# development.

Summary

As we conclude this chapter, remember that the pursuit of being a C# developer is not solely about showcasing technical prowess; it is equally about demonstrating adaptability, collaboration, and a continual learning mindset, all of which are essential soft skills that are indispensable in today's dynamic and collaborative work environments. Keep refining your skills, stay curious, be open to learning, and embrace the challenges, for every interview is a stepping stone to your professional growth in the world of C# development.

In the next chapter, we will equip ourselves with the necessary strategies to confidently navigate the job market, evaluate potential offers, and master the art of salary negotiation as the next natural step in advancing our C# careers.

Part 3: Post Interview

This part provides practical guidance on how to handle the crucial stages following a job interview. It covers strategies for negotiating salaries, understanding job offers, and maintaining communication with potential employers. This part also includes valuable advice and real-life examples for starting a career in C#, offering insights from industry experts and seasoned professionals.

This part has the following chapters:

- *Chapter 9, Negotiating Your Salary and Evaluating Job Offers*
- *Chapter 10, Gaining Expert Insights, Following Up Effectively, and Taking Action*
- *Chapter 11, Launching Your C# Career – Insights*

Negotiating Your Salary and Evaluating Job Offers

After successfully navigating the technical interview for a C# developer position, you might be breathing a sigh of relief. However, this is merely the first milestone on your journey. Your path toward joining a new team is only just beginning. Effective communication following the interview, mastering the art of employment term negotiations, and cultivating professional network connections are pivotal moments that can profoundly shape your career trajectory.

In this chapter, we'll guide you through the pivotal steps that follow:

- The importance of post-interview follow-up
- Effective ways to follow up after an interview
- Building and maintaining a professional network
- Negotiating salary as a C# developer
- Factors to consider when evaluating a job offer
- Tips for making informed career decisions

By delving deeper into various facets, such as the significance of post-interview communication, strategies for effective post-interview responses, the nuances of building and fostering a professional network, and the intricacies of salary negotiations specifically for C# developers, you'll be well-equipped to not only secure your desired position but also thrive in your new role and future career endeavors. Let's dive in.

The importance of post-interview follow-up

Before we dive deep into the specific techniques and methodologies of post-interview responses, it's imperative to understand the gravity of this phase in the recruitment process. This section aims to shed light on why a timely and appropriate post-interview response can often be the linchpin in your job search journey.

In the competitive world of job hunting, especially for a position as sought-after as a C# developer, every move you make can be a deciding factor. Many candidates tend to relax post-interview, believing the bulk of the challenge is behind them. However, the reality is that your actions after the interview can play a pivotal role in the employer's decision-making process.

Expressing gratitude for time spent

Worldwide, especially in business environments, respect and politeness are core values. In a world where every minute equates to money, the time an interviewer devotes to you is a significant investment. Expressing gratitude not only speaks volumes about your appreciation but also indicates your understanding of business processes and the value of time. Such gestures can lay the foundation for a trusting relationship with potential employers. By sending a thank-you note, you not only convey your feelings about the interview but also project a positive image as a potential employee. Moreover, by expressing gratitude, you reinforce the interviewer's memory of you. It's particularly effective when you reference specific topics or moments from the interview. This not only demonstrates your attention to detail but can also pave the way for further discussions and possibly another interview.

I will give you an example of such an email:

Subject: Appreciation for the Interview - Looking Forward to Next Steps

Hi [Name],

Thank you for the interview opportunity for the [position] role.

I appreciate the time you dedicated to our discussion.

The conversation was not only enjoyable but also incredibly informative for my professional growth.

I was impressed by the depth of our dialogue on development topics, discovering new perspectives and ideas that will undoubtedly aid in my career progression.

Your questions inspired me to think more broadly and deeply about future projects.

I look forward to your feedback and information about the next steps in the selection process.

Best regards,

[Your Name]

Reaffirming interest

An essential post-interview step is to reiterate your interest in the position. It might seem obvious, but expressing your enthusiasm signals to employers that you're not just a passive participant in the hiring process but genuinely invested in the outcome. Discussing what attracts you to the company indicates that you've done your homework. Whether it's the company's innovation-driven culture, a particular project you find promising, or the personal and professional growth opportunities they offer, highlighting these aspects can be advantageous. Another key element is showcasing how you can complement their team. It could be your unique experience, specialized skills, or even your approach to problem-solving. For instance, "At my previous job, I worked on a similar project and achieved significant results using technology X. I'm confident my expertise in this area will benefit your company." This approach shows employers that you're not just looking for any job – you aim to be a valuable asset to their organization.

Re-establishing contact

This step is crucial, especially if you feel you could've presented yourself better during the interview or missed out on highlighting key points. Every interview is a unique opportunity to showcase yourself, and sometimes, emotions or stress can cause us to overlook important aspects. Reaching out allows you to rectify any oversights, add to your discussion, or even alter initial perceptions. It also underscores your commitment and interest. For example, if you felt you didn't fully explain your role in a major project due to time constraints, revisiting that topic gives you another shot at conveying that information – for instance, "During our conversation, I didn't elaborate enough on my contribution to project Y. I'd like to clarify that my initiative led to a workflow optimization, resulting in a 20% increase in productivity." Such clarifications can reshape an employer's view of you as a potential candidate, so it's an opportunity you shouldn't miss.

Setting expectations

Every hiring process has its nuances. Sometimes, post-interview, candidates might be left in the dark about the next steps, or employers might provide only a vague timeline. It's essential to understand that you have the right to know what comes next. Not only does this help you plan better, but it also signals your proactiveness and genuine interest in the role. If you're uncertain about the subsequent stages, don't hesitate to reach out to the HR manager or another contact to inquire about the process. You might be curious about the expected decision-making timeframe, any additional interview rounds, or necessary documentation. This approach not only showcases your organizational skills but also your systematic approach to work. Given you might have other plans or interviews lined up, knowing specific dates helps you manage your time and resources more efficiently.

Demonstrating initiative

Employers often seek candidates who show initiative. It not only indicates your eagerness to work but also suggests a capacity for autonomy, a proactive approach to problem-solving, and a readiness to take responsibility. This quality is invaluable in today's dynamic business environments where adaptability and proposing efficient solutions are crucial. By taking the initiative post-interview, you reflect your overall work ethic. It suggests that you're not just keen on securing a job, but also on contributing to the company's success. An employer noting your proactive approach can be assured that you'll apply the same energy to work tasks. The initiative can also be a tie-breaker when an employer is torn between multiple candidates. The one who displays more interest and readiness often has the edge.

In conclusion, the post-interview phase isn't merely a formality – it's a tangible opportunity to leave a lasting impression and strengthen your candidacy for the desired job. Always remember this and seize every chance to present your best self.

Having grasped the critical nature of post-interview responses, you're now primed to delve into actionable steps and methodologies that can amplify the effectiveness of this process. The subsequent section offers a more granulated look at best practices in this realm.

Effective ways to follow up after an interview

Having underscored the paramount importance of post-interview responses, it's now crucial to arm yourself with the know-how to execute it flawlessly. This section will provide a comprehensive overview of tactics, methods, and approaches designed to enhance your post-interview communication prowess.

Effectively following up after an interview is a pivotal step in the job search process. It's not just a formality, but an opportunity to showcase genuine interest in the position, dedication, and the desire to contribute to the company's growth.

Sending a thank you note

At first glance, this might seem like a mere formality, but it plays a much deeper and essential role in communication between the candidate and the employer. Firstly, sending a thank-you note shortly after the interview demonstrates your organizational skills and attention to detail. It signifies that you are taking the hiring process seriously. Secondly, in this note, you can emphasize your genuine interest in the position by pointing out what intrigued you during the conversation or why you believe this job is the perfect fit for you. Thirdly, by recalling specific moments or discussions from the interview, you exhibit your attentiveness and listening skills. Mentioning details discussed with the employer or particular aspects of the job that captured your interest not only emphasizes your enthusiasm but also allows the employer to see that you were attentive and analytical about the information provided. Lastly, a thank-you note offers you a chance to stand out from other candidates. While this practice is becoming more common, not all candidates send thank-you notes after interviews. Taking this step can sometimes make all the difference in the employer's decision-making process.

Addressing shortcomings

Interviews can be nerve-wracking, and it's easy to miss out on certain details or fail to articulate thoughts due to nervousness or other factors. Perhaps you felt that you couldn't answer a specific question adequately or forgot to mention an essential experience or project. By sending a clarifying note or providing additional information, you not only display commitment and professionalism but also show that you value the job opportunity. This also reflects your desire to be fully understood and that you take responsibility for your words and actions. This approach can help employers see you as someone who strives for continuous improvement, evaluates their actions, and is willing to rectify mistakes.

Showcasing additional materials

In today's world, where competition among job candidates is fierce, it's advantageous to have something that sets you apart. Professional materials such as portfolios, work samples, or links to completed projects can showcase you in the best light. A portfolio can visually represent your career achievements, including photos, videos, designs, code, and other significant materials. These materials can also demonstrate your vision, work style, and problem-solving approach. By providing additional materials, you exhibit initiative and a willingness to share, conveying your eagerness to assist the employer in making an informed decision.

Inquiring about status

Communication with the employer doesn't end after the interview. Asking about the status of your application after a certain period not only displays your proactiveness and interest but also underscores your dedication and belief that you're the right candidate for the position. Such inquiries help you stay updated and understand where your application stands. However, it's essential to maintain a respectful tone and not appear too pushy. Your questions should be brief, polite, and to the point to avoid putting undue pressure on the employer. Remember, the primary goal of your inquiry is to gather information, not to pressure the employer for a response.

Giving personal touch

In a world where most communications can seem formal and standardized, a personal touch can truly distinguish you from other candidates. It acts as a bridge between you and the employer, showing that you're interested not just in the position, but also in human-level interactions. When you mention specific moments from the interview or shared interests, it fosters a sense of familiarity and trust. This approach not only strengthens your connection with the employer but also showcases your capacity for empathy and deep understanding. Ultimately, this personal touch might be the added factor that gives you an edge in the hiring process, as employers always appreciate individuals who can establish personal connections and promote harmonious team dynamics.

In conclusion, every interaction with an employer post-interview is another opportunity to leave a positive impression. Each email or message should be well-thought-out, concise, and informative. Your goal is to position yourself as the top candidate in the employer's mind.

Equipped with these potent strategies, you're poised to craft a professional and impactful response after any interview scenario. However, to fully optimize your career opportunities, it's also pivotal to gain proficiency in networking. We will focus on this in the next section.

Building and maintaining a professional network

Transitioning from post-interview strategies, another cornerstone of career advancement is the art of networking. This segment will illuminate the reasons why professional connections are an indispensable asset in today's competitive job market and provide a roadmap to cultivate and nurture these relationships.

In today's era, a professional network has become increasingly significant, regardless of your field of work. For an IT professional, especially a C# developer, networking can be the key to unlocking new opportunities, obtaining referrals, or learning about new technologies.

Starting the network

Many often underestimate the importance of existing relationships in their lives. In reality, our initial contacts in the professional network are those we know personally: friends, family, work colleagues, and acquaintances from university or educational institutions. Each of these individuals may offer unique perspectives, knowledge, or connections that can be beneficial to you. Thus, it's crucial not only to maintain these relationships but also to actively expand your network. Attending professional events, participating in workshops or seminars, and being active on social networks can help you meet new people and establish valuable professional connections. Remember, networking in the modern world is an investment in your future.

Participating in events and conferences

Participating in events dedicated to your field is a pivotal element in building and maintaining a professional network. These are venues where experts, newcomers, industry leaders, and other stakeholders converge to share knowledge, ideas, and perspectives. Not only can you learn about the latest trends, technologies, and methodologies in the industry, but you can also personally meet and interact with individuals who can significantly influence your career. Engaging in panel discussions, workshops, or even informal networking events allows you to establish personal contacts, exchange business cards, and even discuss potential collaborative projects or opportunities. Hence, every conference or event becomes an investment in both your education and your career's future.

Creating social networks

In the contemporary digital age, social networks play a critically important role in professional networking and development. Platforms such as LinkedIn not only enable you to maintain a professional portfolio but also serve as a hub for networking, interacting with industry peers, and exploring new opportunities. It's vital to update your profile regularly, add new achievements and skills, and actively communicate with other community members. Joining groups related to your specialization can help you stay updated with the industry's latest news, discuss topical issues, and discover new career growth opportunities. Also, utilize the network to solicit feedback on your work, seek advice from experienced colleagues, and establish new connections. This way, you not only enhance your visibility in the professional community but also secure a valuable resource for personal and professional growth.

Keeping regular interaction

To keep your professional network active and effective, consistent communication with your contacts is essential. Interactions don't always have to be formal or work-related. Even a simple "How's it going?" or a greeting on a professional holiday can strengthen your ties. Acknowledge the achievements and successes of your contacts by congratulating them or sharing their news. You can also invite them to events, seminars, or workshops that you find intriguing. Conversely, share your updates, professional accomplishments, and career changes. This not only helps you obtain feedback and advice but also keeps your persona interesting in the eyes of others. Regular interactions help keep relationships "alive" and active. And even if you don't see an immediate benefit from a particular contact now, you never know what opportunities this interaction might open in the future.

Reciprocity

No network can exist without the principle of reciprocity. Each of us needs assistance, advice, or support at some point. But it's equally important to remember that we can also be beneficial to others. Actively helping your peers by offering advice, sharing contacts, or simply listening establishes an atmosphere of trust and mutual respect. Such interactions bolster your authority within the network and demonstrate that you're not just seeking benefits for yourself but are also willing to contribute to the community's growth. Moreover, sharing your resources and knowledge might bring you new opportunities. Perhaps a colleague will think of you when a job vacancy or a project perfectly suited for your skills arises. Also, remember the *boomerang effect* in networking: when you assist others, that aid often comes back to you, sometimes from the least expected direction. Therefore, always be open to collaboration and be ready to help – it's an investment in your future and the strength of your relationships in the professional environment.

Empowered with the insights and guidelines from this section, you're well on your way to forging a robust professional network that can be a catalyst for numerous career opportunities. Beyond networking, the ability to negotiate your salary adeptly is equally crucial. This is the subject of the next section.

Negotiating salary as a C# developer

With a burgeoning professional network as your backdrop, it's time to address a topic that's often fraught with anxiety: salary negotiations. This section will delve into the nuances of negotiating remuneration, with a particular focus on the unique considerations for C# developers.

Negotiating a salary can be an integral part of the job search process. For many, it's a moment filled with discomfort and stress. However, by knowing your worth and being well-prepared, you can turn this process into a productive and beneficial one for yourself.

Do market research

Before entering negotiations, it's crucial to understand the market landscape. Being informed and knowledgeable about industry-standard salary ranges for C# developers is vital when you're standing your ground during negotiations. To gauge whether your financial expectations are realistic, research salaries in your area. Consider experience, education, and the specifics of the company you plan to join. Online resources such as Glassdoor or Payscale provide valuable data, but consulting with colleagues and other professionals in your field can also be helpful. The gathered information will not only aid in negotiations but will also show a potential employer that you're a competent and responsible candidate.

Set your expectations

For successful negotiations, you need a clear idea of what you aim to achieve. Establishing specific financial boundaries will give you confidence during discussions with an employer. Start by determining the minimum salary that you'd find acceptable considering your expenses, the cost of living in your area, and other factors. Then, determine the optimal salary – one that would reflect your skills, experience, and contribution to the company. Having these two figures will allow you to approach negotiations more precisely and flexibly. Lastly, consider the possibility of additional bonuses or benefits that might compensate for a lower base salary. Demonstrating foresight and preparation will show the employer that you're serious about your role and value in the job market.

Avoid naming a figure first

In negotiations, understanding the psychological dynamics is essential. Allowing the employer to propose a salary first grants you a strategic advantage. This position enables you to analyze their proposal, compare it to your market research and expectations, and then formulate a counter-offer if necessary. By doing this, you avoid situations where you might propose a figure lower than what the employer was prepared to offer. Conversely, if the employer's offer exceeds your expectations, you can adjust your negotiation strategy accordingly.

Consider other benefits

When negotiating a salary, it's essential to remember that financial compensation is just the tip of the iceberg. Many companies offer a broad range of additional benefits that can significantly improve your overall work experience. For instance, flexible working hours can be invaluable for those with families, and training programs can provide opportunities for skill enhancement or further education. Companies might also offer extra leave days, fitness programs, corporate events, or even relocation support. All these can significantly impact your overall job satisfaction and quality of life. Hence, before making a final decision, thoroughly evaluate all aspects of the offer and compare them against other potential offers.

Be ready to compromise

Successful negotiations often hinge on both parties' ability to find common ground. This doesn't mean you should blindly concede to your demands. Instead, approach the process with an open mind, ready to consider alternative options and offers. Perhaps the employer cannot meet your financial demands, but they can compensate you with additional leave, bonuses, or other benefits. The key is to find a balance between your priorities and what the employer is willing to offer, aiming for a mutually beneficial agreement.

By considering all these aspects, you can effectively negotiate, ensuring a fair salary and benefits that reflect your professionalism and contribution to the company's growth. Armed with this knowledge, you're in a prime position to negotiate a salary that mirrors your skills, expertise, and market demand. Before sealing any job offer, however, it's essential to holistically evaluate the entire package, a topic we'll dissect in the subsequent section.

Factors to consider when evaluating a job offer

Once you've successfully navigated the treacherous waters of salary negotiations, you might find a job offer on the horizon. But how do you discern its worth? This section will elucidate the multifaceted factors that should be weighed when assessing a potential employer's proposal.

Accepting a job offer is always a significant step in your career. Such a decision has far-reaching implications and shouldn't be made hastily. Beyond the core financial package, numerous other aspects need consideration when you're evaluating an offer.

Financial package

This is a central element of any job proposal, determining the offer's attractiveness. It consists of various components that require detailed consideration:

- *Base salary*: Your main compensation for the work you'll provide. It's the figure you rely on for budgeting.

- *Bonuses*: Additional money you can earn for achieving specific goals or exceptional work. It's crucial to understand the criteria for receiving these bonuses and the average bonus amount in the company.

- *Health benefits*: This could include medical insurance, dental insurance, life insurance, and other coverages. It's essential to ascertain the premium percentage covered by the employer and the services included in the package.

- *Retirement plans*: Does the company offer a retirement plan or matching program? What are the terms for participating? How much of your contributions does the company match?

- *Other financial incentives*: These can include stock options, corporate bonuses, tuition reimbursement, or housing assistance.

When considering all these elements, you'll get a comprehensive view of the financial package on offer, allowing you to make an informed decision about the job proposal.

Work-life balance

This is becoming increasingly valuable to many professionals, especially in an age of fast-paced living and high productivity demands. Here are some critical aspects to consider:

- *Flexible schedule*: The ability to start work earlier or later can be a significant advantage, especially if you have personal commitments.

- *Remote work*: Does the company allow working from home or other locations? This can save daily commutes and might enhance productivity.

- *Leave entitlements*: How many leave days are you entitled to annually? What are the conditions for taking these days? Are there additional leave days or public holidays?

- *Sick leave conditions*: If you fall ill or face personal circumstances, what are the company's provisions for sick leave? What portion of your salary is paid during sick leave?

- *Breaks*: What's the company's stance on short breaks during the workday? This can be essential for mental well-being and sustained energy levels.

- *Additional benefits*: Does the company offer childcare programs, gym facilities, meditation rooms, or other means to support a balance between work and relaxation?

By considering all these factors, you can create a picture of how a job will fit into your life and whether it will allow you to maintain the balance you seek. It's not just about the job itself, but how it aligns with your personal values, family needs, and long-term career goals. Ultimately, you can make an informed decision that contributes to your overall happiness and fulfillment both in and out of the workplace.

Corporate culture

This is the company's essence, and it can be challenging to discern at first glance. It encompasses the values, beliefs, norms, and rituals shaping the daily experiences of employees. Here are some key aspects of corporate culture:

- *Team atmosphere*: The vibe you get when you walk into the office. Are people friendly and open? Is collaboration encouraged? Is there open space for interaction or quiet zones for concentration?

- *Innovation stance*: Does the company encourage fresh ideas and experiments? Are there programs to foster innovative projects?

- *Leadership*: What are the primary values and beliefs of the leadership? Are they open to discussions and feedback from employees?

- *Company culture*: The overall culture of a company can greatly influence work-life balance. A culture that values long hours and "face time" may not be compatible with a balanced lifestyle, while a culture that encourages efficiency and results over hours spent at the desk may be more supportive.

Understanding the corporate culture is key to thriving in any work environment. It's the invisible force that can significantly influence job satisfaction and professional growth. As you navigate the company's cultural landscape, remember that aligning your values with those of the company is essential for a harmonious and fulfilling career journey.

Professional development

How does the company support your career growth? Are there opportunities for training and skill enhancement? Recognizing these opportunities is crucial for your long-term career trajectory:

- *Interpersonal relations*: How are work groups and team projects viewed? Is teamwork encouraged?

- *Social responsibility*: What's the company's stance on social responsibility? Are there projects aimed at community support or environmental conservation?

- *Equality and diversity*: How does the company approach diversity and inclusiveness? Are there support programs for minorities?

- *Career mobility*: Does the company offer clear pathways for internal promotions or role changes that can lead to personal and professional development?

- *Work-life harmony*: Are there policies or benefits in place, such as flexible hours or wellness programs, that support a balance between work and personal life?

- *Recognition systems*: Are there formal mechanisms for recognizing and rewarding employee achievements and contributions?

- *Global opportunities*: For multinational corporations, are there prospects for international assignments or projects that can broaden your professional experience?

- *Technology advancements*: Does the company stay on the cutting edge of technology, providing tools and platforms that can streamline work and foster innovation?

When assessing corporate culture, it's vital to determine if it aligns with your values and expectations. This can be a decisive factor in your job satisfaction and productivity in the future.

Opportunities for professional growth

One of the main motivations for many professionals when choosing a job is the potential for career advancement as it reflects the company's commitment to the personal and professional development of its employees:

- *Career ladders*: Investigate whether the company has clear paths for career progression. Understand which positions can be reached from your current role and what requirements must be met to ascend to the next level.

- *Training programs*: Does the company invest in employee training? This could range from internal training sessions, webinars, workshops, or even sponsoring participation in conferences and courses.

- *Mentorship*: A strong mentorship program where more experienced professionals guide and support those new to the field can be invaluable.

- *Feedback loop*: Regular performance evaluations and consistent feedback can indicate a company's commitment to your growth.

- *Diverse projects*: Being exposed to a variety of projects or having the opportunity to take on more responsibility can be vital for development.

- *Horizontal growth*: Besides upward mobility, it's essential to know if you can grow laterally by exploring new departments or roles within the company.

The potential for career advancement within a company is not just about climbing the corporate ladder; it's about the journey of personal and professional development. By assessing and taking advantage of the growth opportunities a company offers, you can craft a career path that is not only upward but also fulfilling and aligned with your personal goals and aspirations.

Workplace location and commute

The location of your workplace and the time spent commuting can significantly impact your daily comfort and overall job satisfaction:

- *Commute time*: Depending on your mode of transportation (car, public transit, walking, or cycling), commuting times can vary. It's crucial to account for peak traffic times and potential delays, especially in larger cities.

- *Commute costs*: If you're using public transportation or driving, daily expenses such as fares, fuel, and parking need to be considered.

- *Remote work opportunities*: With the modern shift toward remote work, many companies offer full-time or part-time remote positions, allowing for time and cost savings.

- *Office environment*: Beyond location, the office's ambiance, amenities, relaxation zones, and meal facilities can greatly influence job satisfaction.

The daily commute and workplace location form the bookends of your workday, framing your professional life with practical concerns and well-being. As remote work reshapes our concept of the office, the traditional boundaries between personal and professional spaces are also shifting, offering new opportunities to redefine what constitutes an ideal work-life balance.

Company reviews and reputation

Reviews and the reputation of a company can offer insights into its internal culture, ethics, and business practices. Reviews and the reputation of a company can offer insights into its internal culture, ethics, and business practices, and can be instrumental in painting a picture of the day-to-day reality of working there. Here are some ways to gauge a company's standing:

- *Information sources*: Utilize websites such as Glassdoor and Indeed, or specialized forums where employees share their work experiences.

- *Review balance*: Aim to see both positive and negative feedback for a well-rounded view.

- *Relevance*: Older reviews may no longer be pertinent as companies evolve; prioritize recent feedback.

- *Context*: Understand the context behind a review. What events or circumstances influenced the individual's perspective?

- *Official responses*: Some companies respond to their employees' reviews, giving insights into how they handle criticism and value their team.

When you're considering joining a new company, it's important to remember that no workplace is perfect. However, with thorough research and gathering ample information, you can make an informed decision that aligns with your expectations and goals. Remember to always trust your instincts and feelings when evaluating potential job offers.

With these considerations in your toolkit, you're better equipped to make informed decisions concerning job offers, ensuring they align with your career aspirations and personal values. However, each decision is just a piece of the broader career mosaic. In the next section, we'll provide holistic guidance on making strategic career choices for long-term success.

Tips for making informed career decisions

While accepting a job offer is a significant milestone, remember that your career is a marathon, not a sprint. It demands numerous pivotal decisions. In this finale, we'll furnish you with actionable advice and strategic insights to navigate these choices, ensuring they align with your overarching career goals.

A career is not just a sequence of jobs or positions; it's a path you choose to achieve both your professional and personal goals. But how do you make the right choices on this journey? In this section, we'll provide some tips to help you make well-informed career decisions.

Labor market analysis

Understanding the labor market is an integral part of career planning. Without grasping current trends and employer needs, your skills or knowledge might become obsolete. Here's how to effectively analyze the job market:

- *Information sources*: Use online platforms such as Glassdoor, Payscale, and LinkedIn to research salaries, candidate requirements, and job descriptions. This will help you identify which skills and knowledge are currently in demand.

- *Industry reports*: Many industry associations and organizations publish annual reports highlighting key trends, challenges, and opportunities. These reports provide valuable context and can help you see the bigger picture.

- *Networking events*: Participating in industry conferences, seminars, and workshops can serve as both a knowledge source and an excellent networking opportunity. Interacting with industry peers can give you insider information and insights into current employer needs.

- *Self-education*: Based on the information gathered, identify any additional skills or knowledge you might need. Consider taking extra courses, obtaining certifications, or focusing on developing specific competencies.

With the rapid changes in technology and business models, regular labor market analysis is essential to remain adaptive and competitive in your career.

Networking

Connecting with the right people and maintaining long-term relationships can be crucial for your professional advancement. Networking can help you discover new opportunities, gain valuable advice, and expand your knowledge base. Here's how to cultivate and maintain these connections:

- *Active participation in professional communities*: Join industry associations, clubs, and groups. They often organize events where you can meet like-minded individuals, exchange experiences, and establish new contacts.

- *Utilize social networks*: Platforms such as LinkedIn not only allow you to maintain an online network but also join interest groups, interact with experts, and stay updated with industry news.

- *Maintain regular communication*: Stay connected with your acquaintances, even if you don't see them often. A simple email, call, or message to share news or ask about their well-being can go a long way.

- *Reciprocity*: Be ready to assist when asked. This could be in the form of advice, a recommendation, or assistance with a task. A genuine willingness to help strengthens relationships and lends credibility to your words in the future.

- *Volunteering*: Volunteering in industry events or educational programs can be a great networking opportunity.

By building strong professional relationships, you can access valuable information, opportunities, and resources that can propel your career forward. Never underestimate the power of networking.

Constructive feedback

Feedback is the foundation of professional growth and development. It helps you identify areas where you excel and highlights opportunities for improvement. Here are some strategies for effectively leveraging feedback:

- *Be open*: When seeking feedback, be prepared to accept both positive remarks and constructive criticism. Avoid being defensive or making excuses.

- *Ask the right questions*: Instead of broad queries such as "What do you think of my work?", pose more specific questions such as "Are there aspects of my project that you believe need improvement?"

- *Active listening*: Listen attentively when receiving feedback. Focus on understanding the core message rather than responding emotionally.

- *Ask for examples*: If you find certain comments unclear, request specific examples or situations to better grasp the critique.

- *Develop an action plan*: After receiving feedback, consider how you can implement the given advice. Create a plan to enhance your skills and competencies.

- *Express gratitude*: Always thank those who take the time to offer feedback. A simple "thank you" or a more detailed appreciation acknowledges the significance of their input and encourages them to share their thoughts in the future.

Remember, feedback aims to foster your growth. Utilize it as a tool for improvement and to attain your career objectives.

Professional development

In today's dynamic world, where technology and industries constantly evolve, ongoing professional development is imperative. It not only keeps you competitive but also opens new avenues for you as a specialist. Here are some areas to focus on:

- *Courses and training*: Regularly seek out learning opportunities, whether it's formal courses, webinars, workshops, or online classes.

- *Certification*: For certain professions, certification is valuable. It validates your qualifications and showcases expertise in a particular area.

- *Professional unions and associations*: Joining these groups grants you access to unique resources, networking events, and learning opportunities.

- *Self-learning*: Always aim to broaden your knowledge. Reading books and articles, listening to podcasts, and exploring new topics or technologies can prove invaluable.

- *Mentorship*: Finding a mentor or becoming one can be a potent tool for professional growth, allowing you to learn from others' experiences and share your insights.

- *Attending conferences and seminars*: Such events not only provide knowledge but also offer networking opportunities with other industry professionals.

Remember, investing in your professional growth is investing in yourself. The initiative you take in this process dictates your future in the professional world.

Adaptability

Adaptability is becoming a key competency in the modern world. The ability to quickly respond to changes and efficiently adapt to new circumstances is not just an advantage but a necessity for today's professionals. Here are some aspects underscoring the importance of adaptability:

- *Technological innovations*: It's crucial to stay updated with new technologies and tools emerging in your field. This ensures you remain competitive and meet current market demands.

- *Changes in organizational culture*: Companies continually adapt, modifying their structures and processes. Your positive attitude toward these changes and swift integration into new work conditions can be a significant asset.

- *Globalization*: Interacting with partners or colleagues from different cultures and countries requires flexibility and the ability to adapt quickly to various communication styles and working methods.

- *Market uncertainty*: Economic downturns, pandemics, and political instability all impact business. Your adaptability helps companies better navigate these changes.

- *Learning and development*: Your readiness to learn and acquire new skills is also an indicator of adaptability. The world is ever-evolving, and you must keep moving forward, continually refining your abilities.

Adaptability is not just about reacting to changes but viewing them as opportunities rather than threats. A positive approach to innovations and alterations makes you an indispensable employee for any organization.

Work-life balance

Work-life balance is a concept that ensures a harmonious blend of professional responsibilities and personal life. It's not just a matter of comfort but is also key to maintaining your physical and mental well-being. Let's delve into its importance:

- *Efficiency and productivity*: A healthy work-life balance helps with maintaining high concentration and productivity. When you have the opportunity to rest and recharge, you work more effectively.

- *Health*: Constant stress and overload can lead to health issues such as high blood pressure, anxiety, or depression. Balancing work and leisure reduces the risk of these problems.

- *Motivation*: When you feel that your job doesn't consume all your time, you'll be more motivated and satisfied with your work.

- *Family and personal life*: Giving time to family, friends, and personal hobbies is crucial. They provide joy and support and positively impact your overall well-being.

- *Flexibility*: The modern world offers many work flexibility options, such as remote work, flexible schedules, or part-time roles. Utilize these opportunities to find the optimal work balance for yourself.

Considering these factors, work-life balance becomes not just desirable but critically important for your career and life as a whole. HR heads always value employees who maintain a work-life balance as it improves overall productivity and team morale.

Ethics and values

Ethics and values form the foundation of every individual's professional actions. They not only define your attitude toward work but also how others perceive you. Let's explore why they are so critical:

- *Long-term reputation*: One misstep can tarnish your reputation for many years. Conversely, if you consistently uphold high standards, your reputation will serve you, attracting new opportunities and partnerships.

- *Trust*: Upholding ethical principles fosters trust between you, your colleagues, partners, and clients. People prefer to work with those they can trust.

- *Personal satisfaction*: Working in alignment with your values brings internal harmony and satisfaction from what you do.

- *Team enhancement*: Ethical behavior can serve as an example to others, stimulating higher overall standards in a team.

- *Long-term success*: Companies and professionals who adhere to high ethical standards often achieve greater and more sustainable success as their partners and clients value reliability and honesty.

By adhering to ethics and values in your work, you highlight your professionalism and commitment to the best standards. HR heads always pay attention to a candidate's ethics as it reflects not only their professional background but also their character and willingness to add value to the company.

Endowed with these guidelines, you're set to steer your career journey with enhanced clarity, foresight, and confidence. Always bear in mind that every choice you make casts a ripple effect on your professional landscape. We wish you unparalleled success in your endeavors, and may this chapter serve as a trusted compass in your career navigation.

Summary

This chapter offered a panoramic view of key competencies and strategies that C# developers should master during their job search endeavors. We underscored how a strategic post-interview response can be a game-changer, influencing an employer's perception and showcasing your commitment and professionalism. The art of networking emerged as a non-negotiable skill, given its potential to unlock a plethora of career opportunities.

Furthermore, we delved into the nitty-gritty of salary negotiations, emphasizing the need for C# developers to ensure their remuneration mirrors their worth in the market. Evaluating job offers demands a holistic approach, considering factors ranging from company culture to growth avenues. As we wrapped up, we emphasized the importance of making informed, strategic career decisions, ensuring a trajectory of growth and fulfillment.

In the next chapter, we'll explore how to follow up effectively, gain expert insights, and take action, guiding you through the practical steps of leveraging the information you've gathered to make informed decisions and initiate meaningful career moves.

10

Gaining Expert Insights, Following Up Effectively, and Taking Action

Embarking on a career in the world of C# development is both an exciting and a challenging endeavor. As one stands at the crossroads, transitioning from learning to application, there's a palpable mix of anticipation and anxiety. C# is not just a programming language; it's an entire universe of opportunities, complexities, and nuances. The road to mastering it, or any craft, is dotted with milestones of understanding, trials, errors, and eventual triumphs. Just as a compelling story has a beginning, middle, and end, your journey toward becoming a proficient C# developer will be laden with tales of rigorous preparations, awe-inspiring successes, invaluable learnings, and exponential growth.

As we conclude this guide, this chapter is structured to provide you with a comprehensive understanding of the following key areas:

- Recap of key concepts and strategies for C# interview success: a refresher on essential concepts to ensure you're primed for any challenge

- Interviews with successful C# developers and hiring managers: a window into the minds and experiences of those at the pinnacle of their careers, offering pearls of wisdom

- Real-life examples of interview experiences and outcomes: illustrative narratives providing a practical perspective of the interview battleground.

- Lessons learned and advice from industry professionals: accumulated wisdom and pivotal advice distilled from years of experience

- Adapting to industry changes and emerging technologies: charting the ever-shifting tech terrain, understanding its implications, and staying ahead of the curve

- The future of C# and career growth opportunities: a forward-looking exploration, illuminating the vast horizon of possibilities

With this roadmap in hand, this concluding chapter aims to stitch together the essence of all we've traversed, setting you on a path to step confidently into the dynamic world of C#.

> **Important note**
>
> In order to assist the author in the preparation of this interview guide, Tanya, Oleksii, Yurii, and Igor agreed to be interviewed and to provide information and other materials to be used in connection with this work, including their personal experiences, remarks, and recollections, which are described in the *Real-life examples of interview experiences and outcomes* section of this chapter.
>
> Meanwhile, the rest of the participants are fictional and their quotes are based on the author's experience.

Recap of key concepts and strategies for C# interview success

As we commence this chapter, let's take a moment to revisit the core tenets and strategies that form the bedrock of your preparation for C# interviews. Reflecting on these will reinforce your readiness and ensure you approach your interviews with the right tools in hand.

Resume

In this section, we'll guide you through crafting a compelling resume specifically for C# developer interviews, focusing on various critical components. Remember, your resume is a direct reflection of your professional persona and should be meticulously prepared to make a strong impression on HR managers.

Refining structure and content

A well-structured resume is your first opportunity to impress. Here's how to effectively organize your information:

- **Heading**: Include your name, contact details, and, optionally, a professional title. Ensure this section is visually clear and easy to find.

- **Professional profile**: Include a brief, impactful summary highlighting your C# expertise, key achievements, and career goals. Tailor this to match the job's requirements.

- **Work experience**: Detail your professional journey, focusing on roles and projects relevant to C#. Use bullet points to describe your responsibilities and achievements in each role, emphasizing your contribution to the projects.

- **Education and certifications**: List your educational background, prioritizing degrees and certifications directly related to software development and C#. Mention any specialized training or courses that enhance your C# skills.

Adapting to the company and position

Adapting your resume for each application demonstrates your dedication and attention to detail.

- **Research**: Before writing, research the company's culture, values, and tech stack, especially their use of C#. This knowledge will help you tailor your resume to resonate with the company's needs.

- **Tailoring**: Customize your resume to reflect the skills and experiences most relevant to the job description. Highlight specific C# skills and projects that align with the role's requirements.

Differentiating yourself

In a competitive job market, it's crucial to stand out. Here's how you can differentiate your resume from the rest:

- **Keywords**: Use industry-specific keywords that align with C# development roles. This not only helps in getting past resume scanning software but also shows your familiarity with industry terminology.

- **Conciseness and clarity**: Keep your sentences short and to the point. Use clear, professional language to make your resume easy to read and understand.

- **Showcasing achievements**: Quantify your achievements where possible, e.g., "Improved system performance by 20% through optimized C# code."

Utilizing GitHub

Your GitHub profile can be a powerful tool to showcase your coding skills and projects:

- **Profile link**: Include a link to your GitHub profile. Ensure your profile is professional, with a clear bio and organized repositories.

- **Highlighted projects**: Feature a few select projects that showcase your C# skills. Provide brief descriptions, your role in the project, and any notable outcomes or learnings.

- **Community engagement**: If applicable, mention your contributions to open source projects or active participation in C# forums and communities, showcasing your engagement and ongoing learning in the field.

Basics of C#

C# (pronounced *C-sharp*) is a versatile, modern programming language developed by Microsoft that runs on the .NET platform. Designed with simplicity and power in mind, it provides developers with a robust set of tools to create a wide range of applications, from desktop to mobile and web-based solutions.

Variables

- **Declaration**: The syntax for creating a new variable, defining its type
- **Initialization**: The process of assigning an initial value to a variable
- **Scope**: Understanding where a variable can be used in the code and how it affects the variable's accessibility

Data types

- **Primitive**:

  - `int`: Whole numbers that can represent values ranging from 2,147,483,647 to 2,147,483,648.
  - `char`: Unicode characters representing a character in 16-bit encoding.
  - `bool`: Boolean values that can be either true or false.
  - `float` and `double`: Floating-point real numbers. Float has 7 digits of precision, while double has 15-16 digits.
  - `byte`: An 8-bit unsigned integer that can hold values from 0 to 255.
  - `short` and `long`: Whole numbers of different sizes. Short ranges are from 32,768 to 32,767, while long ranges can contain values from 9,223,372,036,854,775,808 to 9,223,372,036,854,775,807.
  - `decimal`: Real numbers used for financial calculations with high precision with 28-29 significant digits.

- **Complex**:

  - Strings (`string`): Sequences of characters. In C#, strings are immutable.
  - Arrays: Collections of items of the same type, the size of which is determined upon creation.
  - Lists (`List<T>`): Dynamic collections of elements that can expand or shrink as needed.
  - Tuples (`Tuple<T1, T2, ... >`): Collections of objects of different types that can be used to store different types of data together.
  - HashSets (`HashSet<T>`): Unserted Collections that store only unique elements, and provide fast lookups.
  - Dictionaries (`Dictionary<TKey, TValue>`): Collections of keys and values that help organize data on a key-value principle.
  - Structures (`struct`): Similar to classes but are values, not references. Used for small objects that don't require inheritance or finalization. Examples include `DateTime` and `TimeSpan`.

Conditional operators

- `if`: Used to check a certain condition and execute code if the condition is true
- `else`: Executes code if the condition in `if` is false
- `switch`: Allows executing different code depending on the value of a variable

Loops

- `for`: Used to repeat a block of code a certain number of times
- `while`: Executes a block of code as long as the condition is true
- `foreach`: Iterates through the elements of a collection, such as an array or a list

Arrays

- **One-dimensional**: A collection of elements of the same type accessed using a single index
- **Multidimensional**: Have two or more dimensions; for example, a matrix
- **Lists**: Dynamic arrays to which elements can be added or removed on the fly

Object-oriented programming

In this section, we delve into the core aspects of *classes* and *objects* in C#, exploring their declarations, lifecycle, and interactions, along with the concept of inheritance and related operators.

Classes

- **Declaration**: Every class in C# is a blueprint for creating objects. The class declaration defines variables for data storage and methods to perform actions.
- **Constructors**: Methods that are automatically called when an object is created. They are often used for variable initialization.
- **Destructors**: Although rarely used in C# due to the garbage collector, destructors serve to release unmanaged resources.

Objects

- **Creation**: In C#, an object is created using the `new` keyword
- **Interaction**: Through a class instance, you can interact with its members—methods, properties, and events
- **Destruction**: The garbage collector automatically removes objects that are no longer accessible

- **Inheritance**: Inheritance in C# enables the creation of new classes that derive properties and methods from existing ones, fostering reusability and hierarchical organization in code

- **Base and derived classes**: Through inheritance, you can create a new class that inherits the members of an existing class, adding or modifying them

- `is` and `as` operators: They allow safe type checking of objects and casting between them

Polymorphism

- **Method overloading**: Allows having multiple methods in a class with the same name but a different set of parameters

- **Overriding**: In derived classes, you can change or extend the behavior of base class methods using the `override` keyword

Advanced concepts

This section offers an insightful exploration of advanced C# features such as lambda expressions, LINQ, delegates, anonymous methods, and events, each playing a pivotal role in efficient and expressive coding.

Lambda expressions

- **Syntax**: Lambda expressions use the `=>` symbol to define anonymous functions in a compact style.

- **Usage**: Lambda expressions are particularly useful when working with collections or any other types that support delegates. These expressions are often used in LINQ queries.

Language Integrated Query (LINQ)

- **Queries to collections**: Allows executing queries on various data sources without delving into the details of their implementation.

- **Syntax**: Includes both a query and a method-style syntax for writing queries

- **Usage**: With LINQ, you can filter, sort, group, and aggregate data from different sources

Delegates

- **Declaration**: Defines the type of method that can be represented by a delegate

- **Usage**: They allow the creation of variables that can point to any method with a specific signature, regardless of which class these methods belong to

Anonymous methods

A way to create a method "on the fly" without the need to declare a separate method name.

Events

- **Declaration**: A mechanism that allows an object to notify other objects that a certain event has occurred with it

- **Subscription**: When an object is interested in an event, it "subscribes" to that event

- **Invocation**: The process of initiating an event by the object that generated it to notify subscribers about the event

Design patterns

This section delves into the realm of **design patterns** in software engineering, covering essentials such as singleton, factory method, strategy, prototype, adapter, and decorator patterns, each offering unique solutions for complex design challenges in object-oriented programming:

Singleton

- **Description**: A pattern that ensures the possibility of creating only one instance of a class and provides a global access point to this instance

- **Application**: Used for controlling access to resources, such as configuration managers, logging, or database connections

Factory Method

- **Description**: A pattern that allows delegating the object creation process to subclasses, ensuring flexibility and isolating the code from the specific types of created objects

- **Application**: Used when there are many classes in a system that belong to one group, but they can be dynamically changed or extended in the future

Strategy

- **Description**: A pattern that defines a family of algorithms, encapsulates each of them, and makes them interchangeable

- **Application**: Used when there are different behavior variations of a class and they can be switched on the fly during execution

Prototype

- **Description**: A pattern that allows for creating new objects by copying already existing ones

- **Application**: Used when creating a new instance of a class is resource-intensive or complex and it's more efficient to copy an existing object

Adapter

- **Description**: A pattern that allows objects with incompatible interfaces to work together

- **Application**: Used when there are classes in a system with different interfaces that need to be integrated to ensure their cooperation without changing the code of these classes

Decorator

- **Description**: A pattern that allows dynamically adding new responsibilities or behavior to objects without changing their structure

- **Application**: Used when there's a need to add functionality to objects on the fly, extending their capabilities with wrappers

Preparation strategies

In this section, we delve into proven preparation strategies to equip you with the skills and confidence needed to excel in your C# interviews.

Practice

- **Project development**: Create your own projects to enhance your hands-on experience and deep understanding of C#. This will also help you build a portfolio that you can showcase to potential employers.

- **Participation in hackathons**: These events allow you to work in a team, develop innovative solutions, and compete with other developers.

- **Exercise platforms**: Use platforms such as LeetCode and HackerRank to hone your skills in solving algorithmic problems and preparing for technical interviews.

Theoretical knowledge

- **Official documentation**: Always start with official sources. Documentation from Microsoft is the most accurate and up-to-date source of information about C#.

- **Courses from Microsoft**: These courses are often structured in a way that covers all the material from beginner to advanced levels and often include exercises that involve practically applying knowledge.

- **Books on C# and .NET**:

  - *C# 8.0 and .NET Core 3.0 – Modern Cross-Platform Development* by Mark J. Price

  - *Mastering C# and .NET Framework* by Marino Posadas

  - *C# Data Structures and Algorithms* by Marcin Jamro

- *Hands-On Network Programming with C# and .NET Core* by Tomasz Lelek
- Other books that focus on specific aspects of the C# programming language or the .NET platform in general can serve as a deep source of knowledge and insights for developers at all career stages

Soft skills

In this section, we examine essential soft skills that can significantly boost your interview, such as effective communication and adaptability:

Communication

- **Active listening**: Not just focusing on the words of the interlocutor, but understanding their emotions and motivations. A deep perception of voice tone, mood, as well as unspoken thoughts.
- **Clear articulation of thoughts**: The importance of brief and clear statements, the absence of redundant information, and the ability to persuade.
- **Non-verbal communication**: Understanding and using body language to reinforce or correct one's message.
- **Negotiation skills**: Understanding the opponent's psychology, preparing arguments, and being able to conclude the conversation beneficially for both parties.

Problem-solving

- **Situation analysis**: Studying the context of the problem, the interrelation of its elements, and the possible consequences of decisions
- **Logical thinking**: Applying deductive and inductive methods of thinking to find optimal solutions
- **Adaptability**: Flexibility in decision-making and readiness to change based on changing circumstances

Critical thinking

- **Information analysis**: Distinguishing between facts, opinions, and assumptions. Ability to determine the reliability of sources.
- **Skepticism**: The ability to reject accepted dogmas, ask "why?", and analyze context.
- **Exploring alternative approaches**: Ability to see the situation from different angles and look for unconventional solutions.

Interview simulation

- **Role-playing**: Replicating different interview scenarios, adapting to different types of interviewees
- **Analysis of common questions**: Studying questions that are frequently asked in interviews for various specialties and in different companies
- **Practice responses**: Developing scripts for answers to standard questions, as well as practicing adapting answers to the specific context of the interview
- **Feedback**: Involving professionals to evaluate your behavior and responses during mock interviews

Concluding our recap, it's essential to remember that mastering these key concepts and strategies is just the start. With a solid foundation now in place, you're well-positioned to build upon this knowledge, adapting and growing as you embark on your C# career journey.

In the next section, we delve into the first-hand accounts of C# interview experiences, providing an insightful glimpse into the real challenges and triumphs faced by developers. These stories not only enlighten us with practical knowledge but also showcase the diverse paths individuals take in their journey toward mastering C# programming.

Real-life examples of interview experiences and outcomes

Venturing into this segment, we'll traverse the real corridors of C# interview rooms, exploring genuine experiences and their outcomes. These narratives offer not just lessons but also a window into the practical world of C# interviews, bringing theory into tangible reality.

Every developer has their own unique journey to success. For some, it starts with a fascination with computer games or the development of simple software; for others, it's the desire to solve a specific problem or change the world. I invite you to join our stories and learn more about their initial steps into the world of C#.

Initial steps into the world of C#

How should a beginner developer approach learning C# and what are the most important first steps in this direction? This question is aimed at exploring the best practices for those who are just starting their journey in the world of C# programming.

- Tanya, C# developer

(https://www.linkedin.com/in/tanya-rybina-059a43242/)

I would say that beginners should learn essentials to achieve understanding how their code really works. With a solid understanding of essentials, you can write good, reliable code. They should start from learning about things like data types in CLR, what is stack and heap, OOP principles, SOLID principles, how different constructions like using statement and foreach works and asynchronous state machines. Also, for me, looking how C# works under the hood when it is compiled to IL was very interesting and it helped me better understand how my code works. When you know essentials, you can start learning about ASP.NET, MAUI, and other frameworks that you want to learn.

- Oleksii, full-stack C# developer

(`https://www.linkedin.com/in/oleksii-sokol-44b963197/`)

Everyone can share their successes, but who can share their failures? So I'll start with the failures. C# covers a very large range of technologies and capabilities. My biggest mistake was that I grabbed every job opportunity regardless of the technology stack. Therefore, I advise you to choose a target area for development, and without being distracted by other sweet jobs, improve your highly specialized profile and go for interviews on it. It may seem like it will take a long time, but if you scatter your attention on the entire spectrum of C# opportunities, it will take even more time, and as a result, you will be left with nothing.

- Yurii, C# developer

I do not believe there is a one-size-fits-all approach to learning. Some may find it easier to immerse themselves in books and read, while others may be more productive by taking online courses and learning from them. In my opinion, the first and crucial step would be to find a community where you can discuss what you are learning and learn from others' experiences. This significantly eases and accelerates progress. In addition, it is important not to forget that programming is a practical skill; you can only acquire it through hands-on practice.

In exploring C# interview experiences, we learned key lessons. Tanya highlights mastering fundamentals, Oleksii advises focusing on a specific C# area, and Yurii emphasizes community engagement and hands-on practice. These insights offer a roadmap for aspiring C# developers.

Technical preparation

Technical preparation is a key element in every developer's success. But with the vast amount of resources and information on the internet, how do you determine what's truly valuable? These stories unveil how some successful developers approached their technical preparation and how they keep their skills up to date:

- Tanya:

  I think you can determine which information is really good by the way it's written and who the author is. For example, good articles almost always have detailed explanations that are easy to understand, code samples, and schemes. I always try to find information written by experienced developers. Also, reading official documentation can be useful, but sometimes it is not enough and you want to know more. This is when these articles could be helpful. Books are a valuable source of information, but reading them requires a lot of time. It could be a great thing to do in your spare time.

- Oleksii:

  I would advise you to find an interesting field, but it should be a golden mean between something completely new and something from the dinosaur era. By studying old technologies, you run the risk that this technology will soon be out of support and you will have to learn a new one. Brand-new technologies may be unsustainable, and there will be very few job openings.

- Yurii:

  In preparation, it's important to understand your future role in the team and the specific technologies being used. Often, developers forget that the first call with HR is an opportunity to learn more about the project. Depending on the information gathered during communication, you can determine which technologies to highlight and where to focus less attention.

Tanya and Oleksii's insights on technical preparation reveal two key strategies: Tanya advocates for learning from experienced developers and diverse resources, while Oleksii suggests balancing between emerging and established technologies for a stable career path.

Soft skills and career growth

Soft skills have become an integral part of every professional's career, especially in the IT sector. While the emphasis used to be primarily on technical skills, today, understanding human psychology, effective communication, and teamwork are recognized as equally crucial:

- Tanya:

    Soft skills are very important when it comes to teamwork. I think these are the kinds of skills you could achieve only while working in a team. For me, key elements of good teamwork are understanding each other, being able to solve problems quickly, and the ability to assign tasks correctly among the team.

- Oleksii:

    I also had experience in finding people for the team. First of all, I pay attention to the person as a person. After all, I have to work with them, help them, and consult them on some issues. This person should be easy to communicate with, willing to learn, and able to accept criticism and their mistakes. However, technical knowledge and logical thinking are also important. You need to have a basic understanding of what you will be working with. And logical thinking will help you to easily join the work and master new knowledge.

    I know from my own experience that this is very important now. I had a situation where I passed the interview perfectly, but the team leader was bored and was looking for the same employee. But this is a two-way situation. You also have to evaluate the team you are working with. For me personally, it's not comfortable to work with bookworms, but for someone else it might be the other way around.

- Yurii:

    In one of my previous offices, there was a large sheet with bold letters saying "99% of problems are communication", and it's true! You can write very good code adhering to all architectural patterns, all well-known development principles, code that impresses the Gang of Four, but if it doesn't meet the client's requirements, it's worth nothing. That's why it's important to be able to listen to people, understand what they need, and be able to explain why they don't need what they think they do.

In discussing the role of soft skills in career growth, Tanya, Oleksii, and Yurii underscore their significance in IT. Tanya focuses on teamwork dynamics, Oleksii on personal attributes and logical thinking in team building, and Yurii on communication's pivotal role in meeting client requirements.

Tips from hiring managers

To feel confident during an interview and understand what a potential employer expects from you, it's essential to hear from hiring managers. What exactly are they looking for in a C# developer candidate? Which skills are essential, and how do you establish effective communication during an interview?

- Igor Tis, CEO at A1 Telecom LLC

(https://www.linkedin.com/in/a1telecom/)

> *When hiring, I primarily focus on assembling a team. In this process, soft skills are crucial for me. Hard skills are also important, but still, they are not the primary concern. I pay attention to whether a person is responsible and eager to learn. I am prepared to invest in people and allocate time for their development, but in return, I expect them to actively engage in this process. I believe that such employees are the best.*

- Maxim, technical recruiter:

> *One of the key recommendations I can give candidates is to prepare well for the interview. Research the company, familiarize yourself with its products and technologies. Regarding questions, we often ask about specific situations from a candidate's experience and how they approached and resolved them.*

- Iryna, head of development department:

> *When I conduct an interview, I'm interested in how the candidate thinks and how they approach problem-solving. Technical skills are good, but it's vital for a person to have critical thinking, responsibility, and a desire to grow.*

- Oleksandr, senior tech lead:

> *It's not just about knowing C# inside out; it's about understanding how it fits into the broader ecosystem. I look for candidates who can see the bigger picture, understand the business context, and can collaborate effectively with other departments. I also appreciate when they show curiosity about the latest tech trends and advancements in C# and the .NET ecosystem.*

As we close this section on real-life experiences, it's evident that every interview is a unique tapestry of challenges and opportunities. Embracing these stories, with their highs and lows, can equip you with a deeper understanding and preparedness for your own C# interview encounters.

In the next section, we explore hard-earned insights and guidance from seasoned industry professionals, offering a treasure trove of lessons and advice. Their stories, rich with challenges and achievements, provide a unique perspective, enhancing our understanding of the C# landscape.

Lessons learned and advice from industry professionals

Diving into this portion, we tap into the collective wisdom of industry veterans. Their journeys, replete with trials and triumphs, offer invaluable lessons and advice. It's like standing on the shoulders of giants, seeing further and clearer into the world of C# professionalism.

Work–life balance

In today's fast-paced life, where technology is changing day by day, developers often find themselves under pressure to complete projects on time, learn new technologies, and be constantly available. In this context, striking a balance between work and personal life becomes increasingly important.

Secrets to balance from successful developers

Let's explore how successful developers maintain a healthy work–life balance, focusing on techniques such as setting boundaries, mastering time management, and optimizing their working environment:

- **Setting boundaries**: It's essential to establish boundaries between work and relaxation. Some developers choose to turn off notifications after working hours or set specific times for when they "disconnect" from work.
- **Time management**: Effective planning allows for setting priorities and accomplishing tasks more productively. It also helps you carve out time for relaxation and leisure.
- **Working environment**: Organizing a workspace that promotes productivity can aid concentration and faster task completion.

Recommendations for managing stress and maintaining health

Let's discover key strategies for managing stress and staying healthy, covering essential practices such as regular physical activity, meditation, adequate rest, and maintaining social connections:

- **Physical activity**: Regular physical exercises can help combat stress, enhance mood, and improve overall health
- **Meditation and relaxation**: Relaxation and meditation techniques can be beneficial in reducing stress levels and enhancing focus
- **Rest**: Adequate sleep and regular breaks throughout the day are key to replenishing energy and maintaining high productivity levels
- **Social connections**: Interacting with friends, family, or colleagues outside of work can be a great way to relax and divert from work-related matters.

Evolving with the industry

With the rapid technological advancements, it's essential for developers to keep up with the latest trends and changes in the C# landscape.

Here are some tips for staying updated:

- **Continuous learning**: Dedicate specific hours each week to research and self-study. Subscribe to C# journals, follow industry blogs, and join forums or discussion groups.

- **Attending workshops and conferences**: Networking with peers and experts can provide insights into best practices and upcoming trends.

- **Collaborative projects**: Working with other developers on open source projects can introduce you to new methods, tools, and coding standards.

- **Feedback loop**: Always seek feedback on your code from senior developers or peers. It can be a great way to identify areas of improvement.

Building a strong foundation

While keeping up with the latest trends is crucial, mastering the basics of C# remains paramount.

The key foundations every C# developer should focus on include:

- **Data structures and algorithms**: These are the backbone of problem-solving in programming. They not only help in coding interviews but also in building efficient software.

- **Design patterns**: Familiarize yourself with common design patterns used in C#. This will help you write more modular and maintainable code.

- **Debugging skills**: A significant portion of a developer's time is spent debugging. Mastering tools and techniques can drastically reduce the time needed to identify and fix bugs.

Harnessing soft skills

Technical prowess is just one side of the coin. Soft skills play an equally significant role in a developer's career.

The following are the critical soft skills to develop:

- **Communication**: Explaining technical concepts to non-technical stakeholders is a frequent challenge. Effective communication can lead to better collaboration and project outcomes.

- **Teamwork**: A developer rarely works in isolation. Understanding team dynamics and working well with others can accelerate project timelines.

- **Problem-solving**: Beyond just coding, it's about finding efficient solutions to real-world challenges.

Navigating career progression

C# developers, like all professionals, should be keen on scaling their careers. Here's how you can advance:

- **Specializations**: Consider diving deeper into areas such as C# game development, enterprise applications, or mobile app development using Xamarin.

- **Certifications**: Seek out certifications in C# or related technologies. Microsoft offers various certification programs that can add weight to your CV.

- **Mentorship**: Actively seek mentors in your field or offer mentorship to junior developers. This exchange can provide new insights and perspectives.

Efficient coding practices

Writing code is a craft. The more efficient your code, the better the software's performance and maintainability:

- **Code reviews**: Regularly participate in code review sessions. Giving and receiving feedback can significantly improve code quality.

- **Refactoring**: Don't be afraid to revisit and refactor old code. It's essential for maintaining code health and incorporating new best practices.

- **Automated testing**: Embrace **test-driven development** (TDD). Ensure that your code has adequate unit tests to maintain robustness.

Adapting to remote work

The world is increasingly moving toward remote work. Being proficient in this setup can be advantageous:

- **Digital communication tools**: Familiarize yourself with tools such as Microsoft Teams, Slack, and Zoom. Efficiently using these tools can improve collaboration.

- **Time-zoning**: If working with global teams, be conscious of time zones. Schedule meetings and deadlines keeping in mind the convenience of all team members.

- **Self-discipline**: Remote work demands a higher level of self-discipline. Establishing daily routines and designating a specific workspace at home can aid focus and productivity.

In the world of C# development, the amalgamation of hard technical skills and soft interpersonal skills can lead to unparalleled success. Embracing lifelong learning and fostering a growth mindset will ensure that you remain at the forefront of this ever-evolving field. Let the insights of experts be the guiding light, illuminating your path toward mastery in the C# realm.

Concluding our exploration of expert insights, it's imperative to internalize that the path to mastery is often paved with shared wisdom. May the lessons and advice from these seasoned professionals guide you, acting as a compass in your endeavors within the C# landscape.

In the next section, we delve into the dynamic world of C# development, examining the constant evolution of technology and industry trends. Discover how professionals in this field adapt to these changes, staying ahead in a rapidly shifting landscape.

Adapting to industry changes and emerging technologies

As we pivot to this section, we acknowledge the fluidity of the tech landscape. In a realm where change is the only constant, understanding how to adapt to industry shifts and embrace emerging technologies become paramount. Let's delve into the strategies and foresights that keep C# professionals ahead of the curve.

The modern programming world is always in motion. With the advent of new technologies, platforms, and tools, developers are faced with new challenges and opportunities. Here's a deeper look into some of the main challenges and trends in C# development.

Trends and challenges

Explore the latest trends and challenges in C# development, including mastering CI/CD, adapting to microservices, and integrating with cloud platforms such as Azure and AWS:

- **Continuous integration and continuous delivery/deployment** (**CI/CD**): Automating processes has become a key element of development. C# developers need to master CI/CD tools to optimize their workflows.

- **Microservices**: With the growing popularity of microservice architecture, C# developers must understand how to create and maintain independent services.

- **Integration with cloud platforms**: Cloud solutions, such as Azure or AWS, are becoming increasingly common. Mastery of working with cloud platforms is becoming crucial for the modern developer.

- **Application security**: With the rise in cybercrimes, application security has become a priority. Developers need to be informed about security measures and apply them in their projects.

Adapting to change

Explore how C# developers can keep up with the fast-paced tech industry through continuous learning, community involvement, and adaptation to new technologies:

- **Learning and self-improvement**: One of the keys to adaptation is continuous learning. Developers should keep an eye on new trends, tools, and methodologies.

- **Community participation**: Interacting with peers and attending conferences and workshops can help you acquire new knowledge and keep your skills up to date.

- **Flexibility**: It's crucial to be ready for changes and quickly adapt to the new technological landscape. Being flexible helps developers remain competitive in the market.

Drawing this segment to a close, it's evident that adaptability and foresight are invaluable assets in the tech world. Being anchored in the present while having an eye on the future ensures that you remain relevant and innovative in the evolving panorama of C# and related technologies.

The future of C# and career growth opportunities

Shifting our gaze forward, this section beckons us to the horizon of C# and its evolving role in the tech landscape. In a world where the future is crafted by today's innovations, let's explore the promising trajectory of C# and the expansive career opportunities it presents.

The .NET platform and the C# programming language have come a long way since their inception, evolving and adapting to contemporary development challenges. With constant updates and adaptations from Microsoft and the developer community, exciting innovations can be expected in the future.

Forecasts for future developments

C# and .NET are likely to evolve with deeper cloud integration, expanded cross-platform capabilities, and enhanced support for emerging technologies such as AI, ML, and IoT:

- **Greater integration with cloud technologies**: With the rise of cloud solutions such as Azure, one can expect that C# and .NET will integrate even deeper with cloud services, enabling developers to create efficient and scalable applications.

- **Shift to cross-platform development**: With the launch of .NET 8, Microsoft has already focused on cross-platform development. This trend is expected to continue, making .NET an even more versatile solution for development.

- **Support for new programming approaches**: With advancements in artificial intelligence, machine learning, and the Internet of Things, greater support for these directions in the C# language and the .NET platform can be anticipated.

- **Generative AI and Azure AI integration**: The integration of Generative AI with Azure AI is poised to have a significant impact on various sectors. This integration is expected to influence the development in C# and .NET, leading to a focus on applications that leverage AI's capabilities for content generation, predictive analytics, and personalization. The emphasis will be on creating technologically advanced, yet ethically responsible applications that align with societal needs. This shift underscores the growing importance of AI in software development and the evolving role of C# and .NET in this AI-augmented future.

New technologies or approaches to study

Exploring the latest advancements in .NET 8, this section delves into revolutionary technologies that are shaping the future of C# development:

- **Blazor**: This new technology allows for the development of interactive web applications in C# without using JavaScript. Its popularity continues to grow and might become crucial for .NET web developers.

- **Microsoft Orleans**: A pivotal framework in .NET 8 for creating scalable, distributed applications, Orleans extends traditional C# paradigms to complex, multi-server environments, streamlining the development of cloud-native apps.

- **ML.NET**: This machine learning framework from Microsoft allows for the integration of machine learning models directly into your C# applications.

- **Mobile development**: With tools such as Xamarin or **Multi-platform App UI** (**MAUI**), C# developers can create high-quality mobile apps for various platforms.

- **.NET Aspire**: This is a cloud-ready stack for building observable, production-ready, distributed applications delivered through a collection of NuGet packages.

- **Semantic-Kernel**: This is an SDK that integrates **Large Language Models** (**LLMs**) like OpenAI, Azure OpenAI, and Hugging Face with conventional programming languages like C# and, provide ability to automatically orchestrate plugins with AI.

In addition to these, developers should also keep an eye on any emerging technologies that Microsoft or the broader community introduce. Continuous learning and adapting are crucial in the ever-evolving world of technology. The collaboration between Microsoft and the open source community also suggests that more community-driven enhancements and features will shape the future of C# and .NET, offering a broader set of tools and capabilities for developers worldwide.

As we conclude our journey into the future prospects of C#, it's evident that the language, and the ecosystem around it, holds immense potential. With a blend of dedication, learning, and adaptability, the doors to myriad career growth opportunities in the C# domain stand wide open for you to seize.

Summary

Your journey through the C# interview guide has equipped you with a treasure trove of knowledge and understanding, setting you on the path to not just succeeding in C# interviews but also flourishing in your chosen career. As technologies evolve and the world of C# programming shifts, it will be your adaptability, continuous learning, and passion that will set you apart.

As you move forward, remember the insights shared by experienced professionals and the real-world stories of trials and triumphs and, more importantly, believe in your capabilities and potential. The world of C# offers vast opportunities; it's now up to you to harness them and script your success story. Safe travels on your C# career journey!

In the final chapter, we will consolidate all the insights and strategies discussed, offering a comprehensive wrap-up and additional tips to ensure you're fully prepared to excel in your C# career journey with a robust understanding and readiness for the dynamic field of programming.

11

Launching Your C# Career – Insights

Job interviews in the realm of C# development can often seem daunting. But remember—the interview itself is just a piece of the puzzle. The steps you take afterward can significantly shape your career journey. This chapter aims to be your guiding light on what lies beyond the interview room.

We'll delve into several crucial aspects that can set you apart and pave the path for a thriving career in C# programming:

- **Following up after the interview**: Ensure you leave a lasting impression and establish a continued relationship with potential employers

- **Celebrating your accomplishments and embracing challenges**: Recognize your achievements, big or small, and learn how to tackle obstacles with resilience

- **Building a successful career as a C# developer**: Dive into strategies and practices that can propel your career forward

- **Utilizing the C# Interview Guide as a long-term resource**: Discover how this guide can be more than just an interview prep tool and serve as a continuous learning companion

- **Setting personal and professional goals for your career**: Map out your aspirations and set tangible milestones for your growth

- **Exploring career paths and specializations in the C# ecosystem**: Find out the numerous avenues and niches within the C# world that can resonate with your passion

- **Staying up to date with industry trends and developments**: Equip yourself with knowledge on the evolving landscape of C# and the tech industry at large

With these focal points in mind, this chapter is tailored to provide you with a holistic view, ensuring you're well equipped to not only tackle interviews but also to flourish in your C# career post-interview.

Following up after the interview

As we delve into the first section, we'll emphasize the art of following up post-interview. While the conversation during the interview is pivotal, what you do after can significantly influence an employer's perception of you. Let's explore strategies to ensure you leave a lasting impression and lay the groundwork for a sustained relationship.

Delving into the psychology of celebration

In the rich tapestry of life's experiences, there exists a unique, radiant thread: the act of celebrating. Whether it's completing a challenging project or simply writing a flawless piece of code, every achievement warrants a moment of appreciation. When we take a moment to appreciate our successes, we're not just patting ourselves on the back—we're engaging in a deeply psychological act.

Each time we celebrate, our brain releases dopamine, often dubbed the "happiness hormone." This potent chemical is linked to feelings of pleasure, satisfaction, and motivation. The more we acknowledge and celebrate our achievements, the more we reinforce these positive emotions. Over time, this creates a psychological pattern—a mindset that's inherently optimistic and resilient. This state of mind becomes our shield, empowering us to weather challenges and setbacks with greater ease.

Diverse modalities of celebration

The beauty of celebration lies in its boundless diversity. When you say "celebration," the immediate imagery might be of grand parties or ceremonies. But in reality, some of the most profound moments of recognition are quiet and introspective. Perhaps it's taking a moment to enjoy your favorite pastry, giving yourself a day off to rejuvenate, or diving deep into a hobby you love. The crux of celebration isn't in its grandiosity but in acknowledging the journey and being thankful for the milestones achieved.

Sharing these moments amplifies their significance. Celebrating with colleagues, mentors, or team members not only heightens the joy but also fosters a culture of mutual appreciation—a cornerstone for a thriving, positive professional environment.

Navigating the inevitable ups and downs – understanding the learning curve of challenges

The dynamic tech realm, with its rapid advancements, is no stranger to challenges. But rather than viewing them as roadblocks, it's more constructive to see them as stepping stones—each one paving the way to greater knowledge and capability.

Carol Dweck, a leading psychologist, introduced the concept of the **growth mindset**. She emphasized that intelligence and skills aren't stagnant; with the right attitude, they can be nurtured and enhanced. Through this lens, challenges aren't hindrances. They are opportunities—opportunities to learn, innovate, and evolve. When we adopt this perspective, every hurdle becomes a lesson in disguise, propelling us forward on our professional journey.

Proactive strategies for facing and embracing challenges head-on

Facing a challenge can initially seem daunting. However, with the right set of tools and approaches, what seems intimidating can be systematically addressed:

- **Break it down**: When confronted with a complex issue, simplify it. Segment the problem into smaller, digestible parts. By tackling each segment individually, the larger problem becomes less overwhelming.

- **Seek expertise**: There's immense value in shared knowledge. Approach experienced peers or mentors; their perspectives can provide novel solutions and pathways.

- **Collaborative problem-solving**: Two heads are often better than one. Engage in group brainstorming sessions. The synergy of collective thinking frequently yields innovative outcomes.

- **Lifelong learning**: The tech domain is ever-evolving. Continuous education, be it through formal courses, workshops, or personal study, is paramount. Regularly updating your skills ensures you remain agile and ready to meet and surmount any challenge.

By employing these strategies, one can transform challenges into opportunities for growth, ensuring that each obstacle encountered is not a roadblock but a stepping stone to greater success.

Delving deeper into the art of following up

Emerging from an interview often feels like you've completed a marathon, but in truth, there's still a lap to go. The post-interview follow-up, often perceived as a mere formality, is far from it. It's a testament to your keenness and sincerity toward the position you've interviewed for. More than this, it stands as a reflection of your professional integrity, emphasizing the regard you hold for the interviewer's time and effort. But diving even deeper, it's a demonstration of your grasp on business communication's finer subtleties and decorum.

The essence of timing – harnessing the momentum

Timing, in the context of a follow-up, isn't merely about watching the clock. It's about capturing the essence of the interview while it's still fresh, for both you and the interviewer. The optimal window? Ideally, it's between 24 to 48 hours post-interview. By reaching out within this period, you exude enthusiasm and commitment yet sidestep the pitfalls of seeming desperate.

Meticulously crafting your follow-up message

Underneath an impactful follow-up message lies a trifecta of core principles—expressing gratitude, introspective reflection, and projecting forward-looking insights. While thanking the interviewer lays the foundational brick, to truly set your message apart, you must dig deeper. Forge a note that extends beyond the generic "thank you." Recall what truly stood out about the job or company ethos that resonated with you during the discussion. If any aspect of the conversation sparked a fresh insight or realization afterward, incorporate that. Authenticity is the compass that should guide your words.

Opening doors for expanded dialog

The beauty of the follow-up lies in its potential to be more than just a concluding note—it's an invitation to continue the dialog. Perhaps there's a facet of the job that's caught your fascination, warranting further discussion. Or a certain company practice piques your curiosity, prompting you to seek more clarity. Maybe there's a particular question you responded to during the interview, and upon reflection, you'd like to expand or refine your answer. Utilize your follow-up to articulate these thoughts, showcasing your eagerness to engage and understand.

Strategically emphasizing your compatibility with the role

Concluding our journey on mastering follow-ups, let's shift our focus to an often-overlooked but crucial element: echoing your fitment for the role. This isn't about reiterating what's on your resume. It's about recollecting those moments during the interview when you truly felt a synergy with the role's requirements and the company's ethos. Pinpoint and emphasize those instances. By doing so, you're not merely underscoring your attentiveness, but you're crafting a narrative—one that seamlessly intertwines your professional trajectory with the company's overarching vision, signifying not just a fit of skills but of values and purpose.

Delving into the essence of unwavering professionalism

Launching a career in the C# domain—or any professional arena, for that matter—requires more than technical prowess. Each interaction, especially seemingly minor ones such as follow-ups, becomes a testament to your professionalism. But let's delve deeper. Professionalism isn't merely about selecting apt words; it encompasses the whole spectrum—from the tone you adopt to the aesthetics of your message and even its structure. Aim for a harmonious blend—a tone that, while formal, exudes a touch of warmth. It should come across as courteous yet engaging. Every message is a reflection of your diligence, so thorough proofreading is paramount. What sets a professional follow-up apart is its subtlety; it should radiate understanding, respect, and a keen desire to extend the dialog without appearing desperate.

Deciphering the enigma of unanswered follow-ups

The echo of silence post a follow-up can often be more deafening than an actual critique. Naturally, everyone yearns for some acknowledgment, some feedback. However, silence isn't always indicative of disinterest. There's a myriad of possible reasons: from an overloaded inbox to an internal process delay. Rather than plunging into a spiral of overthinking, equip your approach with tact. Maybe after a week, a gentle nudge or a reminder can be sent. But discernment is key. Sometimes, the most professional stance is to recognize the silence, introspect, and recalibrate your strategies. Perseverance is the mantra, but it should be interspersed with respect and empathy.

Harnessing the power of diverse digital communication avenues

The digital realm has broadened the horizons of professional communication. Beyond the traditional email, platforms such as LinkedIn have evolved into pivotal conduits for professional rapport-building. But how can a C# developer or any professional leverage these mediums post-interview? Consider dispatching a succinct thank you note via LinkedIn, accentuating pivotal discussion highlights. It not only reiterates your gratitude but also underscores your attentiveness. Furthermore, sharing or commenting on content pertinent to the interview's themes can subtly underscore your commitment and knowledge. However, tread with caution. The digital domain demands discretion. Every engagement should uphold the tenets of relevance and professionalism, steering clear of being overly familiar or invasive.

Adopting a panoramic perspective on follow-ups

Detail-orientedness is a virtue, especially when fashioning a follow-up. However, it's pivotal not to lose sight of the broader landscape. Follow-ups, in the grand scheme of things, aren't definitive deciders but facilitators in the job acquisition journey. Their primary role? Keeping the candidate in the interviewer's mental forefront, addressing any residual ambiguities, and cementing a favorable lasting impression. Essentially, the emphasis of a follow-up isn't purely on instantaneous gains. Instead, it's about meticulously crafting and consistently projecting a professional persona, one that potential employers respect and value.

To wrap up this section, remember that the post-interview phase is an integral part of your job application journey. The way you follow up can be the defining factor in differentiating yourself from other candidates. A thoughtful, timely response not only showcases your professionalism but also reaffirms your genuine interest in the role. With the right approach, you can seamlessly transition from being a candidate to a potential team member from an employer's perspective.

As we turn the page from the meticulous art of follow-ups to the vibrant narrative of career evolution, we see a common thread: the celebration of milestones and the strategic navigation of hurdles. This seamless thread weaves together the fabric of professional growth, underscoring the importance of both recognizing our victories and facing our challenges with courage and resilience.

Celebrating your accomplishments and embracing challenges

Venturing into this next segment, we'll focus on the dual aspects of career progression: celebrating successes and confronting challenges. Every milestone, whether it appears grand or minuscule, deserves acknowledgment. Equally, navigating through challenges is an art that demands resilience. Let's dive into understanding the balance of these two facets.

Fortifying resilience for long-term success

Resilience isn't just a buzzword in the realm of personal growth—it's the very fabric that can decide how we handle the multifaceted rollercoaster of our careers. Imagine resilience as the bedrock upon which your professional journey thrives. But how does one cultivate this resilience?

A crucial element in nurturing resilience is the foundation of a reliable support system. Just as a tree relies on the soil and sun, we need a support system comprised of mentors who offer wisdom, peers who share experiences, and friends who lend an understanding ear. These relationships play a pivotal role in helping us navigate the stormy waters of challenging professional times.

Furthermore, the time-tested techniques of mindfulness, including meditation, deep breathing, and grounding exercises, have emerged as invaluable tools. These practices anchor us, providing the stability required during tumultuous career phases. It's also essential to recognize the importance of self-care. Delving into activities outside the workplace, such as indulging in a calming nature walk or exploring hobbies such as painting, can act as rejuvenating respites, offering much-needed boosts to our resilience levels.

The power of reflective recollection on past hurdles

In the midst of pressing deadlines and evolving challenges, it's easy to lose sight of past triumphs. However, revisiting these moments isn't just about nostalgia—it's a strategy for empowerment. Periodically pausing to reflect on past challenges allows us to derive valuable insights. Think of these past adversities not as obstacles but as the very steps you've scaled toward growth. By consciously revisiting, dissecting, and understanding them, we reframe our perspective, viewing challenges not as barriers but as enablers of our evolution.

Striking a balance with well-defined boundaries

Boundless enthusiasm and a spirit that tirelessly tackles challenges are admirable traits. However, they must be accompanied by a clear understanding of one's limits. It's paramount to recognize and respect our mental and emotional thresholds. This understanding paves the way for setting boundaries. Think of these boundaries as your personal guardians, protecting you from overwhelming stress, potential burnout, and mental fatigue. These protective measures could range from assigning specific offline hours, ensuring you take breaks during a hectic day, or even delineating work hours to prevent encroachments into personal time.

Feedback as the beacon of growth and recognition

Feedback, if perceived correctly, is akin to the North Star—guiding, illuminating, and directing our professional voyage. It's vital to not just passively receive feedback but actively seek it. Embrace positive feedback as tokens of recognition and affirmation. On the other hand, constructive criticism, if viewed with an open heart and mind, provides signposts for areas that require attention, enabling us to grow and refine our skills.

Chronicle of professional evolution – documenting milestones and hurdles

In this fast-paced digital age, there's an understated beauty in pausing to document our journey. Whether through traditional journals, diaries, or even contemporary digital portfolios, maintaining a record of your career trajectory is invaluable. This record becomes a testament to your growth—highlighting achievements, underscoring challenges, and elucidating lessons. Beyond its role as a reflective tool, this chronicle serves as a beacon for the future, pointing out areas that merit attention and underscoring the journey's milestones.

Holistic well-being as a pillar of professional success

In the quest to build a successful C# career, the importance of holistic well-being cannot be overstated. This goes beyond the code you write or the projects you complete. It's about nurturing every aspect of your existence—mind, body, and spirit. A balanced lifestyle becomes the foundation for professional excellence. Advise your readers to integrate routines that cater to their mental, physical, and emotional health. Activities such as regular exercise, maintaining a balanced diet, and indulging in hobbies such as reading, music, or art significantly amplify one's overall wellness. When you're balanced, you approach challenges from a place of strength and serenity, and your ability to bounce back from setbacks is greatly amplified.

The role of continuous learning and upgradation

Staying static in a dynamic field such as software development is a sure recipe for obsolescence. Underscore the importance of persistent learning for career longevity. Beyond traditional classroom learning or obtaining certifications, the digital age offers myriad avenues: webinars, workshops, online courses, and even casual tech discussions. Investing in these channels ensures you're always a step ahead, with fresh insights and skills at your disposal. Moreover, this consistent learning not only refines your technical skills but also boosts your self-assuredness, arming you to tackle professional challenges head-on.

Cultivating a growth ecosystem

A lone journey, no matter how talented the traveler, has its limitations. Look beyond solo growth and tap into the collective wisdom of communities. Encourage them to participate actively in forums, online groups, or local meetups centered on C# or broader software development themes. These platforms serve as goldmines of shared knowledge, experiences, and inspiration. By immersing themselves in such vibrant ecosystems, they'll find avenues for collaborative growth, peer support, and innovative solutions to challenges they might face.

Embracing change with agility

In the tech world, change is not just constant; it's rapid. Adaptability becomes a crucial skill. Instead of resisting change or viewing it with apprehension, encourage a perspective shift. Cultivate a mindset of agility—a nimbleness that empowers one to pivot in response to evolving scenarios. This mental pliability can transform perceived threats of change into exciting opportunities, unveiling new horizons of innovation and career growth.

Concluding this section, it's crucial to internalize that both accomplishments and challenges are instrumental in carving out your professional journey. Celebrating your wins fuels motivation, while embracing challenges fosters growth. Harnessing both aspects, you're equipping yourself to navigate the dynamic landscape of the tech world with poise and confidence.

Bridging from embracing change to specialized career development, let's now apply our agile mindset to mastering C# development, where strategic practices are as vital as coding prowess for long-term success.

Building a successful career as a C# developer

As we transition into this segment, we're shifting our focus toward the broader horizon: building a fruitful career in C# development. Beyond just coding skills, there are strategies and practices that can act as catalysts for your career trajectory. Let's delve into these nuances to establish a strong foundation for success.

Deep diving into the basics of C#

Every seasoned developer knows the inestimable worth of a solid foundation. C#, being a versatile and vast language, offers myriad features and tools that might entice newcomers to dive straight into its depths. However, to truly navigate these waters with finesse, one needs to anchor themselves in its basics. Repeatedly revisiting core concepts such as variables, data types, control structures, and **object-oriented (OO)** principles is paramount. As the ecosystem of C# grows and newer tools and frameworks burgeon, possessing a robust foundational knowledge ensures you can weave these into your skill set without confusion or overwhelming adaptation.

The journey of never-ending learning

Just as a river continually flows, so does the stream of knowledge in the technological realm. With C# being at the forefront of many innovations, any developer claiming proficiency in it must dedicate themselves to lifelong learning. It's not enough to be a passive recipient of knowledge. Actively seek out the latest in C#, from emerging updates to nascent best practices. Whether you're enrolling in an advanced online course, attending workshops, or rubbing shoulders with industry leaders at C# conferences, the aim should be clear: continuous growth and evolution. Embrace a culture of curiosity and perpetual learning.

Beyond coding – the art of soft skills and interpersonal communication

A potent code is one thing; articulating its essence to a non-technical team member or fostering harmonious teamwork is another. The C# developers of today need more than just technical acumen; they require a blend of soft skills that are often underemphasized. From clear communication and an empathetic approach to team dynamics to robust problem-solving abilities—these soft skills can often be the linchpin of a project's success. Sharpening these skills isn't just a nice-to-have but a necessity, especially when working in diverse, multifunctional teams. Balance your technical prowess with these interpersonal talents to become a holistic developer.

Building bridges through networking

While lines of code construct programs, connections construct opportunities. The realm of C# isn't isolated; it's a vibrant, interlinked ecosystem. Engaging with fellow developers, industry experts, and enthusiasts brings forth myriad advantages—be it a fresh perspective, job prospects, or collaborative undertakings. How does one build these connections authentically? From participating in local C# meetups, sparking or joining debates on online platforms, to flaunting your skills in hackathons, every interaction is a step toward widening your professional circle. Engage, interact, and integrate yourself into the community.

The two-way street of mentorship

Embarking on the C# odyssey can sometimes be daunting. Having a seasoned traveler—a mentor—to guide can illuminate the path. A mentor doesn't just provide technical guidance but also invaluable insights, shortcuts, and, sometimes, foresight into potential hurdles. But mentorship isn't a one-dimensional journey. Becoming a mentor offers its own set of rewards – the satisfaction of shaping another's journey, refreshing one's own understanding, and the unique perspectives a mentee can offer. Whether you're seeking guidance or offering it, mentorship in the C# community is a bond of shared growth and mutual evolution. Seek out stories or real-life examples, and you'll find countless testimonials of its transformative power.

Broadening your technological horizons

In the dynamic world of technology, expertise in a single programming language, albeit a powerful one such as C#, isn't enough. Think of your technical skills as an ever-growing toolbox. While C# might be the primary tool, integrating others can elevate your craft. For instance, understanding databases isn't just about storing and retrieving data; it's about optimizing backend operations, ensuring data integrity, and crafting efficient queries. Similarly, dipping your toes into frontend technologies such as JavaScript, HTML, or CSS bridges the gap between the backend logic and the user experience, offering a comprehensive perspective on full-stack development. In today's world of ubiquity, familiarity with cloud platforms can empower you to architect scalable and resilient applications. By embracing this wider technological horizon, a C# developer can position themselves as a multifaceted asset in the industry.

Finding your niche in C# development

C# is not a monolith but a mosaic of myriad possibilities. The language serves as the backbone for diverse platforms and applications. For gaming aficionados, Unity offers a playground to craft immersive experiences. Enterprise-level applications value C# for its robustness and scalability. And with frameworks such as Xamarin, mobile application development is at your fingertips. But here lies the perennial conundrum: to specialize or generalize? Specializing lets you dive deep, becoming the go-to expert in a specific domain, while generalizing offers breadth, allowing you to wear multiple hats across projects. It's a choice between depth and breadth, and understanding this balance can help aspiring developers tailor their learning journey and career aspirations.

Your career's showcase – the portfolio

Every artist has a portfolio, and coders are no exception. Beyond the lines of code, a portfolio narrates your story – challenges you've tackled, solutions you've architected, and the impact you've forged. When creating a portfolio, it's not just about listing projects. It's about showcasing your problem-solving prowess, elucidating the intricacies of your implementation, and presenting testimonials that vouch for your skills. A well-curated portfolio resonates with potential employers or clients, often speaking volumes more than a standard resume. It's the bridge between your skills and the world, making the abstract tangible.

Striking harmony between work and life

In the adrenaline rush of coding sprints and project deadlines, it's easy to blur the lines between work and life. But remember – sustained excellence isn't birthed from constant exertion but from rhythmic cycles of work and rest. Punctuate your coding sessions with breaks, allowing the mind to rejuvenate. Engage in hobbies outside the coding realm; they not only refresh you but often offer a new lens to view problems. Prioritize physical well-being; a healthy body is the sanctum for a vibrant mind. Nurturing this harmony isn't a luxury but a necessity for a lasting, creative, and fulfilling career.

The loop of growth – feedback and introspection

Personal growth in a developer's journey isn't linear; it's iterative. It's a cycle of action, reflection, feedback, and improvement. Regular introspection helps pinpoint strengths and areas longing for enhancement. However, the mirror of self-reflection is often complemented by external feedback. Seeking perspectives from peers, mentors, or users can provide insights that might elude self-assessment. And once you gather this knowledge, it's not about brooding but about actionable improvement. Throughout the annals of tech, countless developers have harnessed this loop to refine their skills, leading to career milestones and enriched job satisfaction. Embrace this loop; it's the compass guiding you toward uncharted territories of proficiency.

Wrapping up this part, it's evident that being a successful C# developer is an amalgamation of technical prowess, strategic planning, and continuous learning. As you integrate these strategies and practices into your professional journey, you're positioning yourself to not only adapt but thrive in the ever-evolving world of C# development.

Moving forward, we shift our lens from the foundational aspects of career building to the practical tools that support it. The *C# Interview Guide*, often seen as a key for interview preparation, is also a treasure trove of insights for sustained career development.

Utilizing the C# Interview Guide as a long-term resource

Navigating through this section, we'll reconsider the very resource you're holding: a C# interview guide. While its immediate purpose may seem interview-centric, its utility stretches far beyond. Let's uncover how this guide can evolve into a long-term ally, accompanying you throughout various phases of your career.

Solid grounding and periodic reinforcement

In the realm of software development, the journey begins with a solid understanding of the basics. This guide is crafted to be a lighthouse for both beginners embarking on their voyage into the C# ocean and seasoned developers seeking to revisit their foundational knowledge. The core principles of any language form the bedrock upon which all advanced concepts stand. Whether you're a novice grasping the syntax for the first time or a veteran brushing up before a new project, this guide ensures that the bedrock remains unshaken and clear, offering an anchoring touchpoint for your developmental endeavors.

Transcending the boundaries of interviews

While the title might suggest an emphasis on interviews, this guide's canvas stretches far beyond that. Yes – it's meticulously sculpted to make you ace those interviews, but its essence permeates the everyday life of a developer. It's about the rhythm of regular coding, the art of untangling intricate problems, and the science behind constructing monumental software architectures. This guide is a reflection of real-world challenges and solutions, positioning itself as more than just interview prep; it's a compass for the holistic journey of a developer.

From theory to practice – case studies and grounded scenarios

One can only understand the depth of a river by diving into it. Similarly, this guide plunges into the world of practical scenarios, drawing from a reservoir of case studies that mirror real-world challenges. These scenarios aren't mere academic exercises but reflections of dilemmas and problems developers face in their daily grind. Dissecting these cases arms readers with the analytical prowess and strategies needed to navigate similar waters in their coding voyages, bridging the gap between theoretical knowledge and practical application.

Comprehensive coding repository – samples and excellence paradigms

Code, in its essence, is a tale of solutions told in a structured syntax. This guide treasures a myriad of such tales, presenting a plethora of code samples, design patterns, and distilled best practices of C#. These samples are chronicles of years of experience, refined over countless iterations. They aren't just placeholders; they're embodiments of coding excellence. For a budding developer, they provide direction, and for seasoned coders, they stand as benchmarks of quality, casting light on the nuances of crafting code that's both artful and efficient.

Intensive exploration of niche domains

The world of C# is not flat; it's a multidimensional universe with varied landscapes. This guide recognizes that and dives deep into specific terrains of advanced development. Far from being cursory glances, these sections are rigorous explorations into the intricacies of niche domains. As you advance in your career, the problems you face will demand more nuanced solutions. It's in these moments of challenge that these deep dives come to the fore, shedding light on advanced techniques and methodologies and empowering you to tackle the most intricate of problems with confidence and clarity.

Extensive supplementary materials and deep-dive recommendations

At the end of each section in this guide, you'll encounter a treasure of supplementary materials that serve as gateways to further enrich your knowledge landscape. These bibliographies, which encompass seminal papers, groundbreaking articles, and pivotal books, are not merely tossed in; they have been judiciously selected to elevate your journey. Diving into these resources introduces you to more intricate facets of the domain, carving out pathways to specialized learning and expertise. As you tread these paths, your foundational knowledge is not only expanded but honed to perfection.

Adapting to the times – periodic refinements and enhancements

C# is a dynamic ecosystem, continuously growing and adapting. This guide mirrors that vitality by undergoing periodic refinements to resonate with the latest in the world of C#. From integrating recent innovations and best practices to encapsulating fresh trends, the guide is in a perpetual state of evolution. This undying spirit of adaptability ensures you're not just holding a static tome but a living, breathing chronicle that's always in step with the current beats of the C# realm.

Interactive community engagement and collective wisdom

Beyond the pages of this guide lies a bustling community of like-minded enthusiasts, ever eager to share, learn, and grow. If you haven't yet, dive into this vibrant pool of shared wisdom. Engage, debate, seek clarifications, and offer insights. The advantages of being part of such a collective are manifold – you're exposed to diverse viewpoints, receive timely updates, and can tap into the expertise of seasoned professionals. This guide, in essence, isn't just a standalone entity but a gateway to an expansive knowledge ecosystem.

A canvas for personal insights – annotations and reflections

While this guide offers a structured journey through C#, it also beckons you to paint your narrative. As you traverse its sections, don't hesitate to mark the margins with your musings, insights, or even questions. By doing so, you're not just consuming knowledge but also etching your unique learning trajectory onto its pages. Over time, this becomes more than just a guide; it evolves into a personalized chronicle, capturing the essence of your growth and epiphanies.

Your pocket-sized knowledge companion

One of the standout attributes of this guide is its sheer accessibility. Whether it's resting on your bookshelf, snugly fit in your backpack, or a quick tap away on your digital device, its wealth of knowledge is always within arm's reach. This omnipresence means you're never too far from a quick revision, a deep dive, or a spur-of-the-moment learning session. It's akin to having a wise mentor perennially by your side, ever-ready to guide, challenge, and enlighten, making every moment an opportunity for growth.

To conclude this segment, it's clear that the *C# Interview Guide*'s value isn't confined to just interview preparations. By continually referring to and building upon its insights, you ensure that it remains an evergreen resource, bolstering your knowledge and skills as you journey through the multifaceted world of C# development.

Having considered the *C# Interview Guide* as a pocket-sized knowledge companion, we now turn our attention to the future, where setting personal and professional goals becomes imperative. This next section will guide us through the strategic planning of our career objectives and the importance of establishing clear, actionable targets.

Setting personal and professional goals for your career

Steering into this next section, we'll be honing in on the essence of goal setting. Whether it's the broader strokes of your career vision or the finer details of specific milestones, plotting your aspirations is crucial. Let's dive into the hows and whys of mapping out a structured path for your professional journey.

The critical role of establishing objectives – a deep dive into goal setting

Have you ever found yourself feeling lost or overwhelmed in your career? This often stems from a lack of direction, and that's where the power of goal setting comes into play. Far from being a mere list of wants, setting goals is a transformative exercise that charts the course of your professional voyage. Imagine having a GPS for your career; that's what well-defined objectives offer.

Every goal you set serves a trifold purpose:

- **Catalysts for action**: Like a spark that sets a fire alight, goals ignite motivation. They ensure that when faced with challenges or obstacles, the inner drive doesn't wane. With a clear objective in mind, every hurdle becomes a stepping stone toward that aim.

- **Purpose infusers**: Goals breathe life into everyday tasks. Every piece of code you write, every problem you solve, and every project you undertake becomes a meaningful endeavor, each step moving you closer to your overarching aim.

- **Navigational beacons**: In the vast sea of tech, with its ever-evolving landscape, it's easy to feel adrift. Well-chalked-out goals are like lighthouses, ensuring you remain oriented and steer your ship in the desired direction.

Having established objectives not only steers you through the tempests of tech but also ensures that every milestone reached is a resonant echo of your core ambitions, keeping you anchored and purpose-driven on your professional journey.

Decoding the spectrum of objectives – short-term versus long-term goals

Goals isn't a monolithic term. Think of it as a pair of buckets where one holds your immediate goals and the other contains your grand visions, as set out here:

- **Short-term goals**: These are your immediate waypoints, achievable within weeks to a year. They provide rapid feedback loops, allowing for real-time course correction. Think of them as signposts guiding you on a cross-country drive.

- **Long-term goals**: These are your ultimate destinations – places you envision reaching years down the line. They keep your eyes on the horizon, ensuring you remember the broader narrative of your journey.

It's crucial to see the symbiotic relationship between these two. While short-term goals offer immediacy, long-term visions give context. Together, they craft the mosaic of your professional journey.

A structured approach to objective setting – unpacking SMART goals

Setting a goal is akin to plotting a destination on a map. However, clarity on how to get there ensures the journey is efficient and fruitful. This is where the **SMART** framework shines, refining your objectives and making them actionable and attainable. The acronym stands for the following:

- **Specific**: Broad or vague objectives can lead to confusion. Instead of a generalized aim such as "I wish to excel in C#," specificity would dictate, "I aim to master C# multithreading techniques in the next quarter."

- **Measurable**: Quantifying your objectives gives them substance. "Completing three complex C# projects by year-end" provides a metric to gauge progress.

- **Achievable**: Stretch goals are good, but setting the bar unrealistically high can lead to disillusionment. Objectives should challenge but not dishearten.

- **Relevant**: Align your goals with your broader career vision. If you're aiming for expertise in C# frontend frameworks, a goal could be "Mastering the nuances of C#-integrated frontend tools in 8 months."

- **Time-bound**: A timeline acts as a catalyst, preventing inertia and infusing a sense of urgency. "By the end of this year, I'll be a certified C# specialist" is a goal with a clear finish line.

Harnessing the SMART methodology, particularly in the multifaceted world of C# development, turns aspirations into achievements, translating dreams into reality.

Harmonizing individual dreams with career milestones – the dual track of aspirations

Life can often feel like a tightrope walk, balancing our personal dreams with our professional milestones. On the personal front, we all have those sacred aspirations – maybe it's about creating those irreplaceable family memories, delving into a soul-nurturing personal development course, or losing oneself in a hobby that acts as a sanctuary from work pressures. These dreams anchor us, reminding us of our essence and keeping our spirits alive.

Concurrently, our professional lives beckon with milestones waiting to be achieved. It might be the challenge of mastering the latest C# library or the aspiration to lead and influence in the tech sphere. These career goals fuel our professional growth, giving us direction and purpose.

The magic happens when we intertwine these two tracks, ensuring neither overshadows the other. This harmonization isn't just about career success but encompasses a richer, more fulfilling life journey.

The fluidity of objective setting – the continuous evolution of goals

Setting goals isn't a one-time affair. Imagine planting a sapling; it requires regular care, monitoring, and sometimes, repositioning to ensure it thrives. Similarly, as we grow and the tech landscape evolves, our objectives need revisiting and, often, recalibration.

Life is fluid, and the tech world mirrors this dynamism. An objective set a year ago might seem restrictive today, or maybe the fire that fueled a particular ambition has now dimmed. Embrace this fluidity. Periodically introspecting ensures your goals are not stagnant but are dynamic guides, realigning with your evolving vision and the ever-shifting tech environment.

Gleaning wisdom from external beacons – mentors and peer insights

Imagine embarking on a voyage. While you hold the map, wouldn't guidance from seasoned travelers or fellow voyagers enrich the journey? In our goal-setting expedition, mentors and peers act as these invaluable guides.

Mentors, with their treasure trove of experiences, offer a unique blend of wisdom. They've treaded paths you're now navigating, making them well equipped to offer guidance, share pitfalls to avoid, and even introduce you to shortcuts you hadn't perceived. Their insights can help refine your trajectory, ensuring a smoother journey.

Then there are your peers, comrades in arms, walking parallel paths. They offer a camaraderie born out of shared experiences but peppered with diverse outlooks. Engaging with them can unveil new perspectives, introduce you to unexplored opportunities, and even act as sounding boards for your aspirations.

Remember – while the essence of your goals is deeply personal, drawing insights from these external lighthouses can illuminate your path, making the journey more insightful and the destinations more gratifying.

Crafting a vivid picture of success – the power of visualization

Every traveler benefits from a map, and in our career odyssey, visualization acts as that guiding blueprint. Visualization isn't just about thinking; it's about seeing, feeling, and embodying your aspirations. Tools such as vision boards, filled with evocative images, motivational quotes, and personal symbols, act as daily beacons, galvanizing you toward your aspirations. They crystallize what might be nebulous dreams into tangible targets. In a similar vein, mind mapping acts as a strategic lens, disentangling intricate ambitions into structured, manageable tasks. This visual representation of your journey ensures that each day, you're not just wandering but moving with purpose and passion toward your envisioned success.

Upholding commitment – ensuring goal accountability

The allure of a dream is enchanting, but the path to it demands tenacity. Once you've set those glittering goals, the real task is staying true to them. So, how do we ensure our sails remain steady, even when winds waver? One strategy is to entrust your goals to someone – a mentor or a colleague. When someone else knows of your journey, it fosters a commitment not just to oneself but also to that trusted individual. Periodic reflections, whether they're weekly introspections or broader monthly evaluations, act as your compass, confirming if you're navigating in the right direction. In our digital era, numerous goal-tracking apps stand ready to assist, offering not just reminders but celebrating each milestone, making the process as exhilarating as the pinnacle.

The art of bouncing back – navigating challenges and embracing failures

The route to success isn't a straight highway but often a winding trail with its share of bumps and detours. It's essential to recognize that setbacks aren't barricades but merely bends in the road. Instead of letting failures stifle, let them instruct. Resilience is the art of not just recovering from a fall but rising with added wisdom. Each challenge carries with it a kernel of knowledge, offering insights to enhance strategies, refine approaches, and boost determination. By perceiving challenges as transformative experiences rather than impediments, you infuse your journey with enriching depth, ensuring each phase, triumphant or trying, adds value to your ultimate quest.

Mapping micro to macro – aligning immediate steps with long-term vision

The allure of immediate tasks can sometimes overshadow the grand panorama. However, it's vital to oscillate between the "now" and the "next." Each task undertaken, no matter how minute, should be a stepping stone toward the magnum opus of your career. Maintaining this expansive view ensures that while you revel in the joy of small accomplishments, your trajectory remains aligned with your overarching vision. This holistic perspective acts as a reminder that each effort made today is a brick in the edifice of your future legacy. By consistently mapping the present to the potential, you craft a compelling narrative where every endeavor, big or small, threads into your grand symphony of success.

Closing out this portion, the significance of personal and professional goal setting stands highlighted. By consciously mapping out aspirations and setting tangible targets, you're not just drifting in the vast ocean of C# development but steering your ship with purpose and direction toward desired horizons.

As we transition to the next section, we'll delve deeper into the nuances of C# development, focusing on advanced concepts and how they can be applied to create robust, scalable, and efficient applications. This journey will take us through high-level programming techniques, design patterns, and best practices that are critical for professional growth and mastery within the C# landscape.

Exploring career paths and specializations in the C# ecosystem

As we embark on this section, we'll navigate the diverse landscape of the C# domain. Beyond the foundational skills, the C# ecosystem offers a plethora of specialized avenues. Let's journey through these myriad paths and uncover potential niches that can align with your unique passions.

Delving into the rich tapestry of the C# ecosystem

The world of C# is akin to an expansive tapestry, intricately woven with threads of innovation, flexibility, and power. More than just a programming language, C# stands as a testament to the evolution of software development, demonstrating its prowess in various applications – from simple desktop utilities to robust enterprise solutions. Over the years, C#'s strengths, including its dynamic feature set and adaptability, have propelled it to the forefront of the developer community. This prominence is bolstered by its ever-evolving capabilities and the supportive community that surrounds it. As you immerse yourself in the C# milieu, it becomes evident that each sector, from mobile app development to cloud solutions, presents its unique set of opportunities and nuances.

Venturing into web development with C#

The web, in many ways, is the heartbeat of our digital age. At the nexus of this dynamic world stands C#, empowered by the potent ASP.NET framework. ASP.NET has truly transformed the paradigm of web development by offering an amalgamation of speed, reliability, and adaptability. For developers anchored in the C# ecosystem, ASP.NET presents a unified platform where they can sculpt diverse web solutions, ranging from simple websites to complex web portals. The journey of a C# web developer is a mosaic of varied tasks: designing responsive web layouts, architecting data-driven functionalities, and ensuring that the end user's experience is nothing short of impeccable. The versatility of C# in the web domain serves as a reminder of its vast potential and the myriad of opportunities it opens up for budding developers.

Embarking on a gaming odyssey with Unity and C#

The realm of gaming is where dreams take flight and fantasies come alive. At the core of many of these digital wonders is C#, synergizing seamlessly with the Unity game development platform. Unity's reputation as a leading game engine is enhanced by the adaptability and strength of C#. Whether it's scripting the dynamic behavior of a game character, simulating realistic environments, or establishing intricate game mechanics, C# stands as the linchpin. But venturing into game development with C# isn't solely about coding. It's a multidimensional experience, intertwining art, narrative, sound, and technology. This domain isn't just a profession; it's a passion, a realm where every day is a new adventure, brimming with challenges to surmount and innovations to craft. As you explore the intersection of Unity and C#, you'll find a world teeming with boundless creativity and endless horizons.

The pivotal role of C# in enterprise solution development

In the sprawling world of modern enterprise, software solutions are more than just tools—they are the vital organs that keep businesses alive and thriving. Within this intricate network, C# stands out as an influential architect. Enterprise solutions span a broad spectrum, tailored to meet the nuanced demands of sizable organizations. Think of CRMs that deftly manage and nurture client relationships, or expansive databases engineered to process and analyze colossal datasets with finesse. Or consider

ERPs that act as unifiers, knitting together diverse business functions into a coherent whole. Here, C# showcases its prowess, delivering on multiple fronts. Its inherent adaptability, coupled with top-notch scalability and security, positions it as a favored choice among developers. Further, its seamless synergy with Microsoft's formidable array of enterprise-centric tools means that solutions sculpted in C# are not just efficient but also poised at the cutting edge of innovation.

Journeying through desktop application development, harnessing the power of C#, WPF, and Windows Forms

Desktop applications, in many ways, represent venerable giants of software development. They provide users with immersive, offline experiences, often directly from the sanctity of their workstations or homes. Within this landscape, C# acts as the bedrock, while frameworks such as WPF enhance its creative scope. With WPF at their fingertips, C# developers can weave interactive, visually stunning UIs, replete with fluid animations and intricate data-driven functionalities. On the flip side, Windows Forms offers a more classic touch, channeling the spirit of traditional GUI design but supercharged for swift application crafting. Be it designing a feature-rich graphic suite, conceptualizing an insightful analytics platform, or building an essential day-to-day utility, the union of C# with either WPF or Windows Forms ensures developers can manifest their visions with unmatched clarity and elegance.

Exploring cross-platform horizons with C# and MAUI

The contemporary digital landscape is marked by diversity. With a plethora of devices and platforms in play, the clamor for unified, cross-platform applications has never been louder. Answering this call is **Multi-platform App UI (MAUI)**, backed by the reliability and versatility of C#. Microsoft .NET MAUI stands as a beacon for developers aiming to straddle multiple platforms without getting bogged down by multiple code bases. By leveraging C# at its core, MAUI promises not just universality but also a native look, feel, and performance. This confluence of universality with nativity is transformative. For developers, it heralds streamlined workflows and broader outreach. For end users, it ensures consistent, high-quality experiences irrespective of their device or OS choice. Whether it's spinning up a mobile app that strikes a chord globally or engineering a desktop utility that feels at home on any OS, the combined might of C# and MAUI is reshaping the contours of modern software development.

Embarking on the vast horizons of cloud computing with Azure

Cloud computing, a concept once considered nebulous, has now solidified its presence as the bedrock of modern IT solutions. And right at the epicenter of this colossal shift is Microsoft's premier cloud offering: Azure. More than just a cloud platform, Azure epitomizes the very essence of digital progression, enabling businesses to be nimble, adaptive, and infinitely scalable. As companies worldwide pivot to embrace more malleable infrastructures, Azure stands tall, presenting an abundant suite of services that span the spectrum from IaaS and PaaS to SaaS.

But one might ponder, how do C# developers weave into this intricate web of cloud transformation? This nexus is deeply rooted in Azure's DNA. Being a brainchild of Microsoft, Azure naturally dovetails with the languages and tools associated with the technology behemoth. This positions C# as a quintessential language for shaping the digital constructs within Azure's vast ecosystem. As heralds of this new era, C# developers don't just code; they sculpt, envision, and engineer. They mold scalable web apps, orchestrate virtual environments, weave complex API fabrics, and oversee data sanctuaries in the ether. Beyond mere deployment, their roles extend to fine-tuning, scaling, and vigilant management on Azure. By harnessing tools such as Azure DevOps for seamless integration flows or tapping into Azure Functions for event-responsive coding, C# developers are not mere participants but pivotal architects, erecting solutions that are nimble, robust, and perennially relevant.

Navigating the innovative world of IoT with C#

Beyond the clouds, at the cusp of our tangible reality, lies another tech marvel – the **Internet of Things (IoT)**. Picture a world where mundane objects, be it your coffee maker or city traffic lights, evolve into sentient entities, pulsating with data and intelligence. IoT heralds a future less about isolated devices and more about a cohesive, intelligent symphony, where devices converse, deduce, and autonomously act, amplifying efficiencies and enriching human experiences.

Amid this tapestry of interconnected marvels, where does the C# developer stand? Right at the pivotal juncture of hardware-software synergy, C# crystallizes as a potent enabler in the IoT sphere. Its adaptability, coupled with an exhaustive library repertoire, earmarks C# as the go-to language for curating solutions that dialog with IoT devices. Platforms such as Windows 10 IoT Core amplify C#'s prowess, enabling developers to animate everything from a hobbyist's Raspberry Pi setup to industrial behemoths. The tight-knit collaboration between C# and Microsoft's IoT toolkits ensures that developers are equipped not just to dictate device logic but also to securely oversee, dissect, and represent the voluminous data streams.

But the IoT tale doesn't end here. With edge computing gaining momentum, there's a clarion call to process information closer to its genesis – the IoT device. C# responds with elan, equipping developers to devise edge-centric solutions that crunch data instantaneously, arbitrate real-time actions, and slash latency. As sectors as diverse as farming to telemedicine start embracing IoT's allure, C# developers are not just coders; they are visionaries, etching solutions that merge the tangible with the digital, heralding an epoch of boundless innovation and cohesive coexistence.

Venturing into data science and machine learning with C#

Data science and **machine learning** (**ML**), once dominions largely championed by Python and R, have seen a new player on the block: C#. It's an era where technological boundaries are constantly being pushed, and C# is no exception. With the introduction of potent libraries such as ML.NET, C# is not just knocking on the doors of ML but is stepping confidently inside. ML.NET isn't just another library; it's a robust suite that empowers developers to conceive, nurture, and deploy tailor-made ML models squarely within the familiar terrain of the .NET Framework. This leap means that C# developers aren't just restricted to conventional software development anymore. They can seamlessly weave smart capabilities into their applications, whether it's understanding user sentiments or crafting a sophisticated recommendation engine.

Deep diving into the C# libraries and frameworks ecosystem

C#'s versatility doesn't stop at data science. A treasure trove of libraries and frameworks awaits those who venture deeper into its ecosystem. Consider Xamarin, for example. It's not just a platform but a bridge that unifies various mobile operating systems under the aegis of a single code base. Write once, deploy everywhere – that's the power Xamarin hands to C# developers. Meanwhile, SignalR shines in a different corner, lighting up the world of real-time web applications. It breaks the shackles of traditional request-response models, fostering instantaneous, bidirectional communication between the client and server. By immersing themselves in these diverse tools and more, C# developers can expand their skill sets, unlock new avenues, and truly master the art and science of modern software development.

Harnessing the power of the C# community through networking

A language, no matter how powerful, thrives on its community. C# is no different. There's an entire universe of C# enthusiasts, experts, and pioneers out there. To fully leverage the might of C#, one must dive into this vibrant sea of knowledge and experience. Engaging in C# forums, signing up for hands-on workshops, and marking presence at global conferences are more than just learning avenues. They're platforms to build connections, share experiences, and grow together. Mingling with peers, getting insights from veterans, and partnering with innovators opens up pathways to unseen opportunities and collaborations. Networking isn't just about making acquaintances; it's about planting the seeds for mutual growth and nurturing the spirit of the global C# fraternity.

The imperative of lifelong learning in the C# sphere

The tech world is in perpetual motion, with innovations springing up at every corner. C# sits at this dynamic crossroads, continuously evolving and expanding. With each release of .NET and the emergence of fresh paradigms, the learning curve keeps shifting. For a C# developer, resting on laurels is not a luxury; it's a risk. The thirst for knowledge should be insatiable. Embracing new versions, methodologies, and tools keeps developers not just relevant but ahead of the curve. Committing to lifelong learning isn't just about personal growth; it's about riding the wave of technological advancements, ensuring that one harnesses the best of what C# and its expansive ecosystem unveil.

Wrapping up this exploration, it's evident that the C# world is rich with opportunities. From game development to enterprise solutions, the variety is immense. Identifying and aligning with a niche that sparks your enthusiasm can be the key to a fulfilling and successful career in C# development.

Staying up to date with industry trends and developments

Venturing into this final section, we'll address a vital aspect of any tech profession: staying current. In the fast-paced world of C# and the broader tech industry, evolution is constant. Let's dive into strategies and practices to ensure you're always at the forefront, equipped with the latest knowledge.

Keeping up with the accelerated tech evolution

In the software realm, change is the only constant. Reflecting on the breathtaking pace at which technology advances, one is often left in awe. Within moments, it seems, revolutionary tools and methodologies make their debut, continually altering developers' perspectives and methodologies. These constant shifts paint a vivid picture: the world of technology is not just moving—it's sprinting. And for any developer keen on staying at the top of their game, the sprint is real. Adapting to these changes, absorbing the nuances, and integrating them into one's work is not a mere add-on; it's core to surviving and thriving in an environment known for its relentless metamorphosis.

Staying informed through newsletters, blogs, and reputed websites

In the ocean of information that is the internet, knowing where to fish is paramount. For those steeped in the world of C#, a multitude of newsletters, influential blogs, and specialized websites are the guiding stars. These sources are not just passive information providers; they are curated channels that bring forth the crux of the latest in technology—be it groundbreaking innovations, nuanced best practices, or subtle shifts in the tech landscape. Regularly engaging with these industry stalwarts ensures developers are always in the loop, always tuned in to the heartbeat of technological evolution.

Plunging into the digital hubs of developer communities

Beyond mere information, the digital age gifts us communities—spaces where like-minded individuals rally around common passions. Platforms such as Stack Overflow, GitHub, or even niche programming subreddits are not just websites; they're bustling global town squares of the developer world. Here, ideas are exchanged, challenges dissected, and innovations celebrated. Immersing oneself in these spaces gives developers a holistic view of the industry's landscape, providing insights into both prevailing best practices and the sparks of future trends.

The immense value of conferences, seminars, and workshops

While the digital realm is an ever-flowing source of insights, there's an unmatched richness that conferences, seminars, and workshops offer. These gatherings—whether in a physical auditorium or a virtual webinar—are nexus points of deep knowledge. They bring together thought leaders, industry pioneers, and curious minds. Attendees don't just walk away with nuggets of wisdom; they also cultivate relationships, sow seeds for future collaborations, and sometimes, find avenues that redefine their career trajectories.

Harnessing online courses for continuous skill enhancement

The classroom of the 21st century is not bounded by four walls; it's boundless, spanning the expanse of the internet. Online learning platforms such as Udemy, Coursera, and Pluralsight are gateways to this global classroom. They offer courses that mirror the industry's pulse, ensuring that as technology takes its next leap, developers can leap with it. Investing time in these courses is more than just personal growth; it's about ensuring that one's skills resonate with the industry's heartbeat, ensuring they are always in sync, if not a beat ahead.

Deepening expertise through certifications and specialized training

In the complex mosaic of the software development realm, specialized certifications and training programs are akin to the finer brush strokes that define a masterpiece. Taking the plunge into these programs is not just about enriching one's knowledge arsenal. It's a declaration, a statement that echoes your unwavering dedication to mastery in a specific domain. As the job market becomes increasingly saturated, these certifications have a dual role: they fortify your foundational understanding and serve as beacons, signaling your commitment and proficiency to potential employers and clients. When they seek depth and an assurance of continued learning, these certifications become your advocate.

Enrichment through podcasts and insightful tech discussions

In our fast-paced tech epoch, absorbing knowledge is a multifaceted affair. Beyond articles and books, there exists an auditory realm rich with insights—the world of tech podcasts and video discussions. With industry stalwarts often at the helm, these platforms delve into the nuances of emerging trends, dissect novel technological marvels, and offer forecasts on the software world's evolution. Regular engagement with such resources is akin to attending a global tech symposium from the comfort of your home. It not only broadens your perspective but continually reshapes and sharpens your understanding of the tech sphere's pulse.

The mutual benefits of open source contributions

Open source is more than just freely available code—it's a philosophy, a collaborative odyssey. Delving into open source contributions is both a give and take. While you offer your expertise and innovations to the world, you're rewarded with exposure to state-of-the-art practices, tools, and mindsets. This journey also carves avenues for deep interactions with peers and tech mavens, knitting you into the expansive fabric of the global tech community. Furthermore, these contributions often become the shining stars of a developer's portfolio, illustrating their proactive contributions and unwavering commitment to the tech ecosystem's growth.

Navigating the frontier with beta testing and early tech adoption

In the software universe, the early bird not only catches the worm but often helps shape its trajectory. Delving into beta testing or taking the reins as an early adopter of budding tools places a developer at the forefront of technological evolution. This vanguard position yields twofold benefits: a deep-seated understanding of burgeoning innovations and a possible advantageous footing when these tools hit the mainstream. An early engagement can also morph into a participative role, where one's insights and feedback can sculpt the direction of these emerging tools.

The constructive power of feedback and collaborative reviews

Perfection is a journey, and on this road, reflections and external viewpoints act as signposts. Actively seeking feedback and diving into collaborative code reviews can be both affirming and humbling. It offers a 360-degree view of one's abilities, juxtaposing them against the industry's ever-shifting paradigms. These sessions not only anchor a developer in the present but also chart out paths for future growth. By instilling a culture where feedback is embraced, developers ensure that they're not just treading water but constantly swimming toward the shores of excellence.

Concluding our exploration, the imperativeness of staying updated in the tech realm becomes clear. The landscape of C# and technology as a whole is ever-changing, and being in tune with its shifts ensures not only relevance but also innovation in your professional journey. Your commitment to continuous learning will undoubtedly set you apart in this dynamic field.

To sum up this chapter, the journey of a C# developer extends far beyond the interview room. Post-interview actions, such as following up, can be decisive in job outcomes. Recognizing and celebrating your achievements keeps your morale high, while also understanding the significance of challenges ensures continuous learning. Building a successful career isn't just about the technicalities of C# but also about personal growth and setting clear goals. The *C# Interview Guide* is a companion for this journey, providing valuable insights and strategies. Finally, with the tech industry's ever-evolving nature, staying updated on trends and branching into various C# specializations can offer immense growth opportunities. Remember – every step you take is a building block for a successful career in C# development.

Launching your journey into the world of C#

As we reach the end of this comprehensive guide, *C# Interview Guide*, it's important to take a moment to reflect on the journey we've embarked on together. From crafting a resume that stands out to mastering the intricacies of C# programming, each step has been a building block toward not just landing a job but carving out a successful career in the ever-evolving field of software development.

The journey summarized

We began by laying the foundation with a compelling resume, cover letter, and an online presence that captures your unique professional persona. Then, we did the following:

- We navigated through the nuances of acing the interview, mastering both behavioral questions and technical challenges

- We delved into the fundamentals of C#, establishing the bedrock of knowledge necessary for any aspiring developer

- Our path led us to advanced concepts, where complex ideas became achievable challenges

- We adopted best practices and design patterns, ensuring that our approach to C# is both elegant and efficient

- We explored the depths of C# libraries and frameworks, tools that empower us to craft robust and scalable applications

- We faced technical interview challenges head-on, bolstering our soft skills and expanding our professional network along the way

- We learned the art of negotiating salaries and evaluating job offers to ensure our value is recognized and rewarded

- Finally, we discussed the importance of effective follow-ups and gleaned expert insights that illuminate our path forward

As you close this book, remember that it's not just the end of a reading journey, but the beginning of a new chapter in your professional life. Each page you've turned and each concept you've absorbed has been a step toward your goal of becoming a proficient C# developer and landing the role you've been striving for.

A note of gratitude

Before you set this book aside and turn your full attention to the challenges ahead, I would like to express my deepest gratitude. Thank you for allowing me to be a part of your journey. Your dedication to learning and growing is the very reason this book exists. I hope that the strategies, tips, and insights shared within these pages serve you well as you forge ahead in your career.

Moving forward

Now, take these lessons, apply them with confidence, and embark on your C# career with the knowledge that you are prepared for what lies ahead. Remember—this is not just about cracking an interview—it's about building a future that you're passionate about. Continue to learn, code, and solve problems with the creativity and precision that C# allows.

Your next steps

Implement what you've learned in a personal project or contribute to an open source project to refine your skills.

Connect with fellow readers and C# enthusiasts to build your professional network.

Continue your education, whether through formal classes, online courses, or self-study.

As you move forward, carry with you the wisdom of experience and the courage of conviction. May your errors be few, your successes frequent, and your career in C# be as rewarding as it is prosperous.

With sincere thanks and best wishes for your journey ahead!

Index

Packtpub.com

Subscribe to our online digital library for full access to over 7,000 books and videos, as well as industry leading tools to help you plan your personal development and advance your career. For more information, please visit our website.

Why subscribe?

- Spend less time learning and more time coding with practical eBooks and Videos from over 4,000 industry professionals

- Improve your learning with Skill Plans built especially for you

- Get a free eBook or video every month

- Fully searchable for easy access to vital information

- Copy and paste, print, and bookmark content

Did you know that Packt offers eBook versions of every book published, with PDF and ePub files available? You can upgrade to the eBook version at packtpub.com and as a print book customer, you are entitled to a discount on the eBook copy. Get in touch with us at customercare@packtpub.com for more details.

At www.packtpub.com, you can also read a collection of free technical articles, sign up for a range of free newsletters, and receive exclusive discounts and offers on Packt books and eBooks.

Other Books You May Enjoy

If you enjoyed this book, you may be interested in these other books by Packt:

Clean Code with C#

Jason Alls

ISBN: 978-1-83763-519-1

Master the art of writing evolvable and adaptable code

Implement the fail-pass-refactor methodology using a sample C# console application

Develop custom C# exceptions that provide meaningful information

Identify low-quality C# code in need of refactoring

Improve code performance using profiling and refactoring tools

Create efficient and bug-free code using functional programming techniques

Write cross-platform code using MAUI

Develop cloud-deployable microservices for versatile applications

Refactoring with C#

Matt Eland

ISBN: 978-1-83508-998-9

Understand technical debt, its causes and effects, and ways to prevent it

Explore different ways of refactoring classes, methods, and lines of code

Discover how to write effective unit tests supported by libraries such as Moq

Understand SOLID principles and factors that lead to maintainable code

Use AI to analyze, improve, and test code with the GitHub Copilot Chat

Apply code analysis and custom Roslyn analyzers to ensure that code stays clean

Packt is searching for authors like you

If you're interested in becoming an author for Packt, please visit authors.packtpub.com and apply today. We have worked with thousands of developers and tech professionals, just like you, to help them share their insight with the global tech community. You can make a general application, apply for a specific hot topic that we are recruiting an author for, or submit your own idea.

Hi!

I'm Konstantin Semenenko, the author of C# Interview Guide. I really hope you enjoyed reading this book and found it useful for increasing your productivity and efficiency in cracking C# interviews.

It would really help me (and other potential readers!) if you could leave a review on Amazon sharing your thoughts on C# Interview Guide here.

Go to the link below or scan the QR code to leave your review:

https://packt.link/r/1805120468

Your review will help me to understand what's worked well in this book, and what could be improved upon for future editions, so it really is appreciated.

Best Wishes,

Konstantin Semenenko

Download a free PDF copy of this book

Thanks for purchasing this book!

Do you like to read on the go but are unable to carry your print books everywhere?

Is your eBook purchase not compatible with the device of your choice?

Don't worry, now with every Packt book you get a DRM-free PDF version of that book at no cost.

Read anywhere, any place, on any device. Search, copy, and paste code from your favorite technical books directly into your application.

The perks don't stop there, you can get exclusive access to discounts, newsletters, and great free content in your inbox daily

Follow these simple steps to get the benefits:

1. Scan the QR code or visit the link below

https://packt.link/free-ebook/9781805120469

2. Submit your proof of purchase
3. That's it! We'll send your free PDF and other benefits to your email directly